A PLACE AT HIS TABLE

A PLACE
AT HIS TABLE

*A Biblical Exploration of
Faith, Sexuality, and the Kingdom of God*

Joel Hollier

CASCADE *Books* • Eugene, Oregon

A PLACE AT HIS TABLE
A Biblical Exploration of Faith, Sexuality, and the Kingdom of God

Cascade Books
An Imprint of Wipf and Stock Publishers
199 W. 8th Ave., Suite 3
Eugene, OR 97401

www.wipfandstock.com

PAPERBACK ISBN: 978-1-5326-6712-1
HARDCOVER ISBN: 978-1-5326-6713-8
EBOOK ISBN: 978-1-5326-6714-5

Cataloguing-in-Publication data:

Names: Hollier, Joel, author.
Title: A place at his table : a biblical exploration of faith, sexuality, and the king-dom of God / Joel Hollier.
Description: Eugene, OR: Cascade Books, 2019 | Includes bibliographical refer-ences.
Identifiers: ISBN 978-1-5326-6712-1 (paperback) | ISBN 978-1-5326-6713-8 (hard-cover) | ISBN 978-1-5326-6714-5 (ebook)
Subjects: LCSH: Bible and homosexuality. | Homosexuality—Religious aspects—Christianity. | Marriage—Biblical teaching.
Classification: BS680.H67 H58 2019 (print) | BS680 (ebook)

Manufactured in the U.S.A.   AUGUST 19, 2019

For Heather and Paul. You raised me to seek truth, and I found Jesus. There is no greater gift a parent could pass on to their child.

Contents

Preface

The church is at a crossroads. We find ourselves now in a scary, disorienting, and vitally important moment. Now is not the time to hide, nor is it the time to fight. Now is the time to gather together, to share our stories, to enrich our discussion, and to point one another to Jesus. That's what this book seeks to do.

The focus of this book is on lesbian, gay, and bisexual people (commonly referred to as "same-sex attracted"). I have chosen this focus because it is where I feel most comfortable writing—it resonates deeply with my own personal journey and is where I have dedicated years of my life to research. But the reality is that the experiences you encounter in these pages are lived out on a daily basis by a huge number of other groups, whether they be racial minorities, transgender people, people living with disabilities, or intersex folk. The lived journeys of these people are so often complicated with exclusion, misrepresentation, and distrust. Some of this hardship stems from ignorance. Some of it from ideology, some from theology. Rarely does it stem from a place of hatred, though that is undeniably a factor in too many instances.

The names of the people that you will encounter in this book have been changed to protect their identities. I have also changed some minor details to ensure anonymity. I trust that I have done so without compromising the integrity of their stories.

My prayer for you as you read this book is that you would allow yourself to stand in awe of the majesty of the God that we serve. I pray that you would once again wonder at the beauty of God's embrace, for all of these people—sinners and saints that we are. I hope you will find here words of healing, of clarity, and of comfort.

I present these words not as a treatise to be argued, but as a guide to those seeking answers. I hope that with time, the church may become a safer place of worship for all who would seek God, and I hope that by God's grace, this book might lead us closer to that day.

Read prayerfully, think deeply, love powerfully.

Joel

PART 1

Where We Find Ourselves

1

Preparing the Table

Before I say anything else, I want to make something clear. This is not just a book about sexuality. This is also not a rallying cry for the rights of gay and lesbian people, or a treatise on why any person should believe what I have come to believe. This is not an angry rant and it is certainly not a chance to pit one group of theological concepts against another. If that is all that this book amounts to, I will consider it a failure. Without a doubt, dialogue regarding the LGBT movement and deep theological discussion about sexuality will take place, but ultimately, this is a book about Jesus and his church. As you read these pages, it is my hope and prayer that you would come to a deeper understanding of the God who created this world and the rich plan that has been laid out for humanity. I hope that you will come to appreciate God's word more fully in all of its splendor and that you would leave more confident in handling it for yourself. In the same vein, it is my prayer that you would see this discussion not as an issue that needs solving, nor merely as a series of doctrinal propositions that need articulating. Rather, I hope that you would recognize that what we are talking about are real people, with real stories, serving a real God, with a really big heart.

If you would take a moment, look around you at the state of play in which we find these very real people. It appears now that the battle lines have been drawn; the ideological trenches have been hewn, and with each new blog, book, column, and quip, shots are being fired. As I write this, the incessant barrage of voices surrounding the "gay versus Christian debate" resonates powerfully in my mind. Time and time again, this discussion has been hailed as the watershed standard for which my generation will be known. The question has been put to us over and over—whose side are you on?

On the one hand, a passionate and highly resourced minority who have historically been marginalized has found their voice and been granted a public platform to advocate for recognition and, to varying degrees, acceptance. For the first time in human memory, gay and lesbian people are being heard—and a band of allies has rallied around them. On the other hand, and seemingly diametrically opposed, stands the church with its ancient tradition and divine mandate to uphold a conservative sexual ethic no matter the cost. Eager to demonstrate a deep and courageous love, church leaders are going against the cultural tide, and often at great sacrifice are maintaining a traditional view of sexuality, gender, and marriage.

Why then would I stroll headlong into the battle by writing yet another book? Surely there is enough literature to sate the needs of the encamped for decades to come. Why should I join the movement and put my head above the parapet? Surely we have enough martyrs for the cause. Let me start by saying I do not enter this discussion lightly, and nor do I enter it fully convinced that I should. Indeed, a large part of me wishes that I were never dragged into the discussion in the first place. I have seen firsthand what happens to church leaders whose opinions are not the majority voice. Nevertheless, here I stand with trepidation, ready to lend my somewhat nuanced perspective to those who would listen. With this noted, let me tell you some of the reasons why I don't want to write this book.

I don't want to write this book because I'm scared. It may seem somewhat pathetic, I know, but I'm scared about what people will think about me, say about me, do to me, and, more pressing, to my family. Speaking up with what is deemed by some church leaders to be a dissenting voice will likely open the door on a series of attacks and this is a battle field which I would much rather avoid.

Secondly, I hesitate to write this book because I love Jesus' church, and believe firmly that unity amongst the body of Christ is a beautiful phenomenon. The community of saints who stand together in solidarity as the bride of Christ is something to strive toward on all fronts. The very fact that I am engaging in this discussion at the literary level means that I am deliberately entering into the realm of a significant point of disunity. It is becoming increasingly clear that Christianity is sharply divided. This is not a debate between the faith community and secular society. Nor is it a difference of opinion over two different religious texts. This discussion is playing itself out with great confusion in otherwise united congregations across the Western world. For many people this has become something of a litmus test as to whether or not fellowship is to be extended. As people are coming to differing conclusions, they are also being shown the door. There is no doubt in my mind that this disunity breaks Jesus' heart as the church he paid such a price for turns on itself.

Finally, I fear that in the writing of this book I will inadvertently add fire to the flames and in some measure make it feel as though I agree that this is indeed a matter of central importance to being a Christian. If sheer quantity were our measure of importance, the ever growing mound of literature from all voices in the discussion would seem to suggest that one's view on this topic is the definitive guide to the genuineness of one's faith. In other words, there is the very present notion amongst many Christians today that if you disagree with them on this point, you are preaching a false gospel. If you are traditional in your view, then you are branded as a Pharisee who distorts Scripture in order to oppress minorities that are already marginalized and crying out for community. If you are affirming in your view of gay and lesbian relationships, then you are told that you are preaching that sin is not sin and therefore the gospel cannot be good news. Either way, it is claimed by the opposing side that a false view of sin, and subsequently a false view of the work of Jesus on the cross is being preached, and therefore the gospel is at stake. We will flesh these claims out with significantly more detail as we go along, but for now I need to make it clear that I don't think that one's view of sexuality necessarily reflects, or is even indicative of, their view of the authority of Scripture and their state of salvation. Nor do I believe that one's view in this discussion is intrinsically tied up with their view of the gospel.

All things considered, I am nervous about spilling more ink on a topic that is already hotly debated. That being said, I have clearly set out to articulate my thoughts in these pages, and as such you deserve to know why it is that I am raising my voice and penning these words.

I believe that the Bible is the word of God. I believe that God has revealed himself to humanity through these words. In the Bible we discover God's character; we enter into God's unfolding story of drawing together a people who worship God alone; we encounter a radical grace and an abundant love in Jesus—God's own son. I believe that the Bible is powerful, life-bringing and life-changing. The Bible stands as the highest authority in life, the utmost revelation of true reality. In all things, my conscience is bound to Scripture, and as such I have a strong sense of the need to call attention to any area of church teaching that does not line up with the biblical witness.

Naturally, this call to clarity of truth is made all the more urgent when people are caught up in the mix. Across the past decade, I have had countless conversations with individuals who are wrestling with the interplay between being gay and being a person of faith—either for themselves, or for loved ones. These conversations have often been full of hope and grace, but they have far more frequently been characterized by fear and disillusionment. I am writing this book because love compels me to care for those in my community who are marginalized, whose voices are sidelined and whose lives too often play out as wounded soldiers in a barren no man's land of the culture war in which we find ourselves. Given this, you will find throughout this book a vast array of stories of people who I have encountered in my own journey. As you open up the Bible and seek to understand the profound truths it offers, I hope that these stories will encourage you to work hard, extend grace, and be open to honest conversation.

As far as I can see, very little of the work in this book is original. All of the historical, theological, and cultural exegesis I present has been laid out before in a plethora of rich dialogue and faithful writing. However, my observation is that the "affirming" theological stances are still very much misunderstood and misrepresented, especially amongst my own evangelical tribe. Many loving people thus find themselves unnecessarily ignorant of the points at hand, and even though they have all of the best intentions, the volume of literature out there cripples them. Where does one start? My hope is that this book will serve to make some of these ideas more accessible to those who wish to engage thoughtfully in the discussion. By no means am I the expert, and I am far from the final say. But I do hope that it will serve to point at least some people in a different direction which will begin a trajectory toward what is for many a new way of thinking.

Finally, I am writing this book because I honestly believe that faithful dialogue in this area will result in a greater understanding of the character of Jesus. Whether you find yourself agreeing or disagreeing with the ideas laid out here, by the end of this journey you will have read his word, engaged with his people, and thought deeply about his plan for humanity. As far as I can see, all of these things are healthy spiritual disciplines and all of them will result in a deeper knowledge of God. As a pastor, this is what excites me more than anything else. For me, this journey has been full of heartache and occasionally despair, but as I look back I can see how God has been shaping me, sharpening me, and drawing me ever deeper in faith. I am profoundly grateful that I have had the honor of being on this journey and I pray that the same will be true for you as you read these words.

With all of the above in mind, I have prayerfully come to the conclusion that another book is in order, and so I humbly offer you my thoughts. By way of anticipating who will be reading this, let me take a stab in the dark.

Some of you have come across this book and you would not call yourself a Christian in a million years. You find Christianity outdated at best, and archaic to the core. Perhaps you have had interactions with the church in the past and found it wanting in the domains of love and charity. My hope for you as you enter into this discussion is that you would come to see some things in a different light. My journey of discovering the Bible has been nothing short of astounding as I've come to see a historical Jesus that I simply can't deny. In these pages you will read much about church politics (which trust me, sometimes aren't pretty), historical theology (a rabbit's warren of strange and foreign ideas), and people's lives (which, let's face it, are messy). But through it all you will also encounter Jesus. If I have done him any justice in these pages, then you will discover the most compelling human ever to walk the face of this planet. Perhaps this will spark a far greater journey than you could presently envisage. May I simply invite you to be open to this.

For some of you, you are following Jesus faithfully and are approaching this book with a level of skepticism. Perhaps you have been given it by a loved one, but you are already fairly sure that you know what the Bible says. At great danger of sounding patronizing, let me just say that I was once in that very place. Engaging with new ideas and different theological frameworks can be uncomfortable, to say the least, but that is no excuse for remaining ignorant of discussions that are pertinent to the life of the church of which you are a part. I am in no place to request an open mind or even your passing attention. I would however humbly ask that you consider the ideas presented here for the sake of those in your life for whom this is not just theological musings but rather their lived reality every single day.

Perhaps you come at this book knowing and loving people in your life who are gay, and are tired or disillusioned by the rhetoric of the traditional, conservative church. Maybe you are eager to hear a way forward that both fits with the Bible as your highest authority and gives space for your loved ones to experience the intimacy that you would so long for them to have. My prayer is that this book would serve as a helpful guide in your thinking. My fear is that far too many Christians who have embraced an affirming view of sexuality have done so without thoughtfully and prayerfully engaging with Scripture. They have, for want of a better term, capitulated to prevailing Western narratives of sexuality and in doing so have marginalized the Bible or minimized its claim on their lives. Whilst I understand the temptation to do this, I am convinced that this is not a helpful way forward. Not only does it portray a shallow view of God's word, but in the long run it will (and already has) caused significant damage to the spiritual walks of many gay and lesbian people who already have significant barriers to trusting the Bible as God's authoritative word. Rather than throwing Scripture out, I hope that you can see here that the Bible is profoundly good news for all people, gay and lesbian people included!

And finally, to you who are reading this who find yourselves struggling with unwanted same-sex attraction, I trust that in these pages you will find comfort in knowing that you are not alone. You did not ask for this to be a part of your journey; you did not choose it in any way. With all my heart, I wish that you were not in the position that you are in, because I know something of how desperately difficult this is for you. My prayer is that as you read this book, you would find words of comfort and solace. I hope that you would also find words of conviction and warning, and that God's good plan for sexuality would be both satisfying and enthralling for you. More than anything, I pray that you would take heart in Jesus as you brace yourself for the long journey ahead. The ink in this book will soon fade and the paper it is printed on will tear, but as the days roll on, I hope that these words will remain as another source of comfort for you—one injured sibling to another.

2

In the Interest of Clarity

Let me take a moment to share bit of my journey. As the perfect Sunday school child of a thriving conservative evangelical church, I found myself at a young age surrounded by gentle, gracious men and women who I looked up to and sought to emulate. Immersed in the picturesque mountains to the west of Sydney, and armed with felt-board cutouts and cheesy tape deck tunes, these faithful teachers opened up my mind to discover a creative God. This was a God whose abundance of love led to the greatest of all sacrifices, so that I, rebel that I am, might be declared a child of the most high king. This narrative of self-sacrifice, of created order and steadfast comfort, of extravagant love, and of untold riches resonated with me at a profound level and drew me in to desire more and more of this God of whom the Bible speaks. As I engaged with this God, I discovered not only a sense of security in his grandeur, but also the growing intimacy of a beloved friend. Spurred along by the selfless generosity I saw in my parents and their gospel-shaped witness, I knew from an early age that I was drawn toward ministry, with a great desire to see more and more people encounter the Jesus that I knew.

But as time went on, a sharp divide began to form between how I was presenting to the world around me and the internal monologue that was raging in my mind. Like most people who experience sexual and romantic attraction to those of the same sex, I grew up knowing that there was something different about me, but was unable to put my finger on exactly what that difference might be. It wasn't until early adolescence rolled around that I experienced my first sickening realization that I might, in fact, be gay. Lying in bed that night I wept as I fought back the urge to throw up. I threw the book I'd been reading across the room as though it were cursed, turned off my light, and hid beneath the covers until sleep overtook me. What I could not have known at that time was that that night was just the beginning of a tumultuous roller coaster as I sought to reconcile my sexuality with the all loving, all powerful God that I had come to know. As weeks rolled into months and months became years, my relationship with this God remained vital and central to everything that I did, but now it was different—it was more complex. The rock that I had built my life upon had begun to show signs of cracking. The refuge that I had fled to in the raging floodwaters of life had become the very source of vexed frustration that I now sought to flee from. Strange, isn't it?

The world of Christianity and the world of "being gay" were two mutually exclusive, vitally incompatible terrains, and in my young mind I was sure that one would sooner or later have to give way. The two could not coexist, and for good reason. The models of gay and lesbian behavior that I saw at that time were few, and they were lavishly promiscuous with flaunted sexuality and drug use. In all honesty, as far as I could see, to be gay was on par with being a Satanist. In fact, the latter may have scraped in just on top because the Satanists at least acknowledged the existence of God! By my early teens I had come to the conclusion that because I was gay, I was going to hell. Nobody ever said this to me. I don't remember where I even picked up such a conclusion—chances are something had been mentioned in passing on the television and I'd grabbed hold of it. But it was abundantly clear in my young mind that that was my fate and so I resigned myself to a life of secrecy and shame before facing my maker. Such were the precious musings of thirteen-year-old Joel.

It goes without saying that my story is far from unique. That's not to say that it doesn't have its quirks and idiosyncrasies—it most certainly does—but the experience of growing up gay in the world of conservative Christianity is a well-documented and highly scrutinized phenomenon. Countless young men and women have been through it and their experiences teach us over and over again that it is a journey fraught with loneliness, ostracism, and self-condemnation. As we will see, the vast majority of those who find themselves with unwanted same-sex attraction end up either leaving the church, or being excluded from the church community. Too many give up on Jesus altogether.

This is where my story differs from the vast majority. Rather than running from the church, I threw myself into it. Whilst I had competing desires warring for my attention and affection, I knew to my core I simply could not run away from the God that I had encountered in my childhood years. I had tasted the goodness of this God. At the deepest level, I found that the person of Jesus, though confusing, was simply irresistible. I did what any sane teenager does when they have a life crisis—I read theology.

Though I couldn't articulate it at the time, in those early years of constructing a moral vision for my wayward sexuality, I was building for myself (or rather God was building in me) a theological method that I would later discover had a label—"reformed evangelical." With an unquestioning understanding that God's revealed word was to remain my highest authority, I began by looking up every passage in the Bible that had the word "sex." Whether I was driven by a desire to comprehend the vast biblical witness, or whether I was simply being a teenage boy, is impossible to determine, but one thing became immeasurably clear: God has a lot to say about sex. In fact, God had far more to say about sex than I could possibly have imagined. As it turns out, the Bible is full of it.

After recovering from my initial shock at God's willingness to address such taboo subject matter, I began in my youthful manner to systematize what I was reading. I discovered that sex is good. That sex is a gift from God. I learned that there is good sex and there is bad sex. I discovered that sex had boundaries. I learned that God, being good, had placed those boundaries there for a reason. I saw that God had designed sex to be enjoyed in marriage and any sex that fell outside of this was wrong. Marriage by definition was between a man and a woman. Homosexual sex was off limits as either an abomination or as dishonorable passion that degraded the body. I didn't know exactly what an abomination was, or how gay sex degraded the body, but the clarity of the message was not lost on me.

In a large circus tent at an alternative Christian music festival in my final year of high school, with bare feet and hands raised in worship, I handed my sexuality over to God. I had all but given up attempting to pray that I would be straightened out, and without holding back I spoke the word in my mind that I'd been preparing to say for so many years, "celibacy." Lead me God into a life of singleness for your glory.

The lyrics to the song we were singing spoke of desert places and roads marked with suffering. Over sleepless nights I'd counted up the cost and to the deepest recesses of my heart I understood that following Jesus was worth every sacrifice I was called to make for him. Little did I know that the decision I made that night would set me on a roller coaster ride to become something of a poster child for same-sex attracted, celibate, evangelical Christianity amongst my small tribe of faithful kin. While I never asked for this position, nor sought it out, it was clear that very few people were in the situation that I was in and as the vitriolic debate warred itself on, I was able to bring a pastorally nuanced voice to the table. People came flocking.

Suddenly out of the woodwork I discovered that in my circle of friends alone there were dozens upon dozens of people who were attracted to members of the same sex. For some, I was the first person they ever told. For many it was a secret they planned to take to the grave. Some had been abused as children, though most hadn't. Some were married. Some came out openly as gay and were kicked out of their homes. All of them had serious mental health concerns by the time they stumbled across me. None of them had asked for this. I discovered that in sharing my own personal story of wrestling with the biblical texts and committing to a potential lifetime of celibacy, I was able to naturally provide a small semblance of hope to a band of wounded soldiers that were so desperately in need of light. I was somebody who they could rally around and emulate. Most of all, I was able to point them to the Jesus that I had come to know and love—the Jesus who had sacrificed everything for me, and who now called us to sacrifice all for him.

On the road of celibacy I filled my library with literature which encouraged me on my pursuit. I lapped up Wesley Hill and Sam Allberry. Henri Nouwen became a personal hero and Rosaria Butterfield articulated perfectly exactly what I knew I needed to hear. Yarhouse and Gagnon became my homeboys and The Gospel Coalition sexuality discussion was a permanently open tab on my browser. And yet in the back of my mind, somewhere deep inside, there were questions beginning to surface. I couldn't help but feeling that there was something in this discussion that I'd missed, and that wasn't getting the airtime that it required. For some time I managed to silence these questions, as though fighting off a guilty conscience. I had heard about a growing body of literature from evangelical perspectives that were positing the idea that monogamous same-sex relationships may actually be compatible with a faithful reading of the Bible, but I was readily able to dismiss these as fringe voices capitulating to the hyper-sexualized culture in which we found ourselves.

By this stage I was halfway towards completing my Master of Divinity degree at a conservative theological college. I loved that college. I still love that college. It filled me day after day with grand thoughts about the God that I was preparing myself to serve in full-time ministry. In that space I was surrounded by men and women who sharpened me and carried me. I poured hours into grasping the languages of the ancients, soaking in the rich tapestry of church history, and equipping myself for the weighty task of pastoring God's church. Most of all, I learned how to read the Bible with the respect and diligence that it deserves.

During my time there, I finally plucked up the courage to call upon a number of close friends to assist me in revisiting the theological conclusions that I'd come to as a teenager. I knew that as a matter of intellectual integrity, and in order to better defend my traditionalist readings of the texts, I had to engage with the opposition at some point and there seemed no better time to do so than while I was surrounded by people who would hold me to the text. Over the course of a year I opened up the books again, this time from both sides of the argument.

What I discovered there terrified me. It terrified me because it destabilized me. What destabilized me most was not so much the conclusions that the affirming camp had come to, but rather the way that they had got there. Where I had expected to find a band of liberal quasi-theologians who had thrown the Bible under the proverbial bus, I instead found faithful, intelligent, and sincere Christians using the exact exegetical methodologies that I was being taught in my conservative education. In fact, I remember very clearly one night, sitting in my room poring over the texts and coming to the stark realization that some people in the affirming camp exhibited a far higher regard for Scripture than many who used the Bible to defend a traditional sexual ethic.

Once again, I found myself in the precarious position of presenting an outward appearance of having everything sorted whilst my internal status had undergone what I would later discover was a radical change. My black and white theology had left the building, and in its wake were all manner of confusingly gray tones.

But, I figured, I was biased. Because of my undoubtedly homosexual orientation I was bound to give a greater hearing to those that would legitimate my desires. It's difficult to articulate just how cautious I was around this. Though in my head I intellectually struggled to see the black and white prohibitions that the traditionalist camp had drawn, I knew that my heart was probably more likely to be pulled toward the affirming side. After all, "the heart is deceitful above all things" (Jer 17:9) and in matters such as this, caution was due. And so I resolved to remain celibate, traditional, and safely perched on my trajectory toward my dream job as a pastor in a thriving inner city church.

It didn't take long for things to start coming undone. Like far too many pastors I have spoken to candidly, I hoped that "fake it till you make it" would be enough of a mantra to see me through in this murky world of sexual confusion. But now in a position of greater leadership I was asked to dish out my pastoral advice for gay and lesbian people constantly. Church leaders from across the nation were contacting me for my wisdom on how to best care for people in their congregations and communities. Time and time again I watched people walk away from church. Espousing the most eloquent and well-thought-through traditional sexual ethic I could, I saw young men and women sink further and further into depression. I saw families turn on each other. I saw strong, celibate Christian leaders enter illicit affairs and secret relationships. I saw seekers walk away and young people abandon Jesus. Multiple failed marriages and a thirty-year-old's suicide were the last straws in my increasingly futile attempts to uphold and justify a sexual ethic that I no longer believed was warranted, nor indeed biblical.

To my shame, it took far too long to come to a place where I could say with integrity that it was time to stop being afraid of my heart, and to engage the intellect that God has given me. To this end I resigned from my role as pastor of the incredible church that I had grown to love so dearly and I prayerfully set out to articulate what I came to see a long time ago as a true, biblical vision for gay and lesbian people in our churches. This is what you are now reading. For over a decade I believed, lived, and taught a very different way of thinking, and now, I would like to share with you what I have learned along the way.

Optimistically assuming that you are planning on reading the rest of this book, there are a couple of things that I'd like to make clear before we go any further. As already stated, as far as I can tell, none of the ideas that I put forward in this book are new, or particularly original. Whether you interpret this as a positive or a negative is your prerogative, but wherever possible I will aim to provide you with the original source material. Please don't just take my word for it. As I write this, I am acutely aware that the nature of this world is that the gospel is constantly under attack from any number of directions, and it is the role of the church the be the pillar and buttress of truth (1 Tim 3:15). Further, as leaders in our own spheres and individuals within the church we are called to watch our lives and doctrine closely (1 Tim 4:16). I encourage you to read this book with your Bibles open, and with a readiness to engage with the many voices that are now in this discussion.

Secondly, having spent well over a decade in the traditionalist's "camp," I would like to suggest to you something I constantly am reminded of as I read widely and engage in discussion. In my experience the overwhelming majority of people who call themselves evangelical Christians and who are engaging in this realm are seeking to love well, and love deeply. There are some on the affirming side, and there are many within the secular world, who are more than willing to throw character-slamming bombs that paint the conservative church as an oppressive, power-hungry machine deliberately seeking to marginalize and silence an innocent minority. We have all heard this rhetoric, and were I not in deep personal relationship with many who still disagree with me, I would be tempted to start believing it. I hope that as you read this book, you will find none of that tone. I believe the traditional reading of Scripture in this area is wrong, and I have strong questions for some leaders as to their methods and motives for engagement, but I also know that in my years of urging people toward celibacy I was doing so out of a great sense of love both for them and for the Bible. As such, I hope that my words here will be hued with a level of grace and understanding that is often sadly missing and results in the two groups simply speaking past one another.

Finally, I would like to offer a preemptive apology of sorts. The nature of the discussion that follows is one fraught with emotive subject matter and deeply held personal identities. No doubt there will be language that you come across that may feel clunky at best and offensive to some. For example, whilst recognizing the significant disagreements that there are around these terms, I have chosen to deliberately use the terms *gay and lesbian, same-sex attracted,* and *homosexual* interchangeably. Similarly, I have chosen not to use the term *conservative* as a catchall for those who hold a traditional sexual ethic (partially because I consider myself conservative in many areas!). In this book I will used the terms "traditional" (or "non-affirming") and "affirming" for the two broad Christian views in this discussion. Using labels is often problematic, since one side or both may feel they are being judged. This is not my intention. The use of these categories will, I hope, add definition and clarity in the discussion. These are just three matters of linguistics that come to mind, but no doubt there will be plenty more. While I will try my utmost to not make generalizations or thoughtless remarks, I ask for a measure of grace as you read on.

Having outlined a (very) small portion of my story above, I confess to feeling somewhat exposed. I recognize that sharing this story places me in a position of vulnerability, but I know that in order to do this topic justice, stories like this must be told. But I am not the only one with a story like this. In fact, in offering you this chapter I am simply joining in with the thousands of voices that have already offered theirs. In so many ways, I am standing on the shoulders of the giants who have gone before me, who have braved the cultural storm during much more treacherous weather. It is to these stories that we now turn in the next chapter as we look around us and ask the question "how on earth did we get to where we are today?"

3

Where Are We, and How Did We Get Here?

"We're losing . . ."

These are two words that nobody likes to hear, ever.

Sometimes when these words are spoken, it's not a big deal and not all that surprising—like when my church's mixed netball team takes their halftime break (to be perfectly honest, I don't think they've ever had great cause for optimism). But on other occasions, when these words are spoken, they come with a far greater sense of gravitas—like when a prominent church leader stood up in front of hundreds of his peers to admit that the cultural tide of the "gay agenda" was making unprecedented headway into the pews we were trying so hard to protect, and we were "losing." At points like this we are forced to sit up and take note.

It seems as though church leaders across the Western world are pinching themselves, trying to decide amongst their ranks exactly what went wrong. A short while ago (within my lifetime) engaging in homosexual activity was illegal in much of Australia. Within the space of a few brief decades, what for millennia was deemed by the vast majority of people to be "deviant behavior" has in many countries around the world become a highly acceptable and oftentimes celebrated norm. As we continue our foray into the wide world of sexuality, I think it will be helpful to take a sweeping glance at the historical movements over the past century that have brought us to where we are at today, both within the church and in society broader. In doing this, we discover a few key moments that have radically shaped the cultural tide we find ourselves in.

A Brief History

When it comes to momentous changes in societal norms, few literary publications boast the size of sway that Alfred Kinsey managed to obtain in his dual works on sexuality. As the early decades of the twentieth century came to a close, Kinsey and his team single-handedly put research into sexual behavior on the public agenda, setting in motion the many thousands of further research pursuits that we draw on today. Initially he released a volume titled *Sexual Behavior in the Human Male* in 1948, which was followed in 1953 by its counterpart *Sexual Behavior in the Human Female*. Perhaps the most groundbreaking and controversial assertion to come out of all of his studies was this: most people are heterosexual, some people are homosexual, and some people fall somewhere between the two on a continuum of attraction (bisexual).

For most people reading this in the twenty-first century these findings feel far from radical. The sexual revolution of the '60s and '70s that was precipitated in a large part by Kinsey's research brought the notion of homosexuality into the mainstream consciousness, but it is hard to exaggerate just how profound an impact this categorization (the "Kinsey scale") had on a society which saw homosexual activity as a perverted disorder. While many of his findings were by no means entirely new, and his methodology questionable at best, Kinsey popularized the idea that for some people at least, homosexual activity was a legitimate outworking of their seemingly innate orientation.

Fast forward now to 1973, and the American Psychiatric Association (the world's largest and most influential body of psychiatrists) releases its second edition of the Diagnostics and Statistical Manual (The DSM II).[1] Causing something of a scandal in the conservative world, homosexuality had been removed from this edition as a mental illness and was instead described as a "normal expression of human sexuality."[2] From this point on in the secular professional world, being gay or lesbian was not a disease to be treated, or a disorder to be cured. Rather, it was recognized in the vast majority of scholarly literature to be a naturally occurring phenomenon. We will consider more fully the scientific realm in the next

---

1. To this day the DSM (Diagnostic and Statistical Manual) provides the benchmark for diagnosis and treatment of psychiatric disorders.

2. For a fascinating look at the developments that led to this historic decision, see Bayer, *Homosexuality and American Psychiatry*.

chapter, but for now it is important to note the seismic shift that has taken place within the past sixty years within the scientific community.

Of course, this shift stood in direct opposition to many religious institutions' prevailing traditional views, which saw any form of sexuality that was not strictly heterosexual as a form of brokenness of the created order. Whilst ever there was no discernable genetically based causation that could be pointed to, being gay or lesbian was to be understood as a treatable condition, thus giving rise to the now infamous "ex-gay" movement. Throughout the 1970s, -80s and -90s a plethora of ministries sprung up that promised deliverance from homosexuality. Organizations such as Exodus International became the go-to clubs for those seeking change.[3] Books recounting the experience of people becoming heterosexual flooded the rather niche market.[4] Hopes were high, and for a brief moment, it looked as though there was a tenable answer to thousands of people's deep concerns—it was possible to "pray the gay away."

However, it didn't take long for those hopes to start unraveling. As time marched on, stories began to emerge of those who had undergone reparative therapy and by and large, they weren't the stories that people wanted to hear. First came those who, try as they might, simply could not budge their orientation. Despite intensive therapeutic intervention and extensive, heartfelt attempts to change, their orientation remained a stubborn consistent in their life. After hundreds of hours in prayer, thousands of dollars in therapy costs, and countless nights in shameful agony, these men and women grew disillusioned by the elusive promise of "change" and began publicly recounting their experiences of failure.

Then came the "ex-ex-gay" stories. Pillar after pillar of reparative success began to crumble as those who had claimed change in their orientation came forward to say that either they'd faked it, they'd imagined it, or that it had been temporary and they were now back where they'd begun.[5] The final straw of this movement came when Alan Chambers, CEO of Exodus International, announced the complete closure of the organization and issued a public apology to those who were now calling themselves "ex-gay survivors."

---

3. An umbrella organization for more 150 "ex-gay" ministries.

4. From my own tribe in Sydney, I was particularly enamored by Keane, *What Some of You Were.*

5. This is not to say that no change is possible—we'll examine this more in chapter 4.

And so it came about that by the early 2000s, the growing majority of the traditional church had come to something of the same conclusion that the secular world had come to fifty years prior—enduring, same-sex attraction was a real thing, and it wasn't going anywhere anytime soon. A new solution was required, and it was soon found in an ancient principle. Celibacy.

This is the movement that I so wholeheartedly embraced and espoused for years. Very much in vogue today, its poster figures range from evangelicals such as Wesley Hill[6] and Sam Allberry,[7] to Catholic priests such as Henri Nouwen. Inspired by notions of friendship as discussed by the likes of Aelred of Theroux and C. S. Lewis, they seek to steward their sexuality in a way that balances modern understandings of sexuality with the traditional teachings of the church around marriage.

At this point, I'd like to be quite clear about something. Whilst disagreeing with the underlying theological suppositions, I have deep respect for a great deal of this movement. I respect the way that these men and women seek diligently to live their lives for Jesus. I understand, having been a part of the movement for so long, the genuine desire to take up one's cross and follow Jesus. I admire the sacrifice that they are making in the name of faith. Going against the greater cultural tide takes great courage, and many of the men and women I see in this movement display a level of virtue that few other Christians I know possess.

That being said, as both a pastor and friend to many gay and lesbian people, I have also seen firsthand the damage that this movement can cause. By no means is this damage intentional, but under traditional theology I do believe that it is inevitable. Indeed, I know full well that as a past proponent of celibacy as the only option for many LGBTQI people, I myself have caused deep wounds and perpetuated an ideology which has marginalized so many. To the heterosexual majority of the evangelical world, people like myself (celibate gay Christians) were seen as the answer to the culture war that was and is raging around us; with one foot in the LGB camp and one foot in the Christian camp, we were party to both and friend to all. Realistically, though, we were cripplingly lonely, devastatingly depressed, and vastly misunderstood. Later on we will look at depth into the celibacy movement and discuss its pros and cons, but at

---

6. Hill, *Washed and Waiting.*

7. Allberry, *Is God Anti-Gay?*

this point I just want to acknowledge both the faithful men and women who are part of it, and to note the existence of unintended consequences.

Today's Lay of the Land

And so it is that we have come to the climate of today's traditional, conservative church. From strong denial, to earnestly promising orientation change, to demanding lifelong commitments to celibacy, we have seen momentous shifts in our understanding of, and our response to, gay and lesbian people. In much the same way that technology has advanced rapidly, so too has our understanding of orientation, with the disorienting phenomenon now that those growing up after the 1990s find themselves in a vastly different world to those who went before them. Everything from the rhetoric found in Hollywood to the curriculum taught in our classrooms narrates a story that is profoundly foreign to past generations.

With this historical divide as our backdrop, I'd like to take a moment to look into some of the inadvertent effects of holding to the traditional theology that all homosexual relationships are inherently sinful. As we've already noted, these effects are far reaching and deeply entrenched. This is an area that has in recent years come under intense scrutiny from both affirming Christian groups and from secular psychology associations. Whilst I knew that there was something to be said about the research, I for one spent many years ignorant as to the full magnitude of the picture that it paints.

To this end, here is a sobering statistic—a same-sex attracted person is up to fourteen times more likely to attempt suicide than their heterosexual peers.[8] LGBTQI people have the highest rate of suicide of any other population group in Australia. This is consistent with vast amounts of literature that show that gay and lesbian people who regularly hear negative discourse around gay and lesbian topics (identified in the literature as primarily religiously driven) are far more likely to experience high levels of anxiety and depression.[9] As a reminder, let me point out that the statistics we are talking about here are real people's lives, navigating the crossroads of a faith and a sexuality that seem on first glance diametrically opposed to one another.

8. Rosenstreich, "LGBTI People, Mental Health, and Suicide," 3.
9. Hillier, "I Couldn't Do Both at the Same Time," 81.

When statistics like these present themselves, our prayer of course is that the church would be a safe haven for people seeking hope and that in times of despair, these individuals would find a place of rest in communities of faith. Sadly however, this is not the case. Far from mitigating the turbulence of sexuality, the teachings of the traditional evangelical church are increasingly being seen to exacerbate an internal battle, which, across the board, is taking its toll. To take one example, in perhaps the most significant Australian study of young LGBTQI people, those who reported a religious affiliation were far more likely to self-harm than those who did not.[10]

These statistics line up perfectly with my experience, not only as someone who has been through this journey myself, but also as a pastor walking alongside people. When I hear statistics like these, I can't help but think of people like my friend who, having grown up in church, refuses to set foot in one now. He desperately longs for community and eagerly wants to believe that Jesus loves him. He has told me that he would go back to church in a heartbeat, were it not for his sexuality and the pain that it has caused.

Another friend comes to mind who attempted to take his life after years of failed ex-gay therapy and a subsequent commitment to celibacy; or another who, for the past six years has been seeing a psychologist on a regular basis just to help her face the day; or another who, despite being an active church leader has consistently engaged in random sexual hookups time and time again because he is so desperately lonely.

At this point it should perhaps come as no surprise to discover that the perception of the church from the outside world is now inextricably tied to the issue of the church's sexual ethics. Kinnaman and Lyons's research into deterrents to the Christian faith amongst young people concludes that "the gay issue has become the "big one" . . . surfacing a spate of negative perceptions: judgmental, bigoted, sheltered, right-wingers, hypocritical, insincere, and uncaring. Outsiders say our hostility toward gays—not just opposition to homosexual politics and behaviors but distain for gay individuals—has become virtually synonymous with the Christian faith."[11] What this research is observing is not that all Christians hate gay people, but rather that this is the overwhelming perception of the church from those who are watching on. I remember sitting with

10. Hillier, "I Couldn't Do Both at the Same Time," 84.

11. Kinnaman and Lyons, *Unchristian*, 92.

one pastor who outright dismissed these perceptions as nothing but ill-informed judgments from a prejudiced populace. Somewhat ironically, that very week I sat with someone in his congregation who was wrestling with their sexuality, was severely suicidal, and was terrified of how that pastor would respond if he found out.

These stories scare me, and I sincerely hope that they make you uncomfortable as well, because they are all too real. At the risk of laboring the point, whether you know it or not, there is every chance that these experiences are happening to people you know. People in our congregations, in our youth groups, and Sunday schools are facing this reality. Perhaps you are reading this book because this is your brother, your daughter, your cousin. Perhaps you are reading this because you yourself are facing the daunting reality of being same-sex attracted in a traditional conservative church setting. This is the sobering terrain of today's church.

But it isn't the only story.

If we tilt the camera of our historical narrative just a few degrees to the left or right we discover a whole different set of voices that up until fairly recently have been on the margins of the dialogue. I've known for a long time that this small but persistent group has slowly been gaining momentum but, to my shame, I did a marvelous job at ignoring them for the majority of my life. In a strange plot twist in life's roller coaster, I now find myself to be one of them and to be honest, they make for rather good company. Here at the crossroad of competing voices we begin to see a fork in the road for Christianity. To my surprise, I've found over and over again that this fork is not a choice between liberal or conservative; nor is it a divide between those who hold the Bible as their highest authority and those who have compromised its position. In fact, far from being the devastating chasm that it is so often painted as, I have found that the two competing camps have far more in common than either side often lets on.

So why is it that only now, after millennia of silence from the affirming side, are faithful, Bible-believing Christians beginning to change their mind? I want to suggest three reasons. No doubt there are many more reasons, but I hope that these broad brush-strokes will give something of a framework for how this change has come about.

As we have already seen the generations that are stepping into early positions of church leadership now grew up in a post-Kinsey, post-sexual revolution world. Likewise, the general makeup of our congregations has changed dramatically, with young Christians facing a world that is considerably more hostile toward Christianity, and that no longer takes the conservative doctrines of the church as unquestionable moral truth. This has inevitably given rise to a generational chasm that sees the vast majority of church leaders (of older generations) failing to engage with the questions that the people in their congregations are posing. For people born after the sexual revolution, it is no longer a culturally imbedded assumption that gay and lesbian relationships are inherently evil. Nor is there a prevailing notion of silence on the topic. I have sat with so many people who have told me that they are happy to say that the Bible is against homosexual relationships, but for the life of them they simply can't say why it is that the Bible would offer such prohibitions. They have a law, but no moral backing behind it, and for a generation adept at recognizing moral duplicity, this is proving to be tenuous ground.

Secondly, up until relatively recently, very few people actually knew anyone who was openly gay or lesbian. Today we would be hard pressed to find many people in the West who don't have a relative or close friend who is openly LGB in their orientation. When this relational affiliation occurs, something of a paradigm shift begins to take place as categories, which have been so carefully constructed, are forced to change their shape or take on new meaning. It's easy to call "the gays" heretics and hell-bound when they are "out there." Distance makes ignorance an easy option, and imbibing the stereotype of wayward sexual deviants is viable whilst no one is around to break that mold. But when it is your family member whom you know as a godly woman who is wrestling with unwanted feelings of attraction to members of the same sex, these categories come crumbling down. Excitingly, for many Christians, far from undermining their faith or driving them from the Scriptures, this has forced people to go back to the Scriptures and wrestle with key texts and theological ideas once again. This isn't to say that people are placing their personal relationships in authority over the Scriptures, but rather, their personal relationships are causing them to think about Scripture much more closely, with new questions and fresh lenses.

Thirdly, as people are driven back to the Bible to examine the texts for themselves, they have done so with historically unparalleled access to information. Unlike any age before, the Internet has ensured that there is immediate access to a vast and growing body of literature which, let's face it, isn't the usual stock for the average church library. Congregations are no longer bound to the interpretations of Scripture that their pastors espouse on a Sunday at church, and pastors are no longer relying solely on their limited collection of commentaries. People are discovering the broader range of definitions that many of our Bibles bluntly translate as "homosexual." They are reading the story of Sodom and Gomorrah with newly discovered ancient lenses. They are revisiting the Levitical laws, and armed with a greater contextual awareness, are rigorously reading the texts. In short, more and more people are finding traditional views far less watertight than they had previously thought. The clear prohibitions against same-sex relationships are turning out to be decidedly less clear than they'd been taught, and the positive affirmations of marriage as between a man and woman alone are proving insufficient to exclude their gay and lesbian brothers and sisters from the church.

When I resigned from my role as a pastor of a highly conservative church in order to pursue theology that affirmed the place of LGBTQI people, I wasn't sure how my church would respond. It being an inner-city, highly educated congregation, I had tentative hopes that some people might take the opportunity to ask questions and engage in dialogue. What I hadn't expected was the rallying cries of support that I received in private messages as Bible study leaders, ministry coordinators, and welcoming team leaders all came out of the woodwork to tell me that they'd been reading theology for themselves, and weren't convinced by the traditional church's teachings. So many of them knew gay and lesbian people, and simply could not equate the theology taught by the church with what they saw around them. In much the same manner, they'd read the traditionalist arguments and could not reconcile them with the biblical texts.

This is the story that we now find ourselves in. This is the "watershed" moment in modern church history. The slow opening of the closet doors for gay and lesbian people in our churches has been a long and arduous task, and at the risk of sounding clichéd, too many lives have been lost. I love the church, and in every way I consider it my home. As the bride of Christ it is precious and is to be cherished, honored, and respected. But given the tumultuous lay of the land that we have covered in this chapter, I can no longer stand silently and watch it go down a trajectory that I see to be theologically unwarranted and painfully damaging to so many of its own. When I see within its midst actions that do not reflect the heart of Jesus, I am honor bound to gently point it in a direction that perhaps is more in line with his. To this end, the next chapter will seek to bring some clarity to the discussion around the lived experience of what it means to be gay or lesbian, before diving into the Bible to carefully discern God's will for his people today.

When the church leader I mentioned earlier admitted to the gathering of his peers that "we're losing," he was speaking directly to the fact that a branch of theology that affirmed the place of gay people in the life of the church was gaining momentum. In his mind, this constituted a deep wound that required tactical management and strategic damage control. He spoke about it with disdain and despair. I couldn't help but note the undertones of us versus them in his message.

But, I thought, what if he's wrong? What if the rise in the voices of gay and lesbian people is not a battlefield to be fought, but rather a blessing to be cherished? What if the abundant gifts of LGBTQI Christians I knew were nurtured and their thirsty hearts watered. What if God actually has placed these people in our paths not to fight against, but to learn from?

And so under my breath, inaudible to the people around me, I whispered "You're not losing. You're winning." He may not realize it yet, but I pray that one day he will come to see that homosexual voices are not the enemy. *I* am not his enemy. Rather, I am convinced that when gay and lesbian people are heard, the whole church will be blessed with a deeper understanding of the character of God.

And that's got to count as a win.

4

Just So We Are on the Same Page, What Does it Mean to "Be Gay"?

Ryan is a funny guy. A life-of-the-party kind of guy. You know how some humans have the ability to enter a room and be instantly liked by everybody, without breaking a sweat? Ryan is one of those people. I met Ryan at a church that I once attended and what struck me most about this young man was how happy he seemed to be. He laughed like very few people I know. His smile was contagious, and he had the gift of bringing his joy with him wherever he went.

But I was never naïve enough to think that all was sunshine and roses in Ryan's world. Ryan is a gay man, and after countless conversations with people in his shoes, I have learned that it doesn't take much digging to find a history fraught with challenges. It turns out, had I met Ryan just a few years earlier, I would have found him in a mental health ward having just attempted to take his life for the third time. For this man, being both gay and Christian had not been a possibility, and following the leadership of the church he attended at the time, he undertook intensive therapy to straighten himself out. High on a cocktail of antidepressants and hormone supplements, Ryan committed himself to weeklong fasts, multiple rounds of exorcisms, and around-the-clock prayer. Fully convinced that God promised to heal him of his homosexuality and shamed into thinking of himself as an abomination, Ryan faced the desperate disillusionment that can only come from the dawning realization that you are gay; you are an outcast; you are everything that the church fears—and nothing is going to change that.

I shouldn't have to say this, but here it is: Ryan didn't choose to be gay. Neither did I. Neither of us woke up one day and thought to ourselves, "Hey, I'm going to be attracted to guys today." That would be absurd, and to be sure, I know of no recorded instance where this has been the case, or any scholar who would consistently espouse this. Why would you? If I'm totally honest, I would give almost anything in order to have grown up straight. Ryan's parents and church leaders worked under the assumption that being gay was a temporary, adjustable state. So did Ryan. So did millions of others. Tragically for us, the reality of our "gayness" stubbornly refuses to budge, and so we have been forced to go back to the drawing board in order to rethink two of the fundamental questions that we are going to address in this chapter: How did I end up gay? And can I ever change?

Before we begin, I want to issue a warning. Chances are, you probably won't find the answers offered here particularly satisfying. If you want black and white, you've come to the wrong place. When it comes to sexuality we are constantly walking through all sorts of gray, and as we take a snapshot of the soaring mound of studies in this area, what we do know pales into insignificance in contrast to what still escapes our understanding. With this in mind, let's start with something that at least feels somewhat manageable: what do we mean when we say "gay"?

Defining Homosexuality

I fully recognize that definitions are contested domain, but for the sake of clarity, the definitions I have been, and will continue to be using throughout this book are as follows:

Sexual Orientation: Orientation refers to an enduring experience of attraction toward a specific group of people. A *heterosexual* orientation is toward those of the opposite sex to oneself (hetero=other). A *homosexual* orientation is toward those of the same sex as oneself (homo=same or one). *Bisexual* refers to an enduring attraction to both men and women, sometimes of equal strength, though generally people who are bisexual experience greater attraction to one gender than the other (bi=two). Note in our definition that the experience is described as enduring. This is important as many people can recall times of being attracted to members of the opposite sex, but this does not constitute an orientation per se.

Somewhat confusingly, when we talk about *sexual* orientation, we aren't using the term *sexual* to exclusively speak about erotic arousal (though this is usually present). *Sexual* in this sense is much deeper, also incorporating the ability to experience an emotional and/or romantic attachment—what we might simplistically call "falling in love."

Lesbian: exclusively refers to women who experience a homosexual orientation.

Gay: is an umbrella term that is often used to describe any person with a homosexual orientation, though in many communities it is most commonly associated with men.

Same-sex-attracted: This term seeks to describe the experience of people having a homosexual orientation, without relying on the now somewhat loaded terms "gay" and "lesbian". Here is where things get a touch more complicated. The difficulty with both "lesbian" and "gay" is that over the course of time they have come to mean more than simply "an enduring attraction," and have taken on often far reaching social, political, and cultural connotations that many people (predominately conservative Christians) seek to distance themselves from. When somebody describes himself or herself as "gay," they may well be stating that they have an enduring attraction to members of the same sex; but they may also be describing their allegiance with one or more gay communities; they may be implying that they have chosen to self-identify and sexually express themselves according to their orientation. Many Christians who have a homosexual orientation are, given their theological assumptions, understandably uncomfortable with elements of these identity-laden statements. For the sake of this book, when I use the terms "gay" and "lesbian," unless otherwise stated, I am using them in the strictest sense of enduring attraction.

A Quick Headcount

It is almost impossible to find accurate statistics that show how many people experience a homosexual or bisexual orientation. The only data we have is self-reported and despite enormous strides in removing the shame around matters of sexuality, most analysts assume that there are still a large number of people who, while having a homosexual or bisexual orientation, would never tick a box saying so on any survey.[1] As such, there are wild variations amongst studies attempting to estimate the figures. Further, there is no denying the fact that even the most scrupulous research has elements of bias, and one study's comparison found that pro-gay organizations were likely to report a 10 percent prevalence of homosexuality, while anti-gay organizations were more likely to report this at 1 to 3 percent.[2] That's a huge difference! So what are we to believe?

Remember Alfred Kinsey? He's the one who put research into sexuality on the map. Kinsey's research during the 1940s and 1950s concluded that 8 percent of men and 4 percent of women are exclusively homosexual. Kinsey's sample population was significantly flawed, however, and more recent, far larger studies have put estimates at a much lower percentage. For example, the National Health and Social Life Survey suggested 2.8 percent of males and 1.4 percent of women reported being homosexual or bisexual.[3] Far more studies have placed the figure at somewhere between these, with a much higher prevalence amongst women.[4] Apologies for the lack of precision, but I tend to think it would be safe to conclude that amongst males, somewhere around 1 to 4 percent of the population are gay or bisexual, and amongst females around 2 to 5 percent, with females significantly more likely to report bisexuality.[5]

The Cause

Even at a conservative estimate of 2 percent, we are talking about huge numbers of people. These are people who, confined to the suffocation of the closet, have wrestled with their sexuality day in and day out for decades. Misunderstood by their societies and maligned by their social circles, these people, people like myself, have spent countless nights lying awake asking the question "why am I gay?" But the answer lies tantalizingly out of reach.

1. Ashford et al., *Human Behavior in the Social Environment*, 510.

2. Pruitt, *Size Matters*, 21.

3. Ashford et al., *Human Behavior in the Social Environment*, 510.

4. As discussed in Savin-Williams, *Who's Gay?*

5. Of course, there are many factors that we could explore here that are outside the scope of this book. We will limit ourselves to the most predominant ideas arising in current literature.

And then there are their parents who ask the same questions—"did I do something wrong?" A distraught mother once asked me, "Was I too absent?" A father muses, "Were we too overbearing?" For some the question comes down to blame—if we can put our finger on the cause, then justice can be served or repentance offered. For others, it's a question of prevention—"how do I make sure that my daughter grows up to be straight?" Each year study after study comes forth and as the desperately eager scour the information torrent of our age, clarity remains as elusive as ever. We can however say this: we know more about sexuality than any age before us, and the cumulative research amounts to a considerable leap in the right direction.

In determining the cause of homosexuality, there are two lines of thought that diverged radically in the nineteenth century and continue to do so today. On the one hand, there is the question of nature: biological processes, genetic dispositions, and hormonal influences. This field of study was opened up by Maria Kertbury who (it is claimed) coined the term *homosexual* in 1868 in a bid to demonstrate to the scientific community that some people were "born that way."

Almost simultaneously, another researcher was growing in popularity, asserting that nurture (social, psychological, and cultural influences) was the cause of deviant sexual orientations. As history developed, Sigmund Freud's thesis was adopted with far greater vigor, under the assumption that if environmental factors were the cause, then treatment was a vastly more viable option.

With nature and nurture as our two overarching potential causes, we would do well to now look briefly at some of the prominent theories that are currently circulating. We will assess some of their strengths, and consider some of their limitations, beginning with what has perhaps been the most controversial of them all, the gay gene.

The Gene

Here's the argument: statistically speaking, there is a strong likelihood that you, dear reader, have brown eyes. If you do, congratulations. You are well and truly in with the majority. Spare a thought for the rest of us with blue, green, or hazel eyes, because you know as well as we do that we had no say in the matter—the pigmentation of our eyes was sequenced on our behalf well before we could voice any objection. The same is true for our hair color, our height, the size of our feet, the shape of our noses, and ten million other factors which are determined not by our will, but by our allocated genetic material. What if the same was true for our sexuality? Some factors seem to point in this direction. For example, genealogical studies suggest that there is at least some form of heritability involved, with gay men more likely to have more gay uncles and cousins on their mother's side than on their father's side.[6] This fits with research that has identified a portion on the X chromosome (from the mother) associated with sexual orientation. Further, some studies suggest that there are a number of characteristics that, somewhat strangely, are more common in homosexual people than in the average population. For example, gay men are 3.6 times more likely to have a counterclockwise hair whorl (the spiral shape of hair on the back of the head) than the average population,[7] and are more often left handed (a factor which is largely genetically predetermined).[8]

With the advent of complex genetic mapping, the possibility of locating this gene has for many felt like a very real possibility. But as of yet, no such gene has been located. For many, this lack of location is enough to remove any concept of a gay gene from the equation.[9] This is a premature conclusion, and fails to grasp the complexity of genetics. If we take handedness (a relatively simple trait) as a comparison, we see that scientists are still baffled by how complex a genetic process is involved. Whilst we have identified some genes that we think are pertinent, we still have no clear understanding of the precise genetic material that determines whether somebody is left or right handed. We don't conclude from this lack of clarity that there are no genetic factors at play in this case, and nor should we when it comes to homosexuality. Rather we humbly recognize the limits of our current understanding and continue research in this important field.

One area that is making significant inroads in this field is *epigenetics*,[10] looking at the impact of external factors on genetic material. It has long been recognized that there are many variables (environmental factors, chemical and hormonal balances, diet, drugs, etc.) that have the

6. Hamer et al., "A Linkage between DNA," 321–27.

7. Klar, "Excess of Counterclockwise Scalp Hair-Whorl," 251.

8. Blanchard, "Review of Theory and Handedness," 51–57.

9. As does for example Joe Dallas, past president of ex-gay therapy supplier Exodus International. Dallas, *The Gay Gospel?*, 114.

10. Heil et al., *Epigenetics*, 187.

ability to activate or switch on certain genes. Is it possible that sexuality, as complex as it is, might lie somewhere in this domain?

Prenatal Hormonal Influences

This brings us to our second major theory suggested in current literature. As people researched the prevalence of non-heterosexuality, a curious trend emerged. Men who are gay tend to have older brothers. In fact, the more older brothers a male has, the higher the likelihood that he will be gay. Naturally, this led to a significant body of literature exploring the relationship between fraternal birth order and sexuality.[11] Interestingly, it was found that the mother's ability to produce the hormone testosterone at the precise stage of development in which the baby's brain was being encoded was significantly hindered if she had previously given birth to males. Nobody can be certain as to why this is the case, but many have theorized that her body builds an immune reaction to the heightened presence of the hormone, and thus the development of the baby's brain is in some manner altered. One significant study reported its conclusions in no uncertain terms:

> The fetal brain develops during the intrauterine period in the male direction through a direct action of testosterone on the developing nerve cells, or in the female direction through the absence of this hormone surge. In this way, our gender identity (the conviction of belonging to the male or female gender) and sexual orientation are programmed or organized into our brain structures when we are still in the womb. There is no indication that social environment after birth has an effect on gender identity or sexual orientation.[12]

In other words, if testosterone is not activated, or is lacking during this specific brain developmental phase, the "male-ness" of the baby (including his sexuality) will be, in some manner at least, altered. Of course, this can't possibly account for all people who experience homosexuality. For example, many gay men don't have older brothers, and while the disruption of the hormone at the critical stage may still be present, we are still in the dark as to why. More to the point, it doesn't give us any indication as to why females develop homosexual attraction. As such, most researchers

11. Reviewed substantially in Blanchard, "Review of Theory and Handedness."
12. Garcia-Falguieras and Swaab, "Sexual Hormones and the Brain," 22.

are confident that the above study overreaches the data when it concludes that the social environment has no effect on sexual orientation.

In order to establish credibility for any prenatal or gene-related theory, some researchers have relied heavily on identical twin studies, supposing that the identical genetic material that the twins share would naturally lead to a correlation in sexuality—if one twin is gay, and homosexuality is determined prior to birth, then we would expect the other to also be gay. Some studies have returned significant results in this direction (up to 50 percent correlation),[13] however others have placed the figure much lower (around 20 percent).[14] Either way, given the complexity of the genetic process shown in epigenetics, many are shying away from assessing twin studies with undue weight. Rather, they are acknowledging the fact that while genetics may play a role in determining the sexuality of any given person, it is most likely not the only factor involved. For that, we need to look to the other sciences.

The Parent-Child Relationship

In regard to sexual development, psychoanalytic theories place the parent-child relationship as the primary causation for any non-heterosexual attraction. The early years of a child's life are critical for a huge number of key milestones from language to socialization, from motor skills to empathy. It has long been recognized that disruptions in the first years of life can have ongoing and far reaching implications. When it comes to being gay, this theory suggests that a young boy, for example, consciously or unconsciously patterns his personality after his father. If the father is close and intimate, and demonstrates heterosexuality for the boy, then the boy will follow in his footsteps. If the father is unavailable either physically or emotionally (for example he is a distant father or is physically or emotionally abusive), then the modeling process breaks down and the male identification process is derailed. According to this theory, this often results in a tightening of the relationship between the mother and son, as a compensation for what is lacking in the father figure. The net result is a lack of security in the boy's masculinity as he grows up and a subsequent erotic attraction toward the male figures that he craves.

13. Bailey and Pillard, "A Genetic Study of Male Sexual Orientation," 1087.

14. Bailey et al., "Genetic and Environmental Influences," 524–36.

The most noteworthy studies that hold this as a predominant cause of homosexuality, even amongst the psychotherapeutic community, date back to the 1960s.[15] Very few recent studies maintain that it should heavily inform therapy or intervention.[16] And for good reason.

It is statistically true that there are a significant number of people who report experiencing a distant or cold mother or father, who also identify as homosexual. However, the majority of studies that claim this statistic have been criticized as their sample populations were exclusively patients seeking help, usually for a number of compounding issues.[17] We should therefore recognize that it is also statistically true that the vast majority of people who are gay, lesbian, or bisexual had warm and intimate relationships with their parents. Likewise, it is also readily apparent that the vast majority of people who report distant or cold parents do not also experience same-sex attraction. To this end, a number of studies have shown that adults who were physically abused or suffered neglect as children were no more likely than the general population to identify as homosexual.[18]

The most that we can say in regards to psychoanalytic theories is that there are people who experience both a distant father or mother figure, and who also identify as homosexual. Extending this statement to assume evidence of causation (that distance *caused* the homosexuality) is reaching beyond the evidence available. And yet despite the vital flaws in this assumption, many Christians continue to believe that it is a fundamental factor. The result of this is that many parents of gay people face unwarranted blame and misplaced shame in our churches and communities. Ambiguity is never a pleasant experience, and it is natural that people would seek to place responsibility in parents' hands as a means of restoring clarity. It is my contention that rather than blame, it would be far wiser to offer parents of gay teenagers unwavering support. Rather than questioning their parenting, a far more appropriate response would be to remind them that their child's sexual orientation does not define them, and your community's love for them is not conditional on their attractions.

---

15. The most significant being Bieber and Wilbur, *Homosexuality*.

16. This phenomenon is reported even-handedly by the theologically conservative psychologist Mark Yarhouse, *Homosexuality and the Christian*.

17. Yarhouse, *Homosexuality and the Christian*, 72.

18. Wilson and Spatz-Widom, "Same-Sex Sexual Relationships and Cohabitation."

The Effects of Child Abuse

A second statistically significant factor we need to look at is the correlation between adults who report same-sex sexual activity and who also, tragically, experienced sexual abuse as a child. As I have listened to the stories of gay and lesbian people around me, the ramifications of such abuse of the innocent reverberate powerfully. There is no denying the fact that when the sexual development of a child is disrupted by the violation of their bodies, the process is skewed, and even with significant therapy, the victims experience the impact for decades to come. I have sat with numerous people who have shared just such a journey with me, and it breaks my heart.

Gently, we must look into the claim that those who are sexually abused as children will, or are more likely to, grow up to be homosexual. We must look into this claim because despite its widely held position, there is significant evidence to suggest that the claim is not as simple as it may appear.

In much the same way as psychoanalytic theories, we begin by recognizing that there are many, many people who experience sexual abuse that grow up to be heterosexual. Concurrently, there are many who never experience sexual abuse and grow up to be homosexual. To this end it should be noted that many of the studies that report a strong correlation between adult homosexual orientation and childhood sexual abuse take their sample populations from those who present for therapy.[19] Given that those who seek the assistance of a professional usually have compounding factors warranting therapeutic intervention, this sample population does not accurately represent those who have same-sex attraction.

Indeed, one of the largest studies completed to date that followed a large group of individuals over a thirty-year time period found that amongst women there was no correlation between childhood sexual abuse and adult homosexual identification. This study also found that men who were sexually abused as children were more likely to engage in sexual activity with members of the same sex, but did not adopt a gay identity. Some have concluded from this that their earlier experiences lead them to a place of questioning and exploration without necessarily developing a homosexual orientation. [20]

19. See for example Jones and Yarhouse, Ex-Gays?, 164.
20. Wilson and Spatz-Widom, "Same-Sex Sexual Relationships and Cohabitation."

This is not to say that childhood sexual abuse plays *no* part in sexual development. The question remains as to whether or not the abuse itself is what determines orientation. In the vast majority of cases, we must conclude that abuse, along with parental relationships, play a peripheral role in the establishing of a homosexual orientation.

And so, when all things are considered, I find myself at something of an unsatisfying conclusion. As much as I want to point to a cause of homosexuality, I am forced to concede the fact that the complexity of any person's sexual development is vastly greater than the knowledge that we currently possess. What does seem to be clear is this: natural factors such as genetics and prenatal hormones play a vital role in determining sexuality, being impacted on by a plethora of external factors that are vastly outside of any one person's control. In other words, it is likely that both nature and nurture are intricately interwoven.

Can a Person Change?

Along with a number of conservative Christians, Joe Dallas asserts that God promises to heal people of their homosexuality. Dallas comes to this conclusion by claiming that Paul is stating a change in orientation is in view in 1 Corinthians 6:9–11:

> Do not be deceived: neither the sexually immoral, nor idolaters, nor adulterers, nor men who practice homosexuality, nor thieves, nor the greedy, nor drunkards, nor revilers, nor swindlers will inherit the kingdom of God. And such were some of you. But you were washed, you were sanctified, you were justified in the name of the Lord Jesus Christ and by the Spirit of our God. (ESV)

In order to make this point, Dallas translates "men who practice homosexuality" as "homosexuals" and thus being "washed" and "sanctified" incorporates the process of becoming heterosexual.[21] Even with this flawed translation, this is the only portion of Scripture that could be interpreted in such a way, and the past twenty years of failed ex-gay ministries has seen all but a small handful of theologians reverse their position on the matter. Being "washed" cleanses people of their sins, not their attractions,

---

21. Dallas, *The Gay Gospel?*, 119–22. The translation of this term—"men who practice homosexuality"—is highly contested and will be the subject of our investigation in chapter 9.

and being "sanctified" makes them more Christlike, not "straight." For a theologian to state that God's intention for gay people is to make them heterosexual is to promise that which God does not, and in doing so sets them up for failure from the outset.

This isn't to say that God cannot transform people. He most certainly can! But he does not promise that he will, nor does he demand that homosexual people seek so-called reparative therapy. There are a small number of people who recount change, however as we have already stated, the vast majority of people experience little to none.

Amazingly, in 2009, the American Psychological Association concluded that in the small number of cases where change is experienced, this is rarely in reference to the person's orientation (the direction or strength of their attraction), but rather their change is in regards to their identification. In other words, they are still homosexual but they no longer identify as a gay man or woman—their attractions remain present, but they have chosen to not act out on their attractions in a sexual manner.[22] Most people who hold traditional views of sexuality are now in agreement.

As a side note, I remember a number of people who assured me that in the future I would find a female beautiful enough to "turn" me. Many told me that they hoped that one day I would experience a strong enough attraction to lead to a marriage. Hays[23] (from a traditional theology) and Brownson[24] (who holds an affirming view) both even-handedly approach this topic and warn that unless there is a significant change in a person's orientation, it is almost always unwise for a homosexual person to pursue a heterosexual marriage. Of course, this cannot be a blanket rule, but wisdom should be sought in order to discern a viable path for any individual.

God in the Midst of It All

There are those who spend their days arguing the causes of homosexuality until they are blue in the face. For some on the affirming side, proving that homosexuality is in some way biologically influenced or unchangeable amounts to the conclusion same-sex relationships are perfectly natural (after all, they were "born that way"). For some on the traditional

22. Glassgold et al., *Report of the American Psychological Association*, 54.

23. Hays, *The Moral Vision*, 401.

24. Brownson, *Bible, Gender, Sexuality*, 143.

side, the lack of hard evidence for a clean genetic cause suggests that the attraction is in violation of nature, and thus any person engaging in homosexual sex is an abomination in need of cleansing. As a Christian, I don't buy either argument. Equating biological influence or changeability of desire with moral neutrality without reference to God fails to take into account the standards to which the Christian has been called. For example, just because a heterosexual is born with a desire for sex with women, this does not necessarily mean that all sex with women is morally permissible, nor can we infer that every iteration of heterosexual sex possible is morally wrong—rather, we look for how God has called the individual to express his or her sexuality in this world.

On the other side of the coin, just because a biological cause of homosexuality is not perfectly understood, for the Christian, this cannot form the basis for a moral stance. Even if it were conclusively proven that a homosexual orientation is the outcome solely of human forces, this would not provide us with a sufficient data set to conclude that same-sex acts are intrinsically immoral. This way of determining ethics ultimately suggests that the only sovereignty God has is over the natural world of genetics and prenatal hormones. No, God is sovereign over all aspects of my life, and whether I am gay through genetics or through human actions, God is intricately involved and entirely in control.

When all is said and done, the Christian only has the jurisdiction to bless that which God blesses and condemn that which God condemns. And for those of us who hold his word as our highest authority, we can only claim that God condemns that which the Bible condemns. As such, we turn our attention now to God's revelation, seeking to determine what God's will is for those of us who, like Ryan and myself, are gay.

PART 2

Engaging the Bible

5

On Learning to Read

So far in our venture into the wide world of sexuality we have taken a sweeping glance at the social, cultural, and scientific transitions that have taken place over the past sixty or so years. In broad brush-strokes we've painted a picture of how it is that we have come to find ourselves at something of a fork in the road for both churches and societies the world over. If nothing else, I hope this has served as a helpful orientation into an often confusing and emotionally charged discussion, and that you are now in a better position to grasp the mountainous terrain in which we find ourselves. In many regards however, all of this has simply been by way of introduction, because (at least in my mind) the real work only now begins as we turn our attention fully to the Bible.

For Christians who hold the Bible as their highest authority, science, social trends, tradition, and experience come far down in the ladder of priority when it comes to constructing a reality of what it means to live as a man or woman of God in the world that God created. Rightly so then, it is within the pages of the Bible that the war over sexuality rages most intensely. To this end, we now enter into the largest and most vital section of this book with an analysis of what the Bible teaches (and what it does not teach) about homosexuality.

Initially, and for the sake of clarity, we will begin by outlining the theological methodology I will be using in the rest of the book. Given that I have already shown my hand to be of reformed evangelical ilk, there really should be no surprises here. This will be followed by a series of chapters as we apply this methodology to look at the small number of texts in Scripture that deal explicitly with homosexual activity.[1] Subsequently we will apply this methodology to broader doctrinal discussions regarding marriage, gender, celibacy, and sexuality.

If terms like *theological methodology* and *doctrinal discussions* amount in your mind to a sizeable load of either perplexed boredom or pointless musings, then can I urge you to hang in there! In many ways we have our work cut out for us in the coming chapters, but I assure you that the hard yards are well worth the effort, and I will do my utmost to walk us through this journey in an engaging and clear manner. With all of this in mind, have your Bible open and your mind prayerfully engaged as we seek to discern God's voice.

An Important Distinction

It was a bitterly cold winter's day, but I was inside with a steaming cup of coffee and a good friend. It so happened that this friend had heard somewhere on the grapevine that my understanding of what the Bible says about sexuality had changed and was intrigued as to how I had come to the conclusions that I had, and so I'd offered to meet up with her and begin a dialogue. After a brief introduction in which I told her that, indeed, I did not think that the Bible condemned loving, monogamous same-sex relationships, she opened the Bible. Going straight to Leviticus 18, she pointed to verse 22, which states, as clear as day, "Do not have sexual relations with a man, as one does with a woman; that is detestable." I looked at her in mock surprise as though I hadn't seen that passage before and in my shamefully well-practiced sarcastic manner informed her that she had successfully undermined my years of poring relentlessly over the Bible. If only someone had thought to open Leviticus with me earlier!

It may be simple, but this little vignette demonstrates to me something of the discussion that is currently taking place in so many spheres. On one level, so many people in the church are just entering the realm of sexuality and are looking to the Bible and discovering Leviticus 18 and 20. Passages such as this seem to be unequivocally against any form of homosexual behavior, and so here the discussion ends. But on another level, those who have been in the game for a bit longer (both in the traditional and affirming positions) are wrestling with other questions—questions about the place of Leviticus 18 in Jewish literature; about how Paul

---

1. Gen 19; Lev 18:22, 20:13; Rom 1:24–27; 1 Cor 6:9; and 1 Tim 1:10.

understood the Levitical code; about how Jesus' death and resurrection impacts the manner in which we are to apply these laws in the church today; and the list goes on. These are questions which can dramatically alter how we understand the book of Leviticus as a whole. Much the same questions are being asked of the books of Genesis, Romans, the Corinthians, and Timothy, where other such prohibitions are found.

It may seem like a strange distinction, but it needs to be said that when it comes to any text of the Bible, we aren't simply seeking to understand *what it says* (we've all read the passages) but we are also attempting to work out *what it means*. The words may be there in black and white, and may be readable by a five-year-old, but as we'll see, the task of appropriating them to our lives today is something of a more difficult task. If you are familiar with the rest of Leviticus and its abundance of foreign-feeling rules and regulations, this difficulty shouldn't be surprising to you at all. It's the old "should we all avoid shellfish (Lev 11:12) and mixed cotton (Lev 19:19)?" dilemma.

If you stop and think about it, the task that we are attempting when we read any section of the Bible is a strangely disorienting culture collision that demands an openness to entering into a world that is extraordinarily different from the world of the twenty-first century. As we "do theology" within the safety of our living rooms, we open the pages of the Bible in English and are transported into times and places that we can only scratch the surface of understanding. One moment, our library of canonical literature takes us to the heart of the Ancient Near East with all of its warring tribes and pagan cultic practices; and in the next moment we are in Roman-occupied Israel, engaging with Greek philosophers and church pioneers. One moment we are seeking to understand ancient Jewish marriage rituals, and the next we are reading about first-century methods of execution and burial rites. We move from dowries to death sentences in a matter of chapters. Not only is our current culture radically different from the Bible in terms of era and location, but even within the Bible there are radically different cultures being described.

And yet, throughout it all, we read of a God who is working in time and space, through flawed individuals, nations, and cultures, to bring together a people characterized by justice and worship. The stunning unity of the Bible warrants serious study as we seek to apply it to our lives today. This process of understanding and applying that I have just described is what we call hermeneutics. It is the task of getting our heads around a text in order to discern what it means for us today.

In a strange (perhaps nerdy) way, hermeneutics gets me excited. The process of understanding the character of God and his will for our lives is the task of theology, and has often been described as thinking God's thoughts after him. What greater joy could there be in life than venturing into the very mind of God to grasp the character of the divine and this triune God's plans for our lives today? If all of this seems far too big a task for you, and the thought of moving past *what it says* in ink to *what it means* in my life today feels like an impossible goal, let's take some time now to break it down into some simpler steps. As I've said before, none of this process is new, nor is it unique to the topic of homosexuality. In fact, what we're about to go through is the exact process that pastors do every time they sit down to write a sermon. As we'll see, you already do much of this task intuitively.

With Prayer and Humility

Second Timothy 3:16–17 is the perfect place to start as we consider the task ahead: "All Scripture is God-breathed and is useful for teaching, rebuking, correcting, and training in righteousness, so that the servant of God may be thoroughly equipped for every good work." These words remind us of both the centrality and sufficiency of the Bible. As a Christian approaches the Bible, they do not sit over it as though it were a draft to be corrected, nor do they come in order to critique it or offer suggestions. Rather, the opposite is true. As people seeking to hear from God, we are to sit under the text and allow it to shape our lives.

The Bible unashamedly calls people to do things which are by definition hard. Jesus calls his disciples to deny themselves, take up their cross, and follow him (Matt 16:24). In light of the path that Jesus took, this self-sacrificial act of obedience is one of the overarching rallying cries of the Bible. This is of course based on the premise that Scripture is inspired by God himself, and, as he is the creator who has been proven worthy of worship, the commands offered are not designed to hinder us but rather to guide us and bring glory to God through the radical obedience of the people—first in the nation of Israel, then as the church.

Notice in 2 Timothy, it is Scripture that does the teaching, correcting, and equipping. The Bible itself, through the power of the Holy Spirit at work in people's lives, prepares believers for the good works that God has prepared in advance for them to do (Eph 2:10). To this end, as we engage in God's word, I urge you to do so humbly. Each step of the way, be asking God to guide your thoughts and steps. As you pray and read, be open to new ideas that might challenge dogmatically held beliefs. And most importantly, no matter what conclusions you end up drawing, whether you are heterosexual or homosexual, be prepared to live a life of costly, self-sacrificial obedience.

There's Something in the Context

Imagine you walk past a conversation taking place and you overhear one person say to another, "I just can't believe it!" The myriad options for what this conversation might be about start racing through your mind. What is "it"? And why is "it" so unbelievable? Given this phrase's current usage, it could be that an actual event has unquestionably taken place (for example their stocks have plummeted) and they are expressing devastation; or it could be that something remarkable has happened and they're expressing joyful shock (they've just won the lottery); or, more literally, it may be that there is a concept (such as the existence of extraterrestrial life) that they are struggling to comprehend given the evidence base they are drawing on. Any of these options is equally as viable as the next, until we begin to look at the context. When it comes to reading the Bible, this is exactly what we do. We start to investigate the context in which texts are placed.

Initially, we want to look at the immediate context, the sentences and paragraphs surrounding a passage. Are there repeated words or phrases that might help us in our interpretation? Are there parallel or contrasted ideas or characters that present a better or worse alternative? Is there a sense that what is being spoken about is negative, positive, or neutral?

All of these questions of the directly surrounding context help to ensure that we grasp more fully the text's interpretive scope. For example, Romans 1, by far the most commonly quoted text against any form of homosexual union, has abundant references to idol worship and pagan rites. If we ignore this context, we will undoubtedly miss some sort of relationship between the two that Paul, at the very least, thought important to recount. Likewise, in both Leviticus 18 and 20, prohibitions against having sex with a woman during her menstrual cycle and sacrificing children to the god Molek are placed right alongside homosexual activity (18:19, 21 and 20:4–5, 18). Is there a relationship between these acts?

And if we are to conclude that one, two, or all three of these acts are sinful today and in doing so exclude all same-sex unions, we have to do so knowing full well that they occur in the same paragraph. We will need to be ready to give an explanation as to why that is. We will make many similar observations as we make our way through the texts, so be ready to take note.

But even with all of this, there is every chance that we still wouldn't be able to grasp the full significance of what is being said and would miss its weight. If, for example, we could see that the person who "can't believe it" is indeed holding a lottery ticket, there would still be larger questions we would need to ask in order to get the whole picture. How much have they won? It could range from $20 to $20 million. How many lotto tickets have they purchased before this one? Perhaps they have a gambling addiction for which they are seeking counseling, and in the long term, this will make things worse! Do they have a plan for the money? Are they of a generous predisposition, or are they likely to hoard it for themselves?

As we work our way through the texts that address homosexual behavior, these are the sorts of questions we will next be asking. Much of our work is going to be in considering the text's position in the book, and how both traditionalist and affirming positions have engaged, or failed to engage, with this. We will ask questions such as "what is the overarching message of the book of Romans, and how does chapter 1 fit in to this?" We will look at the lists of prohibitions in 1 Corinthians and 1 Timothy and see how these work in light of surrounding arguments. We will seek to understand how the story of Sodom and Gomorrah fits in the unfolding account of Genesis.

And finally, we will seek to ascertain where these prohibitions fit in in light of the whole biblical narrative. The Bible is, at its core, the story of God who created, redeemed, sustains, and is drawing together a people for his own glory. It is a magnificent piece of literature that has stood the test of time, and continues to break down the boundaries that we would seek to place on God. In light of this narrative, where do the seeming prohibitions against homosexual activity fit, and how are we to apply these today?

As we move through all of these questions that place passages within their biblical context, we will also seek to gain an understanding of the cultural milieu in which the books were written. One of the richest tools that the Protestant tradition has given us is the understanding that the original author and their original audience must play a profound role in our understanding of a passage. As such, an exciting part of the task at hand will be to acquaint ourselves with antiquity. In striving to grasp the biblical authors' understanding of sexuality, we will examine erotic literature of the Greco-Roman and Ancient Near East worlds. In trying to define a number of terms that are pertinent to the discussion, we will undertake word studies of ancient writings. If you haven't already come across them, you will be introduced to a swath of ancient authors whose work will shed light on the discussions that were taking place in society as the Bible was being penned. Having done this, we will be better enabled to disentangle our own cultural assumptions and will protect ourselves from imposing our notions of sexuality onto texts in ways that the original authors perhaps would never have thought likely, or even possible. As Marti Nissinen helpfully suggests, "If we want the Bible and other ancient sources to contribute to today's discussion, the starting point is the sensible hermeneutical principle that there must be a sufficient correlation between the topics discussed today and the ancient sources."[2] This is exactly what this process attempts to ascertain.

While asking contextual questions such as this might seem daunting at first, our analogy with the lottery winner shows us that in fact, we innately ask these sorts of questions every single day. The tools to do so are at your disposal. It is just a matter of doing the hard work of applying those tools to a different set of data.

It is my hope that placing each of these texts in their immediate and broader context will aid in ensuring that we don't fall into the lazy trap of "proof texting" in which we bring together a series of verses that prove our point, and use them to unceremoniously knock down an opponent.[3] As with all studies of the Bible, our goal in presenting any analysis is not to win an argument, but rather to draw us to a deeper understanding of God's word and how the Holy Spirit is working in our world today.

---

2. Nissinen, *Homoeroticism in the Biblical World*, 123.

3. To the disadvantage of all, the six passages that we will spend considerable time in have been used throughout the past several generations in ways that have lacked care and nuance. As such, they have been pejoratively labeled "clobber passages." Far from engaging in rich dialogue, this "clobbering" has simply left people disillusioned and hurt. For a thought-provoking analysis of this effect see Martin, *Unclobber*.

One Step Deeper

Let's change tack for just a moment, because there is one more level of biblical interpretation which we need to embark on, and it's rather vital. In Deuteronomy 25:5, we come across a law that to our minds feels radically strange and intriguingly foreign. It's called the Levirate law. It stipulates that: "If brothers are living together and one of them dies without a son, his widow must not marry outside the family. Her husband's brother shall take her and marry her and fulfill the duty of a brother-in-law to her." It's really quite straightforward in a way. The law commands that in the case of a husband dying, the deceased man's brother is to take the widow as his wife. Deuteronomy is the fifth book of the Bible and acts as something of a conclusion to the Pentateuch, the section of the Torah (the Hebrew canon of Scripture) that outlined the legal codes that would make Israel distinct from the nations around it and mark the Israelites out as the chosen people of Yahweh. This is important because every Jewish child would have grown up hearing the Pentateuch taught over and over again. They would have been deeply familiar with its stipulations and the Levirate law would have been understood and practiced in their community life.

Apparently this was true right up to the time of Jesus. We know this because Jesus addressed this law directly. In Matthew 22:25–28, a group of Sadducees approach Jesus and present to him a hypothetical, saying, "Now there were seven brothers among us. The first one married and died, and since he had no children, he left his wife to his brother. The same thing happened with the second and third brother, right on down to the seventh. Now then, at the resurrection, whose wife will she be of the seven, since all of them were married to her?" Good question! Interestingly, Jesus doesn't use this rather obvious moment to speak out against the practice of polygamy, as one might expect him to (the law makes no distinction between married or unmarried brothers-in-law). Rather, he uses it as a means to teach his listeners truths about the nature of Scripture, about the resurrection, and about the power of God (Matt 22:29–32).

I know of many pastors and theologians who invoke a great number of the Pentateuch's laws, but I have yet to come across any who would suggest that we are still ordered to apply the brother-marries-widow Levirate system to our lives today. To make it awkwardly personal, I have two brothers, both of whom are married. I have a great deal of love for my sisters-in-law, and they are beautiful members of our family. But if one of my brothers were, tragically, to die, I would feel under zero compulsion to "perform the duty of a husband's brother" and take the widow as my wife. In fact, I tend to think that this would be shamefully frowned upon and condemned by most in our church communities.

All of this draws us to the point where we have to ask, if it's clearly stipulated in the Bible, why is it that we do or do not follow it today? What is the exegetical rubric that we are to apply in order to determine if a law still acts as an imperative for the people of God? This is more than simply asking what the text *says*, and it's slightly different to asking what a text *means*. What we are attempting to do in this process is work out what underlying theological, moral, and ethical frameworks are at play. In other words, we are asking the question *why does this law exist?* What is it about the character of God, the nature of humanity, or the state of our world which requires such a mandate to be articulated? We might think of this as the driving moral principle and once again, it may surprise you to realize that we often do this innately as we read the Bible.[4]

If we take the Levirate law for example, it isn't difficult to poke around a bit and discern why this law performed a vital function in the life of a community in the Ancient Near East. The book of Ruth depicts this beautifully. Widowed and facing famine and destitution, Naomi and her daughter-in-law Ruth found themselves at the mercy of Israelite farmers who would leave a portion of their crop for those in need. In an agrarian society where the male represented not only the head of the household, but also the sole source of income, widowhood often signaled certain death unless another man was available and willing to take the woman in. In the middle of this darkening narrative, a relative, Boaz, is summoned to take it upon himself to fulfill the Levirate law and provide protection and security for these outcasts. He does so, and the story ends with great celebration as Ruth and Boaz give birth to a son, an ancestor of King David. Were it not for this law, there is every chance that both Ruth and Naomi would have become fatal victims of the harsh societal state into which they were born.

But if we look further, it is not just the protection of the vulnerable women and children for which this law was created. In all three instances where this law is explicitly articulated or demonstrated through narrative, there is another driving moral principle at work. In Deuteronomy,

4. Brownson refers to this as the "moral logic" of a passage. Brownson, *Bible, Gender, Sexuality*, 9.

the rationale behind the widow being taken in by her brother-in-law is directly stated, that "the first son she bears shall carry on the name of the dead brother so that his name will not be blotted out from Israel" (Deut 25:6). In Ruth, the language of "redemption" for Ruth and Naomi is directly correlated to the offspring that Yahweh would bring about through Ruth's relationship with Boaz, ensuring the perpetuation of the name of the dead (Ruth 4:7–17). And in Matthew 22, the Sadducees interpret the rationale behind the law as being that the one who takes in the woman must marry the widow and raise up offspring for his brother (Matt 22:24).

Whilst the protection of the vulnerable in times of distress was no doubt a part of the rationale behind it, the Levirate marriage law found its greatest driving moral principle in the continuation of the family lineage of the deceased man. In the societal structures of a familial tribe amongst the warring empires of the Ancient Near East, it's not difficult to determine why such a law would have had vital implications. In order for the society to hold its place in the land, procreation and the establishing of family names would have been of utmost importance. Likewise, in a society where land ownership translated directly to survival and government welfare systems were simply unheard of, the protection of the outcast fell largely upon relatives and kinsmen.

If we are able to comprehend that these are our two driving moral principles—the continuation of lineage and care for the vulnerable—then we are now in a much better place to understand the degree to which I would be obliged to marry my sister-in-law should one of my brothers die. That's helpful, isn't it?

Under the new covenant, the sociopolitical establishment of a people of God as the nation of Israel is no longer the chosen modus operandi in growing God's kingdom. Where bloodlines, family heritage, and national identity were key components of the old covenant, the coming of the Holy Spirit upon the Gentiles meant that all people could now call themselves "children of God" and "co-heirs with Christ" (Rom 8:9–17). Thus this driving moral principle as outlined in the Old Testament no longer holds the same sway that it once did.

But what then of the protection of the vulnerable widow? Surely this is still of vital importance to the people of God? Most certainly! But I think that we can all agree that there are other means of achieving this without engaging in matrimony. In a time and place where there are systems and resources at our disposal to ensure that women and children aren't left destitute if "the man of the house" passes away, this system no longer seems to have the mandatory force that it once held. This certainly seems to be implied in Acts 6, where widows were at risk of being overlooked, and the response of the apostles is not to appeal to kinsmen to redeem their brothers' widows, but rather to mobilize a team who would ensure that they were looked after by the body of disciples, the church.

In taking this as a case study, we can see that ancestry and lineage no longer have the imperatival force that they once held. Likewise, care for the widow is able to be appropriated in a wide variety of ways. Given both of these facts, the Levirate marriage system is shown to be a good law of God, but no longer applicable in today's society. This explains why no pastor has asked this of anybody I know, in any church I've been a part of. The driving moral principles are still vital (the growth of God's kingdom and care for the widow) but the application of these to our lives plays out in a vastly different manner.

Let's take one more example before we see how this all relates to the discussion around homosexuality. James Brownson offers a simple case study.[5] In no less than five instances in the New Testament, people who call themselves followers of Jesus are commanded to "greet one another with a holy kiss."[6] Despite these abundantly clear exhortations to kiss one another, there are very few within the contemporary Western church who would practice this ritual as an outworking of their obedience to the Bible. If it were the case that a specific church practiced this today as a matter of course, not only would this make most Christian men and women I know quite uncomfortable, but I tend to think that it would actually undermine the very driving moral principle that it seeks to express.

For the early church (as for many cultures still around the world) a physical kiss was not a sign of exclusive intimacy, but rather an expression of warmth, acceptance, and welcome. It acted in much the same way that a comfortable handshake, a hug, or even a kind smile would in many similar situations.

Are we breaking the rules by not having our greeters kiss each congregation member as they come through the door? Certainly not! Rather, we have identified that the driving moral principle behind the holy kiss is that each member be welcomed in such a way that they feel appreciated, accepted, and at home. We have taken this ancient practice and adapted it to a modern setting. And this is the exact task that we are attempting

---

5. Brownson, *Bible, Gender, Sexuality,* 6.

6. See Rom 16:16; 1 Cor 16:20; 2 Cor 13:13; 1 Thess 5:26; and 1 Pet 5:14.

to work toward in ascertaining the driving moral principles behind any instruction, code, or practice that the Bible talks about.

As I mentioned earlier, I have had numerous conversations with people who have come to the conclusion that the Bible is against any form of homosexual practice, but they simply can't see why this is the case. Perhaps even more disconcerting, there are those in the church who are willing to conclude that God has simply come up with this law, and as he is the all-powerful creator, who are we to question him? Whilst I obviously have no qualm with the statement that God's power is all-encompassing and God's laws to be obeyed, this theological methodology is deeply flawed. It is dangerous territory because the underlying implication of this statement is that God is, in some manner or other, an arbitrary rule-maker, who deliberately places inexplicable boundaries around the people that he claims to be in relationship with. God is not required to adhere to driving moral principles, or at the very least, he is not interested in revealing a working moral rubric to humanity.

If this is the case, then for those struggling with the deep burden that homosexuality naturally brings, it's not too much of a leap before an "arbitrary God" becomes a "capricious God." If he can cause so much pain, simply because he can, without any cause for explanation or justification, then the conclusion that God is fickle or capricious becomes an increasingly viable, and dare I say it, theologically valid conclusion.

Friends, God is not arbitrary, and God most certainly is not capricious. This premise of seeking to grapple with the driving moral principle is based on an understanding that we serve a God who is not flippant with establishing legal codes or fickle in setting forth demands. Rather, this is a God who has revealed the divine character to us in both the "word" (the Bible) and the "Word" (Jesus), and who subsequently acts in accordance with that character. This God may be complex, but this God is knowable. This God may be boundless, but this God does not change. Our assumption in reading the Bible therefore is that the God it reveals is capable of spanning time and cultures and remains altogether consistent in his morality.

We are, in reading the Bible, participating in an extraordinarily complex cross-cultural exercise, and to take any part of Scripture as necessarily mandating certain behavior today under the new covenant without seeking to understand *why* it is articulated by this God in the first place is foolish at best, and damaging at worst. A culturally uninformed reading of the Bible is easy until situations arise where we are forced to reconsider basic assumptions that we've so long taken for granted. This has certainly been my journey when it comes to the experiences of LGB people. For such a long time I took the lazier option of reading the Bible through the lens of the twenty-first-century categories that I wear so naturally. But as I dove further into the cultural mores of the biblical world, as I sought to understand the dynamic societal systems at play, and as I peeled back my own inherent blind spots and assertions, I began to see that all talk of sexuality within the Bible (irrespective of categories of gender and orientation) is deeply imbedded in driving moral principles that I had failed to comprehend or give credit to.

With all of this in mind, prepare yourself now to engage not just with what the text says and means, but also to ask questions about why it is there and how it is relevant to our lives today. How does the text fit not only with the overarching story line of the biblical narrative, but also with the character of God himself? And as we ask these questions, we will seek to peel back our cultural lenses to determine how stipulations which involve same-sex sexual practices are applicable to today's society.

Bringing Your Whole Self to the Table

Up until this point, everything we have discussed in this chapter has been cerebrally driven, dependent on critical examination and cultural understanding. There is one vital element of Bible engagement that I have not yet addressed that plays a peripheral, though genuine role in how we read Scripture. Years ago I read a book that started its discussion on the Bible's approach to homosexuality with the call for people to put their emotions aside and hear what God has to say. The instruction was presented in simple terms and the rubric of understanding was fairly simple—in a discussion laden with deep-seated passions and competing voices, we were to come before the Bible as Scripture and let God do the speaking.

I happened to pick up this book at a time in my life when I was struggling to tie my shoelaces without shedding a tear, let alone engage with a theological disputation on the morality of my sexuality. I came upon this book emotionally spent, and rather than finding a balm for my wounds, I felt as though I was dealt another series of blows masquerading as God's words. Try as I might, I simply couldn't find the means by which to separate my emotions from what I was reading. I began to wonder if this is even possible. I understand that the author was longing for a sense of clarity in his rational reading of the Bible, and he was eager to ensure that our experiences did not dictate our interpretation. However I feel that in this pursuit he missed one vital point—his readership are humans who, I tend to think, are far from rational beings. At the very least, we are not *simply* rational. To separate my emotions from my engagement with any topic that resonates profoundly with my lived experience is to ask me to undertake an impossible task. The author was setting me up to fail with a sterile depiction of God, void of emotional comprehension and held at arm's length at the slightest hint of what might be perceived as deviant emotional responsiveness. Perhaps you, like so many others, have spent years trying to untangle your emotional baggage from your theology, slipping in and out of confusion as you've sought to ascertain God's will for your life. Perhaps you are watching on as somebody that you care for deeply seems to be buckling under the weight of the emotional burden that same-sex attraction so naturally entails.

To this end, as we come now to discuss a biblically grounded theology of sexuality, I am going to ask you to do something that perhaps you have never done before, or even considered an option. I want to invite you to bring your emotions to the table: in all their frailty, brokenness, confusion, and anger. As we engage with God in his word, I want you to register your emotional reactions, not monitor them, but be aware of them. Note how they are impacting your reading. In a pursuit of rationality and unambiguous truth, this is a demanding and oftentimes difficult task, but in my experience there is also great liberation and freedom when we treat God as though he is big enough to handle it.

Never in the Bible do I see God demanding his loved children keep their emotions in check before they approach him. In fact, the opposite appears to be true. Picture Elijah as he stumbles into the wilderness, his life's work in tatters, his loved ones murdered, and a death threat looming over his head. Feeling like an abject, abandoned failure, he cries out to the God he trusted, "take my life, I am no better than my ancestors" (1 Kgs 19:4). In this moment he doesn't gather himself, put aside his gaping wounds, and "listen to God," but rather he cries out with everything he has and tells God that he's really struggling. If you've read the story, you'll know that God's response is not one of stern rebuke, but rather he shows up in the quiet whisper of the gentle wind to comfort Elijah and to encourage him that his task is not in vain.

Likewise, picture Job as he faces the complete devastation now synonymous with his name. As his comforters become his accusers and the time comes for him to face up to God, nothing in the narrative suggests Job must engage with God in an emotionally stable, rationally driven manner. Rather, God embraces the very emotionally charged tumult and harnesses it to show Job what total control of the creation looks like.

Elijah and Job aren't the exceptions. Within the pages of the Bible, not one person passes through life unscathed, and through their cumulative witness, the Bible screams over and over again that God is big enough to handle our cries. These emotions are wild, they are scary, and they are pervasive. They do not determine our theological conclusions, but they do perform a vital task. These emotions drive us to do the work that we would otherwise find onerous and inconsequential. They force us to ask new questions, and protect us from settling for easy one-line answers. Engaging richly with the Bible in today's world takes energy and commitment, and often it is our emotions that provide the drive to undertake the task. Don't be afraid of this—it is a beautiful part of living in God's created world.

And so, with all of the interpretive tools above, the task at hand is to examine sexuality in an informed, theologically rigorous, and biblically sound manner that captures God's heart for this world. The next few chapters will be dense with detail and data, and the path we will be treading is both time-consuming and vital. Brace yourself. Perhaps fittingly, our journey into it all begins at the dawn of time as God breathes life into the very first of the human race.

6

A Rather Good Place to Start

Do you ever stand in wonder at the vast expanse of the ocean? Do you ever feel your heart surge with awe at the majesty of the heavens? In a profoundly moving way, the splendor of the Creator resounds in the cathedral of the universe as this world we inhabit declares God's glory over and over and over. This is the awe that we experience as the curtain ascends on the pages of the Bible. In the opening act of the grand narrative of history, God, in all of the divine's mysterious ways "speaks" and behold, the galaxies are born.

Perhaps this may feel like a strange place to begin thinking about the Bible's view on homosexuality. After all, homosexuality is nowhere to be seen in the creation accounts. But the reality is that Genesis 1 and 2 are at the heart of the debate that is currently raging in the church. If the foundation is sure, the building will stand, and these truly are some of the Bible's foundational texts. The creation narratives that the Bible opens with don't simply answer the questions "how did we get here?" or "where did we come from?" but rather they set us up to ask a far greater question, a question that has plagued every mind since time began: "what does it mean to be human?" As we shall see, the way that we answer this question shapes every aspect of our conception of personhood, including the fundamentals of our theology of sexuality.

In two distinct narratives, the opening chapters of Genesis prepare us to answer this question from two distinct angles. The first chapter tells the story from a grand position as God takes a barren wasteland, forms it into something beautiful, and fills it with all manner of life. The pinnacle of this creation is revealed when God remarkably decides to mirror the triune Godhead into the canvas that has been adorned, creating an "image" in humanity and tasking them with dominion over the land.

The second account zooms in, recounting events that transpire on and after the sixth day, as God brings to life the image-bearers, placing them in the garden prepared just for them. For a brief moment the paradise feels complete, but the narrative takes us into the tragic rebellion that unfolds, and with one fell swoop the stage is set for the redemptive plan that God sets in motion. This is the backdrop of the Scriptures, and in every regard it is the starting place for a Christian anthropology.

Built upon a foundational understanding that Genesis 1 and 2 are vital in our understanding of humanity, the pillars of the church's theology of sexuality have undergone countless transformations over the course of 2,000 years. As with any change, the initial stages have always involved an uncomfortable unlearning process, beginning with revisiting these very narratives. This unlearning process is one that I journeyed on for years before I could even articulate what it was that I was unlearning. In this chapter, we are going to examine the creation stories, see how they have been understood differently in different ages, and, most importantly, assess their efficacy in speaking into the current discussions around gay and lesbian people in the kingdom of God.

Man and Woman

This is where it all begins. Adam and Eve. Male and Female.

For those who argue from a Judeo-Christian perspective that gay unions are inherently outside the ethical realm of the kingdom of God, the creation of two genders culminates in a marriage relationship (a "one-flesh" union, Gen 2:24), which establishes a pattern for all subsequent generations. This pattern is not simply an ideal to strive toward, but rather establishes a mandated boundary system in which anything that does not follow the pattern of "one man, one woman" is understood as a violation of the created order. As such, any permutation of relationship that seeks to fill the one-flesh union but does not fit this prescribed pattern is at best a poor reflection of the garden paradise, and at worst a destructive act of rebellion against the Creator God.

To put a label to this concept, we are talking here about *complementarian* theology. This is the idea that the two sexes are designed in such a way as to complete the other. Under this rubric, there is a vital and immutable fittedness between male and female that is woven deeply into the created order, driven by the concept that men and women are intentionally *different*.[1] In many theologians' minds, it is this *difference* that forms the foundational force that makes the one-flesh union exclusively man and woman. Without difference, the union would not be complete. Without difference, the need for union would be redundant. And without difference, complementarity would not be expressed.

Whether people realize it or not, complementarity is at the heart of almost all theologically derived stances against gay unions. And at its heart, complementarian theology is based upon the notion that males and females are uncompromisingly different. Two questions necessarily arise from these assertions—firstly, what exactly is it about males and females that makes them "different"? And secondly, what is the relationship between this "difference" and the one-flesh union so beautifully portrayed in Genesis 1 and 2? If it is true that difference is what makes a one-flesh union compatible, we would naturally expect to see this reflected in the text.

Defining Complementarian Theology

Here's where we hit our first fork in the road. Amongst traditionalist theologians there is no consensus as to what constitutes the fundamental difference between males and females. There is no doubt that there is difference, but there is no agreement as to its exact nature. This is primarily because there is no statement in the creation narratives, (nor in the rest of the Bible for that matter), that articulates the difference that make man and woman exclusively compatible. As such, we are left to hypothesize.

Emerging in some evangelical circles today is the notion of hierarchy, asserting that embedded into creation is an order of authority, from God the Father, to Christ, to man then to woman. Drawing from 1 Corinthians 11:3 and 1 Timothy 2:11–15, this theological stance assumes an enigmatic differentiation based on both the temporal ordering of creation (Adam was created before Eve) and the fact that Eve was deceived first. Therefore, the thinking goes, man has authority over woman. There are heated debates surrounding this theology, but for our purposes here, the

1. For this argument, see for example Grudem, "Key Issues in the Manhood-Womanhood Controversy."

discussion is rather simple. The limitation of this hierarchical complementarity is that it simply provides no grounded rationale for why male-
female union is the only permutation that a one-flesh union can take. In
fact, asserting the dominance of man over woman gives no data about
how two gay men or a lesbian couple in monogamous relationships are to
interact. Knowing that Adam was created first, and that Eve was deceived
before him, tells us nothing about the inherent morality or immorality of
gay unions. Understandably, in practice this is a minority view amongst
Christians and is countered by a more prominent understanding of difference that revolves around biological and psychological factors.

Under this schema, males and females are like pieces of a jigsaw
puzzle that slot into one another, both metaphorically and literally. For
some this is primarily a "penis-fits-into-vagina" conclusion. For others,
it is primarily procreative potential that is in view.[2] For still others, a
more nuanced form incorporates temperament, psychological otherness,
and gendered skill sets.[3] Each of these theories however raise numerous
dilemmas. For starters, the Bible never speaks of male-female complementarity as a crude coming together of "plumbing." This view is bluntly
sexual, failing to account for the multi-faceted dynamics of any given
relationship. If procreation is on view, then where does that place couples
who know prior to their marriage that one or the other is infertile? Does
this render their marriage somehow lesser? And if psychological fittedness were in view, we have to ask what specific traits does God have in
mind? Gentleness? Steadfastness? Care? Determination? Throughout
Scripture both men and women present with these, and surely such
categories are far too blurry to amount to creation-imperative gendered
traits. It is disastrously simplistic to assume that an allusive set of tem-
peraments could be the distinguishing difference that makes any and all
heterosexual unions somehow more blessed than any and all gay unions.

What all of these theories have in common is that they define male
and female by their distinction, and see Genesis 1 and 2 as explicitly
teaching this. The argument is threefold: Firstly, the creation accounts
present two genders; secondly, these genders are inherently different;
and thirdly, this difference makes them uniquely capable of forming
a one-flesh union. It is this third point that forms the linchpin of the

---

2. Köstenberger and Köstenberger, *God's Design for Man and Woman*, 30.

3. Johnson, "The Biological Basis for Gender-Specific Behavior," 280–90.

non-affirming position. But when placed into the context of the creation narratives, this linchpin proves to be flawed at a fundamental level.

It is Not Good for Man to Be Alone

I want you to have your Bible out as we walk our way through Genesis now, starting with the second account. I want you to closely examine the text, get a feel for the narrative's flow, and grasp the beautiful dynamics that are on display.

We are introduced to our first tension in the narrative almost immediately. We enter into a barren wasteland where no bush of the field is growing and no small plants have yet sprouted up (2:5). Why is this so? It is because God has not yet sent rain to water the earth, and there is no human to work the ground (2:5). The agrarian motif is largely lost on our ears, but to the subsistence farmers of ancient Israel, this would have resonated deeply. Without the partnership of Yahweh and his stewards, how would the land produce its fare?

This first tension is solved in 2:7 when God formed a man from the dust of the ground and "breathed into his nostrils the breath of life, and the man became a living being." God takes the man and places him in a garden of almost mythical beauty that God has prepared for him at the convergence of four great rivers. The man is given the task of working and keeping the land (2:15) and instructed not to eat of the tree of knowledge of good and evil (2:17).

But we quickly discover that paradise without partnership is no paradise at all as God declares that "it is not good that the man should be alone; I will make a helper fit (*ezer kenegdō*) for him" (2:18). Here is our second tension of the narrative—the man that God has brought in to fill the task of tending the garden is alone, and a life void of meaningful interaction is not a life fully lived. Thus, the parade begins.

One by one, the animals that God has formed from the same dust as the man come before him. Adam examines them and names them (2:19). In order to name them appropriately, he must know their nature. And yet, after all the beasts of the earth, the livestock, and the birds have passed by him, Adam still can't find a helper (an *ezer*) who can fill the void of aloneness that he inhabits (2:20). The animals may be formed from the same dust as him, and are most certainly different from him, but they are intrinsically unable to satisfy his longing for partnership. Thus God places him into a deep sleep and forms from a portion of his side another being. God takes this being, who we now discover is woman, and places her in front of the man (2:21–22). Finally, in one of the most profound exclamations history has known, the man proclaims, "This at last is bone of my bones and flesh of my flesh!" (2:23).

This is the narrative of the coming together of the first man and the first woman. What strikes me as I read the text is *not* that Eve is fundamentally different to Adam. There is nothing in the passage to suggest that what makes her such a stunningly suitable fit for the man is a notion of dissimilarity. Indeed, when we read the story in context the exact opposite is seen to be true: the creation of Eve is in direct response to Adam's aloneness. The creation of Eve follows the grand search of Adam's world for someone to fill his void. The creation of Eve is met not with a response of difference, but with a proclamation of perfect similarity. The whole purpose of the narrative is not to demonstrate that Eve is different to Adam, but rather to show that Eve is the *same* as Adam. What makes her such a perfect fit is not that she is unlike him, but rather that she is like him. At last! Someone with the capacity to work alongside him in the task of tending to the garden has been found, having been made from the exact same substance as him. It is their common humanity, not their gendered difference draws that the two together.

This is not, of course, to say that the two people were the same in every capacity—no two people are! But to argue that this passage teaches that the necessary prerequisite for a partnership to form is *gendered difference* (as all theological stances against gay unions do) is to blatantly misrepresent the driving force of the narrative. Difference is glorious, but it is not on display here. Difference may be beneficial, but it is not what makes Adam proclaim of Eve "here is flesh of my flesh and bone of my bones!" If a theologian finds *difference* to be the driving force of the passage, then we can be sure that they have read it *into* the narrative. This is a classic case of taking a phrase (in this case the words "male and female") out of context and theologizing around it, rather than letting the text itself set the intended meaning.[4]

4. A technical note—there are some who have seen notions of gendered difference in the term *kenegdō* ("suitable," [NIV] or "fit" [ESV]) used to describe the *ezer* ("helper") Eve. For example, Sprinkle, *People to Be Loved*, 33. This term is literally a merging of two prepositions *ke* (like) and *neged* (variously translated "before," "opposite," "in the presence of," etc.). It is the only time that we know of where the two prepositions are merged and thus somewhat difficult to define precisely. While it is possible that the term is being used to speak of difference, this not only goes against the entire flow of the passage but is also linguistically difficult to maintain and is not

A Union of Flesh

So strong is the bond that is established between the two newly formed people, that it is fitting to describe them as *echād bāsār* (literally "one flesh"). We often think of this in modern contexts as the romantic courting processes, culminating in consummation through sexual intercourse. Indeed, the very term "one flesh" feels somehow inherently sexual. But the feel of a word is rarely a good way to do theology! It needs to be said that this understanding is anachronistic and would be wholly foreign to the vast majority of societies throughout history. While there may be some overlap of concepts, we have to remember that we are looking at an agrarian society in which marriage was more often than not an exercise in economic pragmatics and diplomacy.[5] When the narrator describes this one-flesh union, we are instantly reminded of Adam's exclamation that the woman is "flesh of his flesh." This is a common analogy in the biblical literature, and when we look at the concept of being united as "bone of my bone and flesh of my flesh" in Scripture, we see that what is being discussed is never sexual unity, but rather the existence of indissoluble kinship (family) ties.[6]

Thus for example, Jacob exclaims of his kinsman Laban "surely you are my bone and flesh" (Gen 29:14); David appeals to the elders of Judah as his brothers, calling them "his bones and flesh" (2 Sam 19:12–13); and similarly Abimelech appeals to his mother's family by stating "remember I am your flesh and blood."[7] Westermann, whose mammoth commentary

---

supported by the ancient manuscripts that we have. For example, the Septuagint (the Greek translation of the Hebrew Old Testament written around the third century BC) quotes Genesis as saying, "but for Adam there was not found a help like to himself." The Apocryphal Tobit (225 BC) similarly states "let us make a helper for him like himself." The most notable lexicon of Hebrew terms simply translates the term "equal and adequate" (Brown, Driver, and Briggs, *Hebrew and English Lexicon*). Even if difference was somehow expressed in the term, it is an ambiguous claim at best, and it is impossible to assert with any confidence exactly what this difference might entail (contr. Sprinkle, *People to Be Loved*, who bases almost his entire traditionalist view of homosexuality in the Genesis account on this term).

5. Westermann, *Genesis 1–11*, 233.

6. It should be noted that the lexical meaning of the term translated "flesh" (*bāsār*) is literally "flesh for kindred; blood relations" or "near of kin" (Brown et al., *Enhanced Brown-Driver-Briggs Hebrew and English Lexicon*). For further discussion of Genesis 2 establishing kinship ties, see Brownson, *Bible, Gender, Sexuality*, 32–34; Cross, *From Epic to Canon*, 8; and Sprinkle, *People to Be Loved*, 30–31.

7. See also Judg 9:2, 2 Sam 5:1, 1 Chr 11:1; and Jordan, *Authorizing Marriage?*, 46.

on Genesis has had an enormous influence on evangelicalism, asserts that the Genesis 2:24 process of leaving one's mother and father to cleaving to one's wife is not describing a sex act, but is rather describing the transition that takes place when a man loosens the strongest bonds that he has hitherto known in order to forge a new, lasting community of life characterized by concern, fidelity, and involvement.[8] Thus it could be said that the pattern is set up for a man to leave one "bone and flesh union" to create another "bone and flesh union."[9] Given the lexical meaning of the terms at hand, and their location in the narrative, it's almost impossible to conclude that Adam and Eve's union is primarily based around sexual compatibility.

This being the case, we can conclude that to describe a relationship as one flesh is not making a statement regarding its *gender*, but rather its *strength*. This makes vastly more sense of Jesus' words when he answers the Pharisees' provocative question about divorce. He counters their proclivity toward flippant severing of the marriage bond by declaring:

> "Haven't you read," he replied, "that at the beginning the Creator "made them male and female," and said, "For this reason a man will leave his father and mother and be united to his wife, and the two will become one flesh"? So they are no longer two, but one flesh. Therefore what God has joined together, let no one separate. (Matt 19:4–6; see also Mark 10:8)

Jesus first orients them into the creation narratives ("have you not read that he who created them from the beginning made them male and female?") and then he slams home his point that a kinship tie is not something to be broken lightly. His double use of the term one flesh is not to emphasize that the man and woman have had sex and therefore can't get a divorce—it is to reiterate that they have entered into a bond that is as strong as the blood ties of an uncle and his nephew, a mother and her child. These ties can no more be severed than the blood that runs through their veins.[10] No other earthly relationship obligates a person to enter into a lifelong union with another individual. By using the term *male and female* Jesus draws the listener's attention back to the very first kinship

8. Westermann, *Genesis 1–11*, 233.

9. So argues traditionalist theologian Gordon Wenham, *Genesis*, 71.

10. The same is true of Ephesians 5:31, where it would be ridiculous in context to think that "one flesh" implies a sexual union. Have a read of it and you will see the strength of the kinship language in view.

union in which the individuals leave their parents' households and create a new indivisible unit. The bond cannot be broken lightly.

This is the same intensity of union that is understood in Paul's quotation of Genesis 2:24 in 1 Corinthians 6:16–17. Here, Paul is reminding the believers that they are vitally and fundamentally united with Christ and as such, they are admonished for their use of prostitutes.[11] Paul rebukes them, "Do you not know that he who unites himself with a prostitute is one with her in body? For it is said, 'The two will become one flesh.'" In contrast, "whoever is united with the Lord [Jesus] becomes one with him in spirit" (6:17). Paul understands that Christians are already spoken for. Their primary kinship tie is now with Christ, so why would they cheapen this union by utilizing their bodies for evil? The two ideas work in parallel, so just as it is possible to "be one" with Christ, it is also possible to "be one" with a prostitute, but they are mutually exclusive states of being. For Paul, the body's resurrection is vitally important and thus the physical body a person inhabits should never be used in a way that compromises the person's life source. In other words, the Corinthian church is being told, don't say with your body what you are unwilling to say with the rest of your life.

One important commentator closes his discussion about one flesh unions by stating, "I don't think that the phrase *one flesh* (or *united*) in itself demands that the marital partners must be opposite sexes. The only clear demand is that the two people leave their former families and create their own new family."[12]

In Our Image

Here is something beautiful: while the second creation account draws our attention to the similarities between two humans and their subsequent kinship union, the first creation account draws our attention to the similarities and differences between humanity and God himself.[13] In my humble opinion, the opening chapter of the Bible stands alone in history as the single most powerful validation of the intrinsic worth of men

---

11. Of course, we can only guess that Paul is speaking about males visiting female prostitutes here. But as Sprinkle notes, Paul could well have come to the same conclusions regarding union of flesh if homosexual prostitution is in view. Sprinkle, *People to Be Loved*, 31.

12. Sprinkle, *People to Be Loved*, 31.

13. Haller, *Reasonable and Holy*, 47.

and women. Having formed the universe and filled earth with life, the pinnacle of this narrative arrives as God speaks once again:

> Then God said, "Let us make mankind in our image, in our likeness, so that they may rule over the fish in the sea and the birds in the sky, over the livestock and all the wild animals, and over all the creatures that move along the ground."
>
> So God created mankind in his own image,
>
> in the image of God he created them;
>
> male and female he created them. (Genesis 1:26–27)

Everyone agrees that to be made in the image of God is vital to a biblical anthropology. All theologians recognize that this points to a profound status of humanity that is simultaneously *unlike* the rest of creation, and *like* God. The perplexing factor emerges when we stop to ask the question "what is it about God that is imaged in humanity?" Clearly humans aren't like God in every way—we are not omnipotent or omnipresent for example—and yet it is clear that at some capacity we share common characteristics.

Much like trying to define "complementary," attempting to discern those characteristics that amount to "imaging" has proven historically to be a contested domain. Some church leaders have understood the term structurally, appealing to the reason, memory, intellect, and will that humans possess.[14] Others (most influentially Calvin) have understood image as referring to the human possession of a soul. Still others have suggested that the functional task of having dominion over the created world is what is captured by the idea of image.[15]

One postulation that was influentially argued by the theologian Karl Barth is the idea that the image of God is reflected in the coming together of male and female. Examining the pattern of language in Genesis 1:27, Barth saw the pluralized pronoun "our" and the repetition of "our image" in conjunction with "male and female he created them" and concluded that the image of God must necessarily be reflected in the fact that there are two genders. In other words, because God is Trinitarian (three in one), this is reflected into his creation (when two become one). Unity in difference. Note that Barth is not arguing that males are created in the image of God, just as females are created in the image of God, but

14. For example, Irenaeus (130–200 AD), Augustine (354–430 AD), and Thomas Aquinas (1224–1274 AD).

15. Clines, "The Image of God in Man."

rather he is stating that when the two come together, they become the image. This view has more recently been espoused by Wayne Grudem as evidence of complementarian theology in the created order.[16]

As a subset of broader relational understandings of the image of God (humans, like God are created with the ability for relationship both horizontally between humans and vertically with God), this complementarian view has led some evangelical pastors to reject all same-sex unions, stating that they not only violate the created order, but they inherently taint the image of God. Many people have soundly refuted this type of narrowly defined thinking, noting that Adam was made in the image of God and was such presumably prior to Eve's creation. Of course, Jesus who never married is the image of God *par excellence*, and we must note the fact that biblical celibacy does not render a person any more or less in the image of God than marriage does. Further, there is universal agreement that at the very least the image of God in humanity is something that *distinguishes* us from the animals who are, safe to say, created male and female in exactly the same manner as us.[17]

Of vital importance, we must also recognize that a far more convincing reading of Genesis 1:26–27 renders Adam and Eve as imagers of God not *together*, but *equally*. In other words, it's not their union that makes them capable of reflecting God, but rather that they reflect God simply because God has designed them to reflect himself. Thus the woman reflects God just as much as the man reflects God. This accounts for the pluralization, "in his image, he created them." While some may be tempted to see within the term *male and female* a universal call for humanity to only and ever prescribe to binary gender norms in marriage, an equally clear reading recognizes the phrase as a glorious pronouncement of the equality of the genders. God did not simply create males as the divine image. No, he created male *and* female to be the image bearers on earth! Neither gender has the upper hand in this world. Both stand before God, equally reflecting glory of their triune maker.

As a Christian, it goes without saying that I long to reflect my creator in all that I do. The fact that I am, and you are, made in the image of God instills within the created order a fundamental shared worth of one another. You have value not because of something that you have achieved, but because of who created your innermost being. And yet

16. Ware, "Complementarity and the Image of God," 74.

17. Whitaker, "Creation and Human Sexuality," 6.

there are those who would seek to take this profound theological truth and limit it to only those whose heterosexuality enables them to maintain a man-woman relationship. Under this guise, those who never enter a heterosexual marriage union will never fully be made in the image of God. If I am honest, it devastates me that so many would use such a beautiful statement of worth and wield it as a sword to condemn people whom I call brothers and sisters.

A Pattern Established?

The Bible is packed to the rafters with marriages. It begins with a marriage, and ends with a glorious wedding ceremony between Christ and the church. In between Genesis and Revelation we read of good marriages and bad marriages, short marriages and long marriages. As those who are traditionalist in their theology are quick to note, every single one of these marriages is between a man and woman.[18] Never are we exposed to a marriage union between two members of the same sex.

There are many voices proclaiming that this itself is clear evidence that gay unions are off the table, anathema in the kingdom of God. It doesn't take a genius however to see the fallacy of this logic. Simply stating that there are no examples in Scripture does not necessitate nonexistence any more than yesterday's grocery list can conclusively tell you my least favorite foods. A far more convincing reading of Scripture would state that Adam and Eve were not only the *first* marriage, but that they provide the *prototype* for marriage. In this sense, they are the first of a pattern that is to be meticulously adhered to by every future generation. For traditionalist theologians, this provides the backdrop for "God's creative intention for human sexuality,"[19] establishing a normative mandate for monogamous, heterosexual marriage.

I used to think that this was a foregone conclusion, but on closer inspection it became abundantly clear that the prototype understanding of Adam and Eve is something of a theological minefield. The danger is not so much in recognizing that they are in some manner types to be emulated, but rather in discerning *which parts of the narrative constitute prototypes*. Here, a strong distinction must be made between those parts of the narrative that are presented as normal (that is, those elements of

18. Recognizing of course that the church is only a woman in an analogous manner.

19. Hays, *The Moral Vision*, 390.

creation that we would expect to see usually expressed) and those that are prescriptive, or normative (that is those parts of the narrative that effectively form mandates for all people, across all cultures, across all times).

It should be clear by now that there is no theologian who claims that *every* element of the creation narratives is normative or mandated. For example, the existence and blessing of singleness throughout Scripture proves that not all people are commanded to form one-flesh unions, despite this being presented as the only option available to humanity in the garden. Are single people violating the created order when they intentionally remain single? Certainly not![20] And yet if we take Adam and Eve as the "prototypes" in every sense, this would be where inevitably we land. Flowing on from this obvious assertion, it's safe to say that subsequently not *all* humans are commanded to "multiply" in the procreative sense, despite the fact that this is one of only three commands that are incontestably given to Adam and Eve in the accounts.[21] More conversations about procreation as a key to marriage will be covered in chapter 11, but for now the question has to stand, how do we determine which points of the creation stories are to be understood as *prescriptive* (normative/ mandated), and which parts are to be taken as *descriptive* of the creation process and thus normally or usually seen within creation?

It is at this point that non-affirming theologians invariably fall back on their established moorings of gender complementarity, one-flesh unions, and the gendered imaging of God. To tie all three together, the argument goes that heterosexuality is the only acceptable expression of one-flesh unions based on the complementarity of the genders and the status of man-woman imaging the relational God. However, as we have established, all three of these moorings fall down of their own accord, being unconvincingly grounded. The genders are most certainly different, but the Genesis narratives provide no category of "complementarity" as understood by non-affirming theologians today. The one-flesh unions form the centripetal force of the narrative, but the Scriptures (and subsequently many scholars today) place no gendered requisites on these unions but rather require that they are the outcome of two people forming a kinship bond of powerful unity, what we would call "family." And, finally, the image of God may indeed be relational in its nature, but it is impossible to conclude from Scripture that in order for this image to be

20. This is evidently the view of both Jesus and Paul (1 Cor 7:8).

21. If this were indeed a normative factor of the Genesis account, then Jesus himself would be branded a failure!

complete, heterosexual marriage must be entered into, or conversely, that gay marriage must be condemned.

In the previous chapter we established that as we go through the Bible we are not simply looking for what the text "says," but we are looking for the driving theological principles that underpin how we apply it today. For those who hold to a non-affirming view of gay and lesbian relationships based on Genesis 1 and 2, the driving principles that are relied upon in the text are perilously flawed, because they are entirely absent. In some senses it boils down to the fact that they are asking the wrong set of questions: however we frame it, Genesis 1 and 2 were not primarily written to form a cohesive and exhaustive defense of heterosexuality. In fact, they weren't designed to address the more nuanced questions of sexuality at all, let alone homosexuality.[22] This stunning portion of Scripture is designed to establish that God is the sovereign creator of all humanity. It places on display God's power over the universe and sets in motion the great narrative of the creation of a people who will act as God's agents within creation. This people, governed by the task of cumulatively stewarding the garden that has been formed, will journey forth into the land not as one man who holds dominion over all, but in a community of families, brought together by their common goal of worshiping the creator God.

With all of this in mind, we ask ourselves the simple question, "Does the Genesis account only allow scope for one permutation of one-flesh unions?" The answer unequivocally is no. The first man and woman are painted as the first kinship union to walk the face of the planet, and while their difference enabled them to be fruitful and multiply, there is no indication that subsequent kinship unions must align with their heterosexual nature. For a long time I held so carefully to an exclusive understanding of Genesis 1 and 2 that forbade the opportunity for gay and lesbian people to have any form of union. If you are anything like me, unlearning something that I have believed to be true for decades is an arduous and destabilizing task, yet the ability to question long-held assumptions is a vital skill in the process of theology. In my experiences, revisiting the text with new insights has been a gloriously enriching experience.

With this in mind, we now dive into a series of scriptural references that look at homoerotic activity in a negative light. There are six texts in all that we will examine over the next few chapters, seeking to

22. Whitaker, "Creation and Human Sexuality," 3.

comprehend the driving theological principles that can inform a faithful, God-honoring hermeneutic for today. My prayer as we do this is that we would not lose sight of the glory of these opening narratives of the Bible. May we stand in awe of the sheer magnitude of the God whom we are seeking to comprehend, holding firm to his divine holiness and infinite grace. And at the end of it all may we stand in worshipful obedience as we follow the radical path of discipleship that Jesus lays before us.

7

The Fate of Two Cities

No matter which angle you approach it from, the story of the twin cities Sodom and Gomorrah is about as dark as it gets. As the sun rises over the plain of the Jordan, the wrath of Yahweh comes swiftly upon the wicked. Burning sulphur rains from the heavens, and the cities with all of their inhabitants are swept up in a furnace of judgment as Lot and his family flee for the hills.

What could precipitate such a violent demise? What atrocity did the people of Sodom and Gomorrah commit to warrant such an outpouring? For a long time I would have answered these questions in much the same way as many traditionalists, by asserting that homosexuality was on display in all of its licentious depravity. The men of Sodom were the epitome of wickedness, and their homosexual behavior was ultimately expressed in their blatant disregard for the created order. It's a dark place to continue our adventure into the biblical world of sexuality, but nevertheless, here we find ourselves! As the first text in the Bible to broach the presence of same-sex sexual activity,[1] Genesis 19 has for millennia played a vital role in the discussions that we are engaging in here.

---

1. There are a few scholars who hold that Genesis 9:20–27 actually recounts the first instance of homosexual behavior, suggesting that Ham incestuously raped Noah whilst Noah was drunk. See for example Gagnon, *The Bible and Homosexual Practice*, 63–69. This has been convincingly refuted, and even if it were viable, given its nature as incestuous rape, it holds little bearing on our current discussion. See Wenham, *Genesis 1–15*, 198–200; and Westermann, *Genesis 1–11*, 484, 488–89.

In fact, though it may seem somewhat extraneous and brief, the story of Sodom and Gomorrah has had a far-reaching impact into Western societies, even making its way into the very courtrooms of our nations with a preponderance of legislative codes enshrining so called "sodomy laws." While sodomy laws have covered a variety of acts deemed by different jurisdictions to be illegal (from anal sex, through to any non-procreative sex acts, including heterosexual), the weight has generally fallen on the side of any form of homosexual behavior. Thus for a large portion of our history, those who found themselves attracted to members of the same sex have been labeled "Sodomites." Perhaps unsurprisingly, this has been the case for the past thousand years.[2]

Growing up in conservative Christian circles, it didn't require a nuanced mind to ascertain the theological force of the fate of Sodom and Gomorrah—homosexual sex incurred the divine wrath of God. As a teenager coming to terms with the nature of who I was, the rhetoric coming from the religious right rung in my mind as an incessant barrage. The AIDS epidemic, having reached its crescendo, was intrinsically linked in my young mind to the story of Sodom. Prominent church leaders whose books I imbibed confirmed my worst fears that "the tidal wave of homosexuality that will drown our children in a polluted sea of sexual perversion . . . will eventually destroy America as it did Rome, Greece, Pompeii, and Sodom"[3] (Tim LaHaye) and "If God doesn't judge America, He'll owe Sodom and Gomorrah an apology"[4] (Ruth Graham). These of course represent something of an extreme view, but nevertheless, these are the voices that had a profound impact on me, and millions of others who shared my story. One author from the traditionalist side who distances himself from the religious far right still sums up his argument succinctly: "the whole incident clearly shows that God takes homosexual sin very seriously." [5]

With this interpretational lens as our introduction, it is appropriate to turn our attention to the text itself in order to critically examine the place that this story has in defining a theology of sexuality. Not exactly a stroll in the park, but a rewarding task nonetheless.

2. For an extensive examination of the history of the term *sodomy* as a reference to homosexual behavior, see Jordan, *The Invention of Sodomy*, 29.

3. Quoted in Petro, *After the Wrath of God*, 32.

4. Petro, *After the Wrath of God*, 32.

5. Morrison, *Born This Way*, 81.

Sodom is first drawn to our attention in Genesis 13:13 and is described as a city of wicked people who are sinning greatly against the Lord. This is in the context of Lot, Abraham's (then called Abram) nephew, choosing to take up residency in the plains surrounding the city. Fast forward some time, and three men visit Abraham—two angels, and the Lord himself in human form. Genesis 18 recounts how Abraham and Sarah take in the three men, approaching them with a deep bow, bringing them water, and preparing bread from the finest flour. The conversation then takes a dramatic turn as Yahweh warns Abraham of the impending destruction of the cities. Abraham pleads that the cities might be spared for the sake of any righteous people that reside there (presumably Abraham has his nephew Lot and his family in mind). Genesis 19:1 picks up the story:

> The two angels arrived at Sodom in the evening, and Lot was sitting in the gateway of the city. When he saw them, he got up to meet them and bowed down with his face to the ground. "My lords," he said, "please turn aside to your servant's house. You can wash your feet and spend the night and then go on your way early in the morning."
>
> "No," they answered, "we will spend the night in the square."
>
> But he insisted so strongly that they did go with him and entered his house. He prepared a meal for them, baking bread without yeast, and they ate. Before they had gone to bed, all the men from every part of the city of Sodom—both young and old—surrounded the house. They called to Lot, "Where are the men who came to you tonight? Bring them out to us so that we can have sex with them."
>
> Lot went outside to meet them and shut the door behind him and said, "No, my friends. Don't do this wicked thing. Look, I have two daughters who have never slept with a man. Let me bring them out to you, and you can do what you like with them. But don't do anything to these men, for they have come under the protection of my roof."
>
> "Get out of our way," they replied. "This fellow came here as a foreigner, and now he wants to play the judge! We'll treat you worse than them." They kept bringing pressure on Lot and moved forward to break down the door.
>
> But the men inside reached out and pulled Lot back into the house and shut the door. Then they struck the men who were at the door of the house, young and old, with blindness so that they could not find the door.

The two men said to Lot, "Do you have anyone else here—sons-in-law, sons or daughters, or anyone else in the city who belongs to you? Get them out of here, because we are going to destroy this place. The outcry to the LORD against its people is so great that he has sent us to destroy it."

So Lot went out and spoke to his sons-in-law, who were pledged to marry his daughters. He said, "Hurry and get out of this place, because the Lord is about to destroy the city!" But his sons-in-law thought he was joking.

With the coming of dawn, the angels urged Lot, saying, "Hurry! Take your wife and your two daughters who are here, or you will be swept away when the city is punished."

When he hesitated, the men grasped his hand and the hands of his wife and of his two daughters and led them safely out of the city, for the LORD was merciful to them. As soon as they had brought them out, one of them said, "Flee for your lives! Don't look back, and don't stop anywhere in the plain! Flee to the mountains or you will be swept away!"

But Lot said to them, "No, my lords, please! Your servant has found favor in your eyes, and you have shown great kindness to me in sparing my life. But I can't flee to the mountains; this disaster will overtake me, and I'll die. Look, here is a town near enough to run to, and it is small. Let me flee to it—it is very small, isn't it? Then my life will be spared."

He said to him, "Very well, I will grant this request too; I will not overthrow the town you speak of. But flee there quickly, because I cannot do anything until you reach it." (That is why the town was called Zoar.)

By the time Lot reached Zoar, the sun had risen over the land. Then the LORD rained down burning sulfur on Sodom and Gomorrah—from the Lord out of the heavens. Thus he overthrew those cities and the entire plain, destroying all those living in the cities—and also the vegetation in the land.

Homosexuality—Front and Center?

Reading the story, there is no doubt that the people of Sodom elicit the wrath of God, the likes of which is rarely seen elsewhere in Scripture—it is swift and it is total. Likewise, there is no doubt that the men of Sodom sought to have sex with the two men who were Lot's visitors, engaging in homoerotic behavior that presumably was not out of character for the city's inhabitants. Indeed, the presence of this illicit sexual behavior seems to be at the core of the evil perpetrated by the men.

Textual links with Genesis 6:4–6 add weight to this, where another form of illicit sexual activity (between women and "sons of God") is directly correlated with wickedness of the human race that leads to the act of total destruction in the flood.[6] In both stories there is a righteous man and his family who narrowly escape a cataclysmic judgment intrinsically tied to a wickedness which pertains in some measure to unnatural sexual relations.

As we move into the New Testament, there is a pertinent reference in Jude 7 in which Sodom serves as an example of the condemned because they "indulged in sexual immorality (*ekporneusasai*) and pursued unnatural desire." Robert Gagnon concludes that while the reference to sexual immorality is ambiguous, it probably refers to homosexual acts.[7]

Further, the idea that sex between men is the impeachable offense of Sodom certainly seems to be the view of some noteworthy Jewish scholars of the first century.[8] Both Philo of Alexandria and Flavius Josephus condemn the homoerotic behavior of the Sodomites as against nature (*para physin*).[9] Philo is particularly vehement in his condemnations, asserting that:

> . . . not only in their mad lust for women did they violate the marriages of their neighbours, but also men mounted males without respect for the sex nature which the active partner shares with the passive; and so when they tried to beget children they were discovered to be incapapble of any but a sterile seed.[10]

Given these intertextual associations with homoerotic behavior, there seems to be good reason for Kevin DeYoung to state that "We are right

6. Gagnon, *The Bible and Homosexual Practice*, 75.

7. Gagnon, *The Bible and Homosexual Practice*, 87.

8. As discussed in the previous chapter, examining ancient literature outside of the Bible is helpful in understanding the sociocultural factors that would have governed the authors' writing, and sheds light on interpretations over time.

9. Nissinen, *Homoeroticism in the Biblical World*, 93. *Para physin* forms a key philosophical and theological concept of the centuries surrounding Jesus' birth. We will be exploring this concept more as we engage with Romans 1 in chapter 10.

10. Philo, quoted in Loader, *Sexuality in the New Testament*, 207. Interestingly here, Philo understood the logical progression from same-sex intercourse was male infertility. Given his aversion to any sexual act that didn't involve a procreative element, this appears to be the driving moral principle for Philo.

to see homosexual practice as one aspect of Sodom's sin and as a reason Sodom and Gomorrah were destroyed."[11]

And yet despite these voices that seek to place the burden of the text under the helm of homosexuality, and despite the vast quantity of literature over the past several hundred years that has added weight to this interpretation, it may surprise some to discover that this has not been the universal view of the church for most of its 2,000-year history. In fact, a rich literary tradition from both Jewish and Christian heritage shows that this has been something of a *minority* interpretation and moreover, most modern critical scholarship has distanced itself greatly from any such association.

To this end, when discussing homosexual relationships as displayed in the modern West, prominent traditional theologian Richard Hays concludes, "The notorious story of Sodom and Gomorrah . . . is actually irrelevant to the topic." And further, "The gang rape scenario exemplifies the wickedness of the city, but there is nothing in the passage pertinent to a judgment about the morality of consensual homosexual intercourse."[12]

How is it that one story can elicit such a polarity of views? In order to unpack the answer to this question, we need to visit a few other passages of Scripture and some ancient sources, which shed further light on the sin of Sodom.

An Ancient Interpretation?

From the literature we have available to us (which is a surprisingly large amount), Philo, mentioned above, was the first to directly assess the sin of Sodom as attempted homosexual intercourse. This is significant because a traditional dating would place Philo some 1,500 years after the writing of Genesis 19.[13] How was Sodom viewed in these intervening years? Scattered right throughout the Old Testament, New Testament, and ancient sources there are abundant references to the city of Sodom.[14]

11. DeYoung, *What Does the Bible Really Teach?*, 35.

12. Hays, *The Moral Vision*, 381.

13. There are some scholars that would argue that Genesis was not written until much later, but even at its latest estimate, Genesis would have been completed some 600 years prior to Philo.

14. Deut 29:23,32:32; Isa 1:9–10, 3:9, 13:19; Jer 20:16, 23:14, 29:18, 50:40; Lam 4:6; Ezek 16:46–56; Amos 4:1–11; Zeph 2:8–11; Matt 10:5–15; Luke 10:12, 17:22–29; Rom 9:29; 2 Pet 2:6; Jude 7; Rev 11:8.

We know from the unanimity of these texts, and with great accuracy, the sin (or rather sins) Sodom was condemned for.

The book of Isaiah for example opens with a scathing indictment on the sins of Jerusalem, pejoratively labeling the city as "Sodom" (Isa 1:10). In this chapter the city is condemned for its failure to seek justice, correct oppression, care for the orphan, and plead the case of the widow. Murder, theft, hypocritical worship, and lack of care for the poor are all listed. Sexual sins (much less, homosexual sins) are nowhere in the picture.

Or we could take Ezekiel as another example. Writing from the Babylonian exile sometime in the sixth century BC, Ezekiel addresses the city of Jerusalem with the most strident condemnation available to him, by comparing God's holy city with the city of Sodom itself:

> Behold, this was the guilt of your sister Sodom: she and her daughters had pride, excess of food, and prosperous ease, but did not aid the poor and needy. They were haughty and did an abomination before me. So I removed them, when I saw it. (Ezek 16:49)

Ezekiel provides an interesting case study given the fact that the vitriolic diatribe dished out in the surrounding chapters is littered with pornographic imagery, describing Jerusalem as a (female) prostitute with uncovered nakedness, "playing the whore" with untold lovers. Ezekiel clearly isn't afraid to invoke sexualized language, and yet when it comes to the sin of Sodom, this is nowhere to be seen.[15] Rather, Sodom is condemned for arrogance and apathy toward the poor despite its prosperity.

Zephaniah, Amos, and Jeremiah all progress in a similar vein.[16] The sin of Sodom is seen as a cumulative lack of care for those within society who are marginalized, for a lack of justice, and for a disregard for the

15. Gagnon (*The Bible and Homosexual Practice*, 83) sees in the term *abomination* (*tô'ēbâ*) a clear reference to the homosexual proscriptions of Leviticus 18:22 and 20:13, and therefore contends that Ezekiel was condemning same-sex sexual acts in Sodom. Given that this term is used 117 times in the Old Testament, and only twice as a referent to homoerotic activity, and given the fact that Ezekiel uses this term thirty-nine other times only ever to describe idolatrous or heterosexual adulterous behavior (e.g., Ezek 22:11), this interpretation is a far stretch. Further, if *tô'ēbâ* here did refer to Sodom's homosexual behavior obscurely referenced in Leviticus, we would expect to find it again mentioned when Jerusalem's sexual behavior is explicitly described in Ezekiel 22:10–11, which, of note, has much stronger parallels to Leviticus 18 and 20. There is however no such condemnation. To conclude that homosexual behavior is in view in Ezekiel 16 is exegetically untenable.

16. Zeph 2:8–11, Amos 4:1–11, Jer 23:14.

alien and stranger in their midst.[17] According to the Old Testament, these are the sins of Sodom.

When we turn to the New Testament we find a similar story. For example, Jesus himself provides us with a further nuanced understanding of Sodom's sin. As Jesus prepared to send out the twelve (Matt 10:5–15) and the seventy-two (Luke 10:1–12), he encouraged them to enter a town and locate a person who could take them in as guests for the duration of their stay as they proclaimed the good news. If nobody would fulfill the task of hospitality, then the sent ones were to wipe the dust off of their feet and proclaim that it would be more bearable for Sodom on the day that Jesus' kingdom comes (Matt 10:15; Luke 10:12). Jesus saw in Genesis 19 a failure of the citizens of Sodom to take in the strangers in order to care for them.

This "inhospitality" reading of the narrative is reflected alongside xenophobic vices in the apocryphal book, Wisdom of Solomon, written sometime in the first century BC:

> There had been others [Sodomites] who refused to welcome strangers when they came to them, but these made slaves of guests who were their benefactors. There is indeed a judgement awaiting those who treated foreigners as enemies; but these, after a festal welcome, oppressed with hard labor men who had earlier shared their rights. They were struck with blindness also, like men at the door of one good man." (Wisdom of Solomon 19:13–15, NEB)[18]

All of these ancient interpretations of the text take us away from understanding the sin of Sodom as sexual, and lands us with a clear understanding that Sodom was condemned for its arrogance, disregard for justice, and in part, its flagrant contempt of hospitality. This fits neatly with the Ancient Near Eastern conceptualization of homosexual rape used as a means of humiliation and dominance over another man. We will explore this at length in the next chapter, but for now it is important

---

17. This disregard for the stranger and contempt of hospitality is most certainly the driving principle behind the tragic parallel story of the Levite and his concubine in Judges 19. The use of the Levite's concubine as a substitute for the mob having sex with the man demonstrates clearly that the men were not interested in exclusively homosexual behavior but rather were intent on shaming the man who entered their town.

18. While the Apocryphal books are not considered by the Protestant tradition inspired by God, they provide extremely valuable insights into the cultural milieu of their time.

to note that it is highly doubtful that *all* the men of Sodom (a point which 19:4 stresses) were motivated by homoerotic arousal, but rather asserting their power and strength over the men who had entered their territory was their true intention.[19]

Further, while it was noted above that Josephus and Philo view homoerotic behavior as a vice of the Sodomites, they read into the narrative their own understanding of homosexual behavior as they witnessed in first-century Roman-occupied Israel—with overtones of pederasty and with sharp distinctions between "active" and "passive" (effeminate) males.[20] Josephus for example adds to the story a typical Greek flair,

> Now when the Sodomites saw the young men to be of beautiful countenances, and this to an extraordinary degree, and that they took up their lodgings with Lot, they resolved themselves to enjoy these beautiful boys by force and violence.[21]

Nowhere in Genesis 19 is there any indication of the age or appearance of the two men that entered Lot's house, but as the expression of homosexual activity that Josephus would have been exposed to in his society, he understandably read this *into* the narrative.[22] Given his apparent disregard for the text, it is difficult to take him as an authoritative exegete.

As noted by Gagnon, however, Jude 7 still appears to contend that homosexual behavior was central to the sin of Sodom.[23] Read in its context, this too proves to be a shaky assertion at best. The key phrase in this discussion, "pursued unnatural desires," literally translates more

---

19. Regele, *Science, Scripture, and Same-Sex Love*, 127; Nissinen, *Homoeroticism in the Biblical World*, 49.

20. Nissinen, *Homoeroticism in the Biblical World*, 93. Pederasty in the Greco-Roman world was a common social practice in which young boys were taken in by older men in student-mentor relationships, usually understood to include a sexual relationship. Pederasty and "active/passive" notions of sexuality will be discussed at length as we examine ancient understandings of homosexuality in following chapters.

21. Josephus, *The Works of Josephus*, 41.

22. To be clear, Josephus certainly did not see this as the only, or even the main, reason for Sodom's destruction. Rather, as he notes in *Antiquities*, it was Sodom's arrogance and hatred of strangers that brought them judgment.

23. Gagnon, *The Bible and Homosexual Practice*, 87. 2 Peter 2:7 is the only other place in the New Testament where a sexual interpretation of Sodom is seen. Here the term *sensual conduct* is utilized. Given that Peter had a plethora of terms he could have employed to describe same-sex sexual activity, the ambiguity of this term makes it doubtful that Peter was convicting them solely on homoerotic behavior.

accurately to "departed after a different type of flesh."[24] This statement directly follows another example of pursuing different flesh cited in Jude 6 which references the pre-flood Genesis narrative of fallen angels having sexual relations with human women (Gen 6). The logical flow of the argument is a reversal of relations: angels having sex with women followed by men having sex with angels (which is precisely the narrative of Sodom).[25] This makes much greater sense of the term *different type of flesh*, where homosexual behavior (which would be "similar flesh") is a possible, though confused interpretation at best.

Prominent church fathers Tertullian (second century AD), Origen (second to third centuries AD), and Jerome (fourth to fifth centuries AD) all wrote extensively about the nature of the sin of Sodom, but none of them link this with homosexuality at all, despite addressing same-sex sexual behavior elsewhere in their works.[26] Rather, once again Sodom is condemned for its arrogance, its violence, its inhospitality and disregard for the marginalized.

Reclaiming the Message of Sodom

Even with all of the diverse contextual features we have now covered, there are still some from within the traditionalist camp who perplexingly hold that this story presents itself as a moral indictment against all forms of gay and lesbian unions. Gagnon, who is commonly upheld as the foremost authority in sexual ethics from a traditionalist perspective, concludes his discussion around Sodom and Gomorrah like this:

> . . . the height of the town's evil was epitomized by the attempt to rape visiting strangers and a resident alien, and worse still, sexual intercourse with males: emasculating Lot's guests by treating them not in accordance with their nature as males, but as females to be penetrated in anal sex.[27]

24. Davids, *The Letters of 2 Peter and Jude*, 52.

25. For further examination of this letter, see Bauckham, *Jude and the Relatives*, 187; and Nissinen, *Homoeroticism in the Biblical World*, 92. This interpretation is reflected in the pseudepigraphical works *The Testament of Naphtali* and *The Book of Jubilees*, both attesting to the ancient understanding of Sodom's sin being the interspecies sex of humans with angelic beings.

26. Carden, *Sodomy*, 129–34.

27. Gagnon, *The Bible and Homosexual Practice*, 90–91.

Perhaps I am alone in this, but I find it astonishing that Gagnon would so readily assert his theology of a hierarchy of sins, establishing that sexual intercourse with males is "worse still" than the gang rape that so nearly played out in the story. This sort of theological process is somewhat alarming given the influence of Gagnon's work in this field. Not only does it fail to understand the text in light of its ancient interpretations, but it also fails to engage at the hermeneutical level we spoke about in previous chapters, seeking to determine if there is a sufficient correlation between the ancient text and the realm of sexuality as it is currently discussed today.[28]

In other words, we have to ask the question, "Does Sodom and Gomorrah provide us with a sufficient hermeneutic to address the loving, monogamous, self-giving relationships that I see in so many of the lesbian and gay communities around me?"

On the one hand, we have to offer a loud and clear "no." The narrative of Genesis 19 recounts a violent attempted gang rape of two angelic beings. The cities' destruction follows years of rebellion, which culminates in this scene. Even if we were to concede against the interpretational weight of Scripture that homosexual practice was the reason for their ultimate annihilation, the only sin that we could condemn here would be violent rape intended to humiliate its victim. To contend that this story thus offers a sound defense of a traditionalist view of sexuality is akin to concluding that because heterosexual rape is condemned in the Bible, all heterosexual sex is inherently evil.

However, on the other hand, I also wish to suggest that there are some things that, as a society, we need to take heed of from this narrative. Sodom has gone down in history as a place of violence, of oppression and disdain for the alien and stranger in their midst. For these reasons, God in the bounds of infinite wisdom saw fit to take action, raining fire upon those who would so flagrantly assert their dominance over others. The driving moral principle here is patently obvious. God takes seriously our treatment of the marginalized, the poor, the outcast, and the alien. How we relate to those who come into our sphere of influence who are seeking shelter, fleeing from violence or escaping oppression, must matter to us, because it matters to God. Violence, humiliation, sexual license, and wickedness play no part in God's kingdom. As God's people it must always be our honor to uphold the goodness of God's design for humanity before a watching world.

28. Nissinen, *Homoeroticism in the Biblical World*, 23.

8

The Abomination

Let me give you something of an insight into my life, a snapshot of what is going on in my world. As I write this, a society-wide debate is raging over the legitimacy of gay relationships. On a government level, legislation amendments are being proposed and constitutional rights are being scrutinized to the nth degree. At a grassroots level, hundreds of thousands are being mobilized to lend their voice to both sides of the debate. Millions of dollars are being poured into lobby groups, pitting a "conservative" (usually religious) worldview against a "progressive" (often secular) narrative. For the most part, in my Australian context, debates like this play themselves out with civilized decorum, and the marginal vitriolic voices play a smaller, though nevertheless aggressive, part.

But as with all things, there are wheels within wheels, and within the societal cogs of this debate, a secondary debate is playing itself out in the many church circles. For the church, the "threat of homosexuality" is no longer an abstract concept that has its home amongst the raging pagans "out there." Indeed, it has permeated its way into the very congregations that have for so long seen themselves as buttresses of truth against the sexual mores of our age.

Needless to say, between the societal tumult and ecclesiastical roller coaster, I find myself confronted with countless voices professing their judgment over my sexuality on an almost minute-by-minute basis. The net result of such a public and all-pervasive debate over such a private and intensely personal matter is a strange existential whiplash. Like many in my position, I feel caught up in the middle. If this were war, I would argue that I have one foot in both camps because I love them both. Both would argue that I have one foot in each camp because I'm a traitor. Needless to say, if I had it my way, I wouldn't choose this.

If we continue with this war motif for just a moment, the verses we are looking at in this chapter constitute the weapon of choice for the armies encamped on both sides. Posted on placards and whipped out in any given battlefield, Leviticus has proven itself to be a potent grenade on so many levels.

For those who wish to mock the Bible and undermine its validity, the language of abomination and the archaic death penalty for gay sex come across as a relic of an ancient, misogynistic legal code that society has moved on from long ago. To be fair, it's not hard to make Leviticus appear quaint at best and diabolically oppressive at worst.

On the other side of no man's land, for those who seek to maintain that homosexuality is not part of God's intended design, Leviticus 18:22 and 20:13 stipulate some of the harshest terms in all of Scripture and simply cannot be ignored. The verses present an unquestionably negative condemnation of homoerotic activity, and, as far as sound bites go, the term "abomination" is practically begging to be lobbed over the barricade.

For those who have been living under the proverbial rock, here are the verses in question:

> You shall not lie with a male as with a woman; it is an abomination (Lev 18:22, ESV).

> If a man lies with a male as with a woman, both of them have committed an abomination; they shall surely be put to death; their blood is upon them (Lev 20:13, ESV).

I'll be the first to admit that these verses come across as unquestionably clear. This being the case, our first task is rather straightforward though somewhat counterintuitive, as we seek to demonstrate that the application of these verses to the twenty-first century is *anything but* clear. Oddly enough, this is a rather simple task. Most people already agree that Leviticus is a complex beast of a book. The far greater task is what follows as we read the book of Leviticus as a whole, within the canon of Scripture, ascertaining its driving theological, cross-cultural principles that must inform our lives today. We're talking about Leviticus, and I apologize from the outset—this chapter is going to be dense, but hang in there, it's worth it!

What Am I Looking At?

The book of Leviticus has simultaneously inspired and perplexed both Jewish and Christians theologians for millennia. At its core, a large portion of the book can best be described as a *holiness code*, outlining for the nation of Israel how they are to live as God's chosen people in the promised land that they are preparing to enter. As a stipulation of the covenantal agreement between Yahweh and Abraham's offspring, it reflects other ancient treaties of the time between reigning kings and vassal (conquered) nations, outlining the obligations of the people (the laws) and the assurance of God's provision (both materially and spiritually).[1]

The vital theological weight of the book is found in the repeated call for the people of Israel to "be holy" as Yahweh their God is holy (Lev 11:44–45, 19:2, 20:7), a status that is achieved through a complex set of ceremonial functions (1:1—10:20), cultic (temple) practices (8:1—10:20), avoidance of anything deemed "unclean" (11:1—15:33) and a plethora of ritual laws (16:1—25:55). The difficulty of application to our modern setting is in determining which of these functions, cleanliness standards, and ritual laws are to be maintained today. For example, there are stipulations around the uncleanness of meat from camels, pigs, rabbits, shellfish, and chameleons (Lev 11); there are instructions for how to dismantle a house if mold is found in it (Lev 14:43–45); if a man is found to have a skin disease on his head, he is to wear torn clothes, let his hair be unkempt and cry out "Unclean! Unclean!" whilst living alone outside the camp (Lev 13:38–26); fields are not to be sown with two types of seed and clothing woven of two types of fabric is not to be worn (Lev 19:19). The one thing we can say with clarity about Leviticus is that it is certainly not intended to be directly applied to today as a formal set of legal stipulations. How then do we determine which (if any) stipulations still apply today? With this question in mind, let us look more closely at the section of Leviticus in which homosexual activity is mentioned, chapters 18—20.

Whilst identifying a watertight structure of the book remains elusive, the verses that pertain to our topic are found in a discrete section, clearly bound by the call for Israel to be defined by its distinction from the nations surrounding it. Have a look at the words that come before and after both of our verses:

---

1. Sklar, *Leviticus*, 30.

And the Lord spoke to Moses, saying, "Speak to the people of Israel and say to them, I am the Lord your God. *You shall not do as they do in the land of Egypt*, where you lived, and *you shall not do as they do in the land of Canaan*, to which I am bringing you. *You shall not walk in their statutes*. You shall follow my rules and keep my statutes and walk in them. I am the Lord your God.

(Lev 18:1–4, ESV)

Do not make yourselves unclean by any of these things, for *by all these the nations I am driving out before you have become unclean*, and the land became unclean, so that I punished its iniquity, and the land vomited out its inhabitants. But you shall keep my statutes and my rules and *do none of these abominations*, either the native or the stranger who sojourns among you (*for the people of the land, who were before you, did all of these abominations*, so that the land became unclean).

(Lev 18:24–27, ESV)

You shall therefore keep all my statutes and all my rules and do them, that the land where I am bringing you to live may not vomit you out. *And you shall not walk in the customs of the nation that I am driving out before you*, for they did all these things, and therefore I detested them. But I have said to you, "You shall inherit their land, and I will give it to you to possess, a land flowing with milk and honey." I am the Lord your God, who has *separated you from the peoples*.

(Lev 20:22–24, ESV)

Thus, the instructions that we are looking at in 18:22 and 20:13 are best conceived of as commands for the nation of Israel to, in some manner or other, be distinguishable from the pagan nations around them and identifiable as the people of Yahweh. As 18:26–27 makes clear, the things that Israel are to avoid are those things that cause the Land itself to become unclean, otherwise known as "abominations."

Understanding "Abomination"

What a word! The Hebrew term *tôʿēbâ* has been interpreted in a few different ways. The ESV and KJV translate it almost always as "abomination"; the NIV prefers "detestable thing"; the Holman bounces between "detestable" and "abomination" (HCSB); and the NRSV adds "abhorrent" to the list. While these are decisively negative, many scholars and pastors alike have rightly raised questions not so much at the word itself, but at what it is applied to throughout the Old Testament. The word *tôʿēbâ* is used 117 times in the Hebrew Scriptures and a cursory glance at the way that the term is used shows that it is impossible to attribute a direct correlation between the Hebrew term *tôʿēbâ* and the notion of "sin" as that which is always and universally opposed to the will of God.

For example, for the Egyptian people, dining with an Israelite was considered *tôʿēbâ* (Gen 43:32). Similarly, it would have been considered *tôʿēbâ* to the Egyptians for the Hebrew people to worship Yahweh whilst in the presence of Pharaoh (Exod 8:6). Perhaps most noteworthy, for the Egyptians, the very profession of shepherding rendered a person *tôʿēbâ* (Gen 46:34). Likewise, for Yahweh and his people, rock badgers, pigs, and hares were all considered *tôʿēbâ* (Deut 3–8). It is evident that the term itself cannot be directly translated as a theological equivalent to sin, leading some to conclude that "if the act was identified as *tôʿēbâ* it did not therefore mean that the act in question was inherently, objectively or eternally an immoral offense or a violation of God's will."[2] As Ancient Near Eastern literature shows, the term in and of itself does not necessarily carry ethical or moral implications, but rather points to strong social boundaries and areas of cultural taboos which were unacceptable for a society's self-identification.[3] The English term *abomination* rightly carries negative associations, but it fails to capture the vitally social aspect of this richly laden term.

Given that distinction from the nations around them constitutes such a large theological drive for the Israelite people, it is no surprise then that in the Old Testament the term *tôʿēbâ* (with its emphasis on social boundaries and taboo cultural practices) is applied in abundance directly to the presence of idolatrous worship of the gods of foreign nations.[4] As we read the Scriptures, we discover that in the vast majority of cases the term *tôʿēbâ* is very closely tied to the temple rituals of the Egyptian people (whose land the Israelites have left) and the Canaanite people (whose

2. Martin, *Unclobber*, 90.

3. For extended examinations on the cultural boundary marking nature of *tôʿēbâ*, see Gnuse, "Seven Gay Texts," 75–77, and Bird, "The Bible in Christian Ethical Deliberation," 152.

4. Nissinen, *Homoeroticism in the Biblical World*, 43.

land the Israelites are entering). This cultic (temple) association is the word's usual usage.[5] For example, Deuteronomy 27:17 declares "Cursed be the man who makes a carved or cast metal image, an abomination (*tôʿēbâ*) to the Lord, a thing made by the hands of a craftsman, and sets it up in secret." Likewise, in Ezekiel 5:11 God declares "Surely, because you have defiled my sanctuary with all your detestable things and with all your abominations (*tôʿēbâ*), therefore I will withdraw."

The abundance of such usages gives any reader strong reason to think that when Leviticus invokes the term *tôʿēbâ*, it may contain in at least some measure undertones of idolatrous behavior as a corollary of the cultural activities of their surrounding nations which Israel are to avoid.[6] Of course, idolatry, according to Yahweh, is always sinful. Indeed, in Leviticus 20:13 the *tôʿēbâ* committed is sufficiently significant so as to warrant the death penalty. This understanding of the term *abomination* and its unquestionably dire consequences has given countless scholars pause to consider exactly what was being condemned when the author speaks of "lying with a male as with a woman." To understand this further, we need to zoom out and look at the context in which we find our texts.

Two realms of context will be covered. First, we will examine whether or not there are elements of cultic practices at play, and secondly, we will unpack the intrinsically patriarchal nature in which the laws are found. Combined, these vital factors will inform a more nuanced understanding of the driving theological principles at play here.

As a Man Lies with a Woman

As we have already seen, the principle focus of the Holiness Code is that Israel be distinct from the nations around them, set apart for God's glory. Everything described within the code is designed to separate them morally, culturally, and politically from the peoples with whom they come in contact. See those Egyptians? You are to look different. See those Amalekites? You are to be distinct. They worship other gods, but you, Israel, are to worship Yahweh. In doing this, you will be holy, as God is holy. A natural question to ask then at this point is "what were those nations up to?" As it happens, history has preserved great slabs of cultural data

5. For other examples, see Deut 7:26; 1 Kgs 11:7; Isa 44:19; Jer 32:25; Ezek 5:11, 18:12.

6. Gnuse, "Seven Gay Texts," 76.

about the practices of the people of the Ancient Near East. We have their lore and their laws in surprising detail. We have stories and poems and pyramids and stones. We know a great deal about their trade routes and their social customs. More pertinent to our discussion, we know an awful lot about their attitudes toward the sexes and toward sex—marriage rites, concubinage, sex slaves, rape of war prisoners, lists of punishments for illicit sex acts. We have their dowry lists and divorce provisions—from Mesopotamia to Assyria we have it all . . . One thing however is conspicuously absent. In all of the literature that we have, there is not one mention of consensual, committed, monogamous homosexual unions in the lands surrounding Israel. Not one.[7]

That's not to say that no sex acts between two men were taking place. They most certainly were. But when the words "as a man lies with a woman" were penned in Leviticus, it would seem that there was nothing even remotely similar to what we would conceive of today as faithful, same-sex relationships. Rather, all of the evidence suggests that homosexual sex was intrinsically tied to one or both of two concurrent cultural realities, either to cultic, idolatrous worship or to patriarchal notions of power and shame. What does this tell us then of Leviticus?

Leviticus chapters 18 and 20 are commonly mistaken to be lists of vices concerned purely with sexual ethics. They contain repeated lists of people with whom sex cannot be had. However on closer inspection this does not do the texts justice. Chapter 20 lists the vices in order of severity of punishment (death penalty through to infertility), while chapter 18 lists them thematically, grouping together similar acts. Many scholars have noted that when we take a closer look at the verses surrounding the prohibitions around homosexual activity in 18:21–23, we find exactly what we would expect to find given the strong cultic associations with the term *tôʿēbâ*. We find two other acts thematically tied to idolatrous temple practices of the Canaanite people. Sacrificing of children to the god Molech was viewed by the Israelite people as a particularly abhorrent behavior (see, for example, 2 Kings 23:10 and Jeremiah 32:35.) Though some specifics are still debated, infant sacrifice amongst the Canaanite people was a well-documented practice, and brought the harshest of condemnations in the Levitical code (Lev 20:2–5). Likewise, the Israelites understood the existence of sex acts with animals representing various

7. Brownson, *Bible, Gender, Sexuality*, 270. Nissinen's discussion of *Horus and Seth*, and *The Epic of Gilgamesh* provides an even-handed analysis of homosexual themes present in Mesopotamia. Nissinen, *Homoeroticism in the Biblical World*, 20–30.

pagan deities, and the place that this had in cultic practices.[8] The fact that women are mentioned here, whilst being noticeably nonexistent as active participants throughout the rest of the chapters, further separates this as an act which is distinct from the general sexual vices.

Why is it that these laws were placed thematically together in chapter 18? One vital clue to this is perhaps located in the unfolding narrative of Israel. The covenant outlined by God in the book of Leviticus repeatedly came with a dire warning:

> But you shall keep my statutes and my rules and do none of these abominations (*tôʿēbâ*), either the native or the stranger who sojourns among you (for the people of the land, who were before you, did all of these abominations, so that the land became unclean), lest the land vomit you out when you make it unclean, as it vomited out the nation that was before you.

(Lev 18:26–28, ESV)

The covenantal promise was that God would bless Israel abundantly if they remained faithful to him, but should they stray from Yahweh's statutes, God would remove this blessing, and they would be removed from the promised land. Almost from the moment of entry, there is a downward spiral of rebellion as Israel turns to foreign gods, and history recounts the exiles that subsequently occurred. Naturally, when we read the histories of Israel and the denouncements of the prophets, we would expect to see the Levitical law being held up as a litmus test for why Israel is handed over to her enemies. Therefore, working backwards, the history of Israel becomes an interpretational key to the book of Leviticus because the two work hand in hand. What is condemned in Leviticus would be condemned in Israel's history. What is upheld in one, would be upheld in the other. If faithful, caring same-sex unions were being prohibited in Leviticus, then we would expect at some point in Israel's downward spiral that these would be historically evident and decried. If however there were some form of idolatrous edge to what is being condemned in Leviticus, we would expect to find relics of the cultic practices of the nations around them. The latter is what we discover, with striking linguistic parallels to Leviticus 18:20–28:

> For they also built for themselves high places and pillars and Asherim on every high hill and under every green tree, and

8. Gnuse, "Seven Gay Texts," 76.

there were also male cult prostitutes (*qĕdēšîm*) in the land. They did according to all the abominations (*tôʿēbâ*) of the nations that the Lord drove out before the people of Israel.

(1 Kgs 14:24, ESV)[9]

High places were the geographical markers for foreign gods. Even Yahweh utilized mountains as symbolic of his presence (think Mount Sinai). These male cult prostitutes, *qĕdēšîm*,[10] provided sexual temple services, offering their bodies to both women and other men for same-sex intercourse as a means of worship of the foreign deities thought to be present on the high places.[11] Aside from the gang rapes discussed in the previous chapter, the *qĕdēšîm* are the only examples of non-heterosexual intercourse in the entire Old Testament. As the direct quotation shows, for the author recounting Israel's demise they are intrinsically linked to the Holiness Code established in Leviticus 18. Of course, this by no means provides evidence for what the author of Leviticus had in mind when the document was penned, but it does give an insight into how the authors of 1 and 2 Kings understood the term "with a male as with a woman." There was no sense of faithful, mutual relationship and nor was there a desire to honor Yahweh with their bodies. Rather, these male cult prostitutes were using their bodies to appease and entice gods who were no gods at all. If this is what Leviticus is indeed condemning, then it is a far stretch to conclude based on these verses that all same-sex unions are inherently evil.

It's by no means conclusive, but it does seem possible that cultic rituals were in view here—at the very least this was evident for the authors of 1 and 2 Kings. But even if we were to pass the idolatrous concepts in Leviticus 18 and 20, we are still left with a plethora of interpretational difficulties that those who hold a traditional view of sexual ethics far too often fail to engage.

9. The same condemnations with similar wording are proffered in Deuteronomy 23:17–18; 1 Kings 15:12, 22:46; and 2 Kings 23:7.

10. Translated "sodomites" in the King James Version.

11. For a thorough examination of the existence and sexual practices of the *qĕdēšîm* in Israel's history, see Gagnon, *The Bible and Homosexual Practice*, 100–10.

Three Types of Law?

When it comes to Leviticus, there is a long history of attempting to categorize the laws it contains so as to determine which laws are still applicable to us today. By far, the most common approach has been to categorize them under three distinct headings: *civil laws* outline the legal societal codes for how Israel was to conduct itself; *ceremonial laws* pertain to the temple (or tabernacle) practices—sacrifices, cleansing rituals, and religious festivals; and *moral laws* (summarized in the Ten Commandments) reveal the ongoing, eternal will of God.[12] Under this schema, civil laws were disbanded by the New Covenant's Gentile inclusion and thus are no longer applicable. Ceremonial laws acted as shadows of Christ's work and were thus fulfilled by his life, death, and resurrection. Moral laws on the other hand continue to remain applicable to today and hold their weight across all cultures. For those who hold a traditional view of sexual ethics, the Levitical prohibitions against homosexual activity fit into the "moral" category.

While this approach to Leviticus is appealing in its simplicity, at the end of the day its simplicity is its greatest flaw.[13] How do we determine which law fits where? Is the command to not murder a moral issue or a civil issue? And what about the Sabbath? Though this is patently clear in the Ten Commandments, it is scarcely practiced by Christians today without significant modification. Prohibitions against worshiping foreign gods would most clearly fit under ceremonial laws, and yet nobody is arguing that idolatry is an appropriate behavior according to God today. When it comes to sex acts, most people would initially consider these to be moral issues, but both Leviticus 18 and 20 state that illicit sexual activity results in uncleanness (a distinctly ceremonial term), which is then punishable with a range of sentences (such as death)—suggesting they fall under civil law. See the confusion?[14]

---

12. See Bayess's short work, *Threefold Division of the Law*.

13. Barker, *Deuteronomy*, 77.

14. This confusion is made even greater when we consider the plethora of underlying rationales given by both traditional and affirming theologians for why various sex acts are prohibited. For some, the spilling of semen is the reason for the prohibitions, and therefore they represent a moral issue (Milgrom, *Leviticus 17–22*, 1568). For others, the mixing of bodily fluids (semen with menstrual blood or feces) created ceremonial uncleanness (Bigger, "Family Laws," 202–3). Yet others argue that continuation of the family line is of primary importance and thus the prohibitions may be fundamentally civil (Melcher, "The Holiness Code," 98–99).

Ultimately, the greatest failure of this way of thinking about the Levitical law is that it is simply not how the Bible itself understands the law—the civil laws *are* deeply moral. Likewise the moral and ceremonial laws were branded into their civil code (hence they were punishable). The vast disagreements about what laws should fall under what umbrella show that by their very nature, these categories fail to grasp both the unity and complexity of Leviticus.[15] As Brownson states, "Indeed, the entire distinction between the ceremonial (bad and irrelevant) and moral (good and binding) probably gains more of its energy today from low-church Protestantism than it does from anything in the New Testament itself."[16]

The Law After Christ

If you're still with me, and you are starting to feel somewhat confused, let me offer you this encouragement, you are in good company. In fact, you are experiencing something of the question that has plagued Christianity since its inception. One of the most heated discussions in the early church was how to interpret the Old Testament laws in light of Christ's work. The ushering in of the Gentile believers into the kingdom of God under the New Covenant signaled a dramatic shift as Jewish Christians felt the pull to continue in their deeply engrained rituals, while the new converts from multi-ethnic origins found these ancient strictures impossible to live by. Acts 15 recounts the drama of the debate.

The tension is this: Christ has set us free from the law (the Old Testament), and we are to no longer let ourselves be burdened again by its yoke of slavery (Gal 5:1). Indeed, for Paul, the Old Testament is the "law of sin and death," and a "curse" from which Christ has redeemed us and brought life (Gal 3:13; Rom 8:2, 10:4). How then can we apply with good conscience the Old Testament to those who are in Christ, the New Covenant?

In Acts 15, amidst the tumultuous spread of the gospel to the nations, the gathered council of apostles and elders writes a letter to the Gentiles, seeking unity amongst the churches. In it, they assert that the Old Testament does not bind Gentiles, but they implored the new, non-Jewish converts to abstain from just four things: food sacrificed to idols,

---

15. For a critique of this way of viewing the law, see Schreiner, *40 Questions*, 91–94.

16. Brownson, *Bible, Gender, Sexuality*, 184.

from blood, from the meat of strangled animals, and from sexual immorality (Acts 15:29). That was the year 49 AD.

Two things need to be noted about this list in order to determine its applicability to today. Firstly, sometime around 57 AD, Paul wrote in his letter to the church in Corinth that no food, including food sacrificed to idols, was to be considered unclean for Christians to eat (1 Cor 8—10). Apparently for Paul, the strictures of the Jerusalem council were clearly to be interpreted as binding only for a short time—they in no means were demanding that believers under the New Covenant were to be bound indefinitely to the legal codes. We see this in the church's current apathy toward a medium rare steak—it may be unappealing to some, but we aren't committing sin by eating beef that still has some blood in it!

Secondly, the term translated "sexual immorality" in Acts 15:29 is the term *porneia*, which is an exceedingly broad term, seemingly used here as a catchall term for sexual sin. There are some who attempt to equate this term directly with the sexual vices outlined in Leviticus 18 and 20, but that fails to account for the strictures around having sex with a woman during menstruation (Lev 18:19, 20:18). By no means is this act sinful by any church's teaching today. The early church's teaching on how the Gentiles (which is most of us) were to relate to the Levitical law simply does not provide us with a rubric by which we can apply its prohibitions of same-sex sexual activity to our life today.

It's Sex, Therefore It Matters

And so where does this leave us? Chances are, it is a stretch to apply the Levitical laws in question to faithful, mutually giving, same-sex, monogamous relationships. But even if against all the odds that's what they are addressing, we come across insurmountable barriers in applying them to today when we look at Christ's work in abrogating (doing away with by fulfilling) the Old Testament law. At this point, we inevitably enter the realm of pop theology, which surprisingly is vastly more common than we'd perhaps like to admit. In fact, it's probably the most common exegetical method amongst Christians, and it goes like this, "some things in Leviticus just feel more inherently important than others; murder, lying, sex, theft etc. and as such, those things should still apply today." I'll be honest. This is how I treated Leviticus for most of my theological journey.

The idea that sexual sin "feels more important" than others is hardly a sound hermeneutical principle, but I would like to suggest that it does on some level have a portion of merit, because sex *is* important. It's a beautiful part of the creation that God has given us, and as I look around at people whom I encounter every day I am reminded that sexual sin has far reaching ramifications. It makes sense that as people who long to protect our families and communities, we would be cautious with sex—it is a dangerous thing to distort that which God has created beautiful.

Indeed, for many theologians it is the beauty of this creation as described in Genesis 1 and 2 that stands as the final pillar upholding Leviticus as applicable to today. Most people who hold to a traditional view of sexual ethics assert that Leviticus places strictures around homosexual activity because of God's creation of male and female. To put it in the theological terms we've already covered, Leviticus is encoding gender complementarity into Israelite law. Under this rubric, complementarity is intricately woven into all of creation, with the duality of male and female coming together in marriage being the only acceptable place for sexual expression. Gagnon (who, as mentioned earlier, is often described as the foremost authority on homosexuality from a traditionalist perspective) puts the matter like this: "The particularly 'abhorrent' character of homosexual intercourse . . . is to be traced to its character as a flagrant transgression of the most fundamental element of human sexuality: sex or gender . . . such an act constitutes a conscious denial of the complementarity of male and female found not least in the fittedness (anatomical, physiological, and procreative) of the male penis and the female vaginal receptacle."[17] In other words, the reason that homosexual sex is so sinful is because it doesn't fit the heterosexual intentions God had for his creation in Genesis.

We have already covered the idea of gender complementarity and will continue to do so throughout this book as it is a key concept, but here our interest is to determine if this is the driving theological principle that is at play in Leviticus 18 and 20. For Gagnon, the "anatomical, physiological, and procreative fittedness" of the penis and vagina is the driving reason for why God would prohibit same-sex erotic activity, even in the context of committed, loving relationships.

There are a number of vital flaws in maintaining this position as a viable exegetical rubric for our chapters. If we look at them again in

17. Gagnon, *The Bible and Homosexual Practice*, 139.

their context, we see that the vast majority of the sexual acts that are prohibited in Leviticus are strictly between a male and a female (in fact, all but two). We see prohibitions against sex with female family members, with in-laws, and with women who are already married. There are laws that prevent a man from having sex with both a mother and her daughter, and laws that expressly forbid taking one's brother's wife to bed. All of these laws are exclusively related to male-female sex and as such fall well within the bounds of "gender complementarity." The prohibitions clearly exist for a reason, but their *raison d'etre* is most certainly not to maintain a strict gender binary of sexual practices. Given that these are the laws that dominate Leviticus 18 and 20, it is an exegetical stretch to isolate two verses and then claim that Yahweh was somehow invoking Genesis 1 and 2 for these alone.

Concurrently, if gender complementarity were the driving theological principle prohibiting same-sex sexual relationships, then we would fully expect the same standards to apply to women (i.e., lesbian sex) as to men. As it stands, not only Leviticus, but the entire Old Testament is imperviously silent on the matter, and the New Testament contains just one reference that many have interpreted as lesbianism.[18] While it may be argued that in the cultural milieu of the day, rules which applied to men would also be assumed to apply to women, this assertion is patently untrue. We see this instantly in Leviticus 18:17 and 20:15–16, where men and women are distinctly treated separately in regards to bestiality. In every other law here, men alone are being addressed. Can we conclude from this silence that God has different standards for males and females? Certainly not! But it does give us good reason to question the assumption that anatomical fittedness is the driving force behind the list of prohibitions.

We can add to this the interpretational rubric that ancient commentators used when discussing Leviticus 18:22 and 20:13. Reading the Torah from within their Greco-Roman context, Josephus and Philo (both Jewish) once again saw in these verses the practice of pederasty (men taking younger boys as sexual partners) and condemned the practice in no uncertain terms. While procreation was the end point that they saw in sexual activity,[19] the most immediate threat of pederastic activity was

18. Rom 1:26. As we shall see, a number of scholars have questioned this interpretation.

19. Nissinen, *Homoeroticism in the Biblical World*, 93–95.

the danger that the practice brought about feminization of the boy. Thus, Philo states:

> Much graver . . . is another evil, which has ramped its way into the cities, namely pederasty. In former days the very mention of it was a great disgrace, but now it is a matter of boasting not only to the active but to the passive partners, who habituate themselves to endure the disease of effemination, let both body and soul run to waste, and leave no ember of their male sex-nature to smolder.[20]

And of those who are the elder in the relationship, he remarks:

> He sees no harm in becoming a tutor and instructor in the grievous vices of unmanliness and effeminacy by prolonging the bloom of the young and emasculating the flower of their prime, which should rightly be trained to strength and robustness.[21]

Here, Philo is condemning the same-sex sexual practice that he witnessed in front of him, pederasty, and the effeminate nature that it brought about. Notice the lack of concern regarding the supposed complementarity of the genders. In the Jewish mind, the concern was not primarily that the men did not anatomically fit together, but worse, they were at risk of becoming effeminate, when they should instead be becoming manly in "strength and robustness." The great danger of pederasty, according to these authors, was not that they failed to engage in complementary sexual practices, but that in the act of being penetrated they gave up their superior status as men, and took on the inferior position of women. Steeped in their ancient patriarchy, this was by and large the viewpoint of ancient Jewish and early Christian writers and, whilst entirely misogynistic to our modern ears, was the prevailing attitude of both Ancient Near Eastern civilizations and Greco-Roman antiquity.[22]

We are speaking of course of societies in which women were often considered the property of men, with far fewer legal rights and a deeply inferior status.[23] To be a woman was to be a second-rate citizen, and thus, to take on the sexual role of a woman (to allow oneself to be penetrated) or to force another person to take on the sexual role of a woman (to penetrate a man) was seen as a heinous crime—unless, we should note,

20. Philo, *Works*, 499.

21. Philo, *Works*, 501.

22. Nissinen, *Homoeroticism in the Biblical World*, 95–97.

23. Gagnon, *The Bible and Homosexual Practice*, 100.

the man in the receptive role was already of a socially lower status (for example, a slave).[24] To be sure, while rising above much of the misogynistic rhetoric of Israel's neighbors, Leviticus can hardly be described as a manifesto on women's rights.[25] Women (when they are addressed) are almost always spoken of in regards to their husbands or fathers, and as such are seen as objects of honor or shame for the man. Many scholars agree that this is why lesbianism is not included in this list—when there is no male in the picture, it is impossible to lose male honor.[26]

This is the stark sociocultural backdrop of the writing and early interpretation of the book of Leviticus. Far from providing a thorough critique of this cultural milieu, Leviticus seems to assume its existence. We may not like it, and we certainly don't agree with it, but for society at large at the time, for a man to allow himself to be penetrated by another man (whether in a cultic, temple setting or not) was not a matter of anatomical complementarity, but rather of shame at taking on the inferior role of a woman.[27] So much of God's good law to his people protects women in ways that far outdo the nations around Israel, but we also must recognize that there is an unassailably patriarchal thread within Israel that shows itself so strongly in Leviticus.

Of course, at the end of the day, it is impossible to conclude with certainty whether or not the prohibitions against same-sex sexual behavior in Leviticus find their loci of force in the notion of complementarity. The author simply does not state *why* such behavior was deemed wrong for the people of Israel and as such those who would assert this notion are forced to admit that it is *assumed* knowledge in the author's intention. Given the complete silence about the so-called fittedness of male and

24. As Nissinen (*Homoeroticism in the Biblical World*, 26–28) notes, this is particularly apparent in Babylonian and Assyrian legal codes. According to the Middle Assyrian Laws, "if a man has sex with his comrade [i.e., rapes his social equal], and they prove the charges against him and find him guilty, they shall have sex with him and they shall turn him into a eunuch."

25. For example, see Leviticus 19:20–21: "If a man sleeps with a female slave who is promised to another man but who has not been ransomed or given her freedom, there must be due punishment. Yet they are not to be put to death, because she had not been freed. The man, however, must bring a ram to the entrance to the tent of meeting for a guilt offering to the Lord. With the ram of the guilt offering the priest is to make atonement for him before the Lord for the sin he has committed, and his sin will be forgiven."

26. Nissinen, *Homoeroticism in the Biblical World*, 43.

27. In our discussion of 1 Corinthians 6:9 and 1 Timothy 1:10 in the next chapter, we will flesh out this cultural phenomenon to a greater degree.

females, and the nonexistence of references to such a profound theological concept throughout the entire book of Leviticus, it is safe to say that this assumption does not stack up under the evidence.

A Society-Wide Identity Crisis

As we come toward the end of our venture into the book of Leviticus, we would do well to stop and consider the two driving principles that we have explored. Far too often this book of codes and commands is brushed over as a relic of a time long gone, for a people long dismissed. As we have seen, its strictures are strangely foreign and its prohibitions often feel archaic and arbitrary. But as I will say over and over again, God is not arbitrary. In the book of Leviticus, we see a God who is deeply engaged with creation, establishing a people of worship, ushering in peace and justice amongst the nations. It is the very distinction of the people of Israel that would eventually pave a way for God to enter into the world with all the trappings of a human, opening up the blessings of an abundant God to all who would call upon his name. With this overarching narrative at the forefront of our minds, we are able to make some sense of what we are reading.

Firstly, God is a jealous God, protective of his people and deeply concerned with the holiness of Israel. The refrain that binds our understanding of Leviticus is the call for Israel to be distinct from the nations, to mark themselves off as holy (separate) for the reputation of Yahweh. On a day-to-day basis, this meant that they were not to eat the same foods as the nations around them (hence pork was off limits). At a societal level, they were to physically arrange their encampments around the tabernacle (and later, temple) to show their unified allegiance to the one true God who brought them up out of Egypt. And at all levels, above all things, they were not to whore themselves out to the gods of the nations around them. Were they to do this, they would be rendered *tôʿēbâ*, abominations amongst God's own people. The link between the homosexual acts decried in Leviticus and their cultic heritage seems readily apparent, and here we find a timeless, cross-cultural hermeneutic that can help us understand homosexuality today. Relationships that center on the manipulation and appeasement of false gods are off limits for the people of Yahweh's kingdom.

Further, as stated above, even if we are entirely off the mark with this understanding, under the law of Christ it is impossible to simply take any given law within Leviticus and apply it to our situation today. The cultural backdrop of Leviticus was deeply engrained with the concern to protect male honor. The cornerstone of gender identity was found in the distinction between the *active male* and the *passive female*, and for a man to be penetrated was a crossing of those boundaries. The extent to which disgrace was brought upon the man is readily apparent in the literature of the time.

This shame-honor culture served a vital purpose in the life of the ancient Israelites: nomadic, engaged with enemies on all sides, and endlessly struggling against the harsh elements of the wilderness, the people of Israel (like all fledgling nations) faced the chronic danger of a population shortage.[28] Strictures around sexuality had a strong stabilizing role to play in the nation, clearly defining familial boundaries and establishing a mechanism by which reproduction could be encouraged.[29] It's possible that the shame of the gender role-crossing of the male becoming effeminate through penetration protected the people from the destabilizing effects of sexual behavior outside of the strictly delineated codes. In ancient Israel, these codes relied heavily on adopting the Ancient Near Eastern patriarchal structure of society. Does that mean that we too should adopt a society or church culture in which women are intrinsically of less value, or men with effeminate qualities are deemed second class? Of course not! So too it would be exegetically foolish to apply the Ancient Near Eastern models of homosexual behavior to our current concepts of faithful unions. Rather, we would do well to recognize Leviticus for what it is—a time-bound code, encased in rich history, which revealed how God's chosen people were to live in a specific era.

As we will see later, the ancient world knew nothing of the concept of enduring homosexual orientation as we understand it today, nor did it have any model of loving, exclusive, and mutually self-giving same-sex relationship. Naturally, Leviticus is repelled by the same theological principle that repels Christians today. It would appear that the same-sex activity they saw was either a capitulation to the idolatrous gods surrounding them, or a deeply intentional shaming of a fellow human being. As somebody who longs for Jesus to be glorified, it infuriates me when

28. Gnuse, "Seven Gay Texts," 76.
29. Gnuse, "Seven Gay Texts," 76.

I see his name being dragged through the mud. As a man who longs to see people recognize God as their loving, creating Father, I am saddened when I see so many rejecting the Spirit's work in their lives, preferring to chase after the gods of this world. In the end, these gods who our society pursues will be shown for what they are—no gods at all. Those who would seek to label all homosexual unions an abomination based solely on the words of Leviticus must ignore a preponderance of contextual factors that suggest that there is more going on here than a simple, timeless prohibition.

When we see this, we see a God who is deeply involved in the life of his creation. Against those who would see God as a distant deity, unconcerned with the things of this world, Leviticus reveals to us Yahweh, as one who is intimately participating in the story of this world. Read the book in the context of the continued failures of the nation of Israel, and it won't take long to discover the pressing need that all of humanity has for a savior—one who would embody the spirit of the law perfectly, fulfill its obligations, and ultimately redeem us from its power. Leviticus sets the scene for the greatest chapter in the history of creation as God steps onto earth and achieves just that. And so with this, we turn our attention to the age of the New Covenant, and the glorious life of the people of God as the church.

9

A Tale of Two Words

In my mind, the pillars were beginning to fail. Cracks were appearing in my carefully constructed traditional understanding of sexuality. The theological constructs I had held and taught for so long were beginning to crumble around me. If Genesis could not hold the theological weight I was asking it to bear, my first column was in danger. If Sodom and Gomorrah were not fateful condemnations of same sex behavior, another column was straining under the weight. And if Leviticus failed to shed the light I was expecting on the situation, a third pillar was coming under question. But as I turned to the New Testament, I found a sense of clarity. Three times in the New Testament, gay and lesbian sex was condemned, and seemingly in no uncertain terms. In fact, in two of these instances the word *homosexual* itself was used. Surely this clarity would be enough to establish an internally consistent theology that could hold up under scrutiny.

Perhaps it comes as no surprise to you that more pillars were about to come down, with 1 Corinthians 6:9 and 1 Timothy 1:10 (two verses which non-affirming stances rely upon to build their case against gay unions) being the next to topple. In this chapter, we are diving headlong into a cultural and linguistic analysis of these two key texts, and to mitigate against any potential boredom, I thought we'd start this chapter with a game.

It's called "What do these three things have in common?" It's simple. Here is a list of three facts, and you have to work out what characteristic they all share. Here we go:

1. The other day at the beach, wearing a hat and sunscreen, I read my Bible, and spent some time in prayer.

2. My brother has long hair.

3. At church on Sunday, my friend Sarah asked me why I thought following Jesus is so important.

If you're creative, you can probably think of a few commonalities, but the answer I'm looking for is this: according to the book of 1 Corinthians, Paul (the author) would have been uncomfortable, and potentially horrified that I, as a Jesus follower, would allow these sorts of things to happen. In fact, not only did he disapprove of the above, he went out of his way to make sure that others did as well, penning a letter in which he rebuked the Corinthian church for just such practices.[1]

And yet here is a peculiar thing. Despite the clear mandates that Paul lays out in his letter, I have no current church leader demanding that I remove my hat when I pray. I also have no intention of telling my brother (a faithful Christian) to cut his hair short, and if Sarah asks me the same question next week, I certainly hope that a long and fruitful conversation would unfold.

Now, some would argue that by and large, today's church has ignored Paul on these points, preferring to move on from these rules to forge new, more appropriate (read "modern") ones. I don't think it's quite as simple as that. In fact, to suggest that people have ignored Paul here is to ignorantly discount a sizeable library of theological debate and rigorous discussion on these matters. Rather, over the years, historians and theologians alike have by and large come to recognize that Paul was situated in a political, cultural, and religious era that was vastly different from ours. When Paul stepped out of his front door on to the dusty city streets of Ephesus, or walked alongside a donkey in the ancient metropolis of Rome, or debated stoic philosophy in the Acropolis of Athens, the world that he inhabited was immeasurably foreign to our minds today.

1. Before you write me off on these points, read Paul's words for yourself:

1. "Every man who prays or prophesies with his head covered dishonors his head" (1 Cor 11:4).

2. "Does not nature itself teach you that if a man wears long hair it is a disgrace for him, but if a woman has long hair, it is her glory?" (1 Cor 11:14).

3. "As in all the churches of the saints, the women should keep silent in the churches. For they are not permitted to speak, but should be in submission, as the Law also says. If there is anything they desire to learn, let them ask their husbands at home" (1 Cor 14:33–35).

Why is this relevant? In many Protestant (especially Reformed, evangelical) circles, there is a stated theological method that seeks to take any given text at face value—we call it the "plain reading" of a passage. The three sentences above demonstrate rather clearly however that the phenomenon of a plain reading of Scripture is rather more enigmatic than we would often like to admit. The reality is that everything that we read in the Bible is filtered by 2,000 years worth of theologizing through social, cultural, and political data, culminating in a strangely personalized framework situated somewhere in the twenty-first century. Whether we like it or not, this framework is radically informed by our class, gender, family history, education, and political persuasions. I'm not saying this is a good thing—it's just a thing. If all my years in theological education taught me one thing, it is that those who hold that there are plain readings of a text are, in a strange way, misguided. There are "informed readings," and there are "more informed readings," but nobody approaches any text entirely neutral. One of the tasks of the careful Bible reader is to be informed of the world that the biblical authors lived and breathed. Only then will we begin to understand why my brother's hair would place him on the outside of faithfulness, and only then will we be able to appropriately apply this text to other long-haired males today. You'll notice that when we do this, we aren't ignoring the passage, nor are we changing the *interpretation* of a passage. We are re-examining the *cross-cultural meaning* of the text (the driving theological principle), and in doing so, clarifying what it was that the Holy Spirit saw fit to inspire all those years ago.

For countless pastors, scholars, and theologians, it has been this detailed, carefully researched process that has led them to reexamine the prohibitions outlined in 1 Corinthians 6:9 and 1 Timothy 1:10. In fact, a sizeable amount of ink has been spilled into this topic, and what we are going to cover below is a crude summary of decades of work. Our task is twofold. Firstly, we will attempt to place the prohibitions into their contexts, and secondly, we will look at what the prohibitions Paul puts forward would actually have meant to Paul himself. In the ESV, the passages that we are looking at are as follows:

> Do not be deceived: neither the sexually immoral, nor idolaters, nor adulterers, nor μαλακοι (*malakoi*), nor ἀρσενοκοιται (*arsenokoitai*), nor thieves, nor the greedy, nor drunkards, nor revilers, nor swindlers will inherit the kingdom of God. And such were some of you. But you were washed, you were sanctified,

you were justified in the name of the Lord Jesus Christ and by the Spirit of our God. (1 Cor 6:9–11, ESV)

Now we know that the law is good, if one uses it lawfully, understanding this, that the law is not laid down for the just but for the lawless and disobedient, for the ungodly and sinners, for the unholy and profane, for those who strike their fathers and mothers, for murderers, the sexually immoral, ἀρσενοκοῖται (*arsenokoitai)*, enslavers, liars, perjurers, and whatever else is contrary to sound doctrine, in accordance with the gospel of the glory of the blessed God with which I have been entrusted. (1 Tim 1:8–11, ESV)

I have left the words that pertain to our current discussion in their Greek so you can see them clearly. Initially we must point out that despite the first passage using two distinct words (*malakoi* and *arsenokoitai*) and the second passage only using one (*arsenokoitai*), the ESV translates them both exactly the same, as "men who practice homosexuality." As we'll see, this odd interpretive decision does not reflect clarity about what either word means, but rather significantly betrays the lack of scholarly consensus about just how these words should be rendered into English. But before we get into these details, our exegetical methodology demands some context!

Church, Church, Oh Messy, Messy Church

I've seen my fair share of messy churches. I've seen division and I've seen power struggles and it's not pretty. It hurts. 1 Corinthians is a deeply personal letter to a deeply troubled church. Paul, having planted the church some years before, writes to the divided and dissenting converts to call them to faithful living and gospel unity. It's the sort of letter that comes as a slap in the face, a deserved wake-up call to a group of believers who have forgotten that they were called into fellowship with Jesus Christ.

The divisions in the church are starkly evident from the outset, with Paul condemning their quarrels and proclivity toward factionalism. In 1:11–17, we see that the Corinthian church, a mix of Jewish and Gentile believers, have taken on the city's infamous model of patronage, lining themselves up between various leaders. This system necessitates a division amongst the believers, rendering them in Paul's mind mere infants in Christ, for since there is jealousy and quarreling among them, are they not worldly? (3:3). By contrast, Paul impresses upon them that the stun-ningly beautiful wisdom of the cross, revealed by the Spirit, is that "you yourselves are God's temple and God's Spirit dwells in your midst . . . God's temple is sacred, and you together are that temple" (3:16–17).

This call to unity echoes right through the book, culminating in chapters 11—14, where Paul outlines the practicalities of this oneness, emphatically condemning their divisive abuse of the Lord's Supper, and urging them to pursue and employ spiritual gifts that edify the whole body. All of this is tied together by the oft-quoted love passage of chapter 13, where he urges the believers to follow "the most excellent way."

Scattered throughout the letter, Paul addresses a number of pastoral instances that have been reported to him, urging the Corinthian church to strive for holiness, deal with sexual immorality, ensure devotion in their marriages, and avoid idolatry. We will cover a number of these topics throughout this book, but notice as you read the letter (which I encourage you to do) that Paul repeatedly draws these issues back to the central call of the book—the unity of believers and their duty to uphold their brothers and sisters with the love of Christ.

It is in one of these moments of repetition that we find our first passage. Paul has spoken harshly against the fact that the people of God are publicly displaying their disunity by dragging one another to court (6:1–7), and he decries that this sort of behavior renders them "already defeated" (6:7). In order to show them just how dastardly this behavior is, Paul summons up a comparable "vice list" characterizing those who will not inherit the kingdom of God (6:9–10). Vice lists are common right throughout the New Testament and are a staple of Greco-Roman litera-ture.[2] They are a potent rhetorical device used to epitomize those who are universally counted as immoral. In Paul's case here, his aim in doing this is to locate people in his world who are "wrongdoers," point to them and say "Look! See those people? That's what you were. You were as bad as them before you met Jesus. Now you know a better way, so stop taking each other to court!"

Recognizing the rhetorical device Paul is using here is vital in lo-cating the theological force of the passage. Far too often, people from both sides take 1 Corinthians 6:9 by itself, radically losing so much of its meaning. In making this point, it is important to recognize the mecha-nisms which actually enable the rhetorical use of the vice list to work.

2. For thoughts on how vice lists were commonly utilized in extant literature, see Elliot, "No Kingdom of God for the Softies?"

For example, the vice list can *only* fulfill its function if it is universally agreed upon amongst the recipients of the letter that those within the list are acting in grossly immoral ways (hence he states "do you not know"). Paul makes no effort to defend his statements here and nor does he seek to define them; rather he assumes that his audience is wholeheartedly on board with his condemnations. If on any of these points there was disagreement as to their morality, Paul's driving theological point regarding unity amongst the believers would be severely debilitated.

Secondly, in order for this universal recognition of immorality to actually hold its weight, there had to be a reference point that the audience could visibly see and be readily acquainted with. In other words, the rhetorical function of the vice list is lost if Paul condemns a sin that nobody in the church had ever heard of, witnessed, or felt the force of. Paul's vice list here is not random. Each category is chosen strategically so that the recipients of the letter could read it, resonate with it, recognize its abhorrence, and then compare it to their current divisive behavior. Thus, in the list that Paul gives, the consensus of understanding must always be universal. For example, when the audience received the letter, every person would have known what greed is. They could shake their head in disapproval because they saw it in action, and felt the force of its destruction. Likewise, everyone was in agreement about what idolaters and swindlers were—in the city of Corinth they were surrounded by them.

But here's where things get interesting. Obviously when the Corinthian church received the letter from Paul, there was equal consensus as to what the *arsenakoitai* and *malakoi* actually were. They could experience them in their realm of existence. Equally, for the list to function, there was universal consensus that the *arsenokoitai* and *malakoi* were inherently immoral. The trouble for us lies in the fact that nobody in antiquity thought to systematize either of these words into a dictionary and their usage elsewhere is maddeningly elusive. As you'll see, we simply don't have certainty as to what they were referring to. Any teacher or preacher who tells you otherwise is either pulling the wool over your eyes, or hasn't spent time acquainting themselves with antiquity. Somewhat frustratingly, providing a list of easily recognized immoral behaviors, Paul had no need to tack on a definition of what he is actually referring to. Thus, there's no footnote supplying examples of *arsenakoitai-ish* behavior, and we can glean almost nothing from their immediate context.

With this in mind, we must now dive headlong into one of the most detailed analyses of two Greek words that most of you are likely to ever bother reading.[3] The path there may be windy and the scenery a touch mundane, but I for one am convinced that a foray into some etymology pays rich dividends! As we noted at the outset, we are on our way to a more informed reading. I know for myself, comprehending the following unlocked new doors.

Malakos: A Word with Many Meanings

Initially, it is worth noting that the term *malakoi* in 1 Corinthians 6:9 is translated a couple of different ways, depending on which Bible you are reading. As we have seen, the ESV collapses it in with *arsenakoitai* to mean "men who practice homosexuality."[4] Other mainstream interpretations take somewhat more nuanced approaches, such as "passive homosexual partners" (LEB), "male prostitutes" (NRSV and NIV 1984), "perverts" (CEV), and "the effeminate" (NASB).

Malakos and its derivatives appear five other times in the New Testament.[5] Three times it has the meaning "affliction" (ESV) or "sickness" (NIV), and the other two times it is in reference to clothing, translated "fine" (NIV) or "soft" (ESV). In literature of the time, the term is somewhat common and usually carries this latter meaning, characterizing something that is soft or delicate.[6] When applied to men, it seems to always be a pejorative label, insinuating that the individual was either weak and sickly, morally lax, or exhibited traits deemed "feminine."[7] Thus for

---

3. I hasten to add this clarifier: it is exceptionally rare that we have words in Scripture that we struggle to interpret with pinpoint accuracy. Often there are nuances that are lost in the transition from Hebrew or Greek, but I want to point out that on the whole, our English translations are astoundingly accurate. In questioning some of our current interpretations of these two words, I am in no way implying that the Bible is unreliable.

4. The NIV takes a similar route, translating the two together as "men who have sex with men" and including a clarifying footnote that separates the two into "passive and active participants in homosexual sex." In instances such as this one can only assume that the term "passive" is a crude euphemism for "penetrated" in regards to anal sex.

5. Matt 4:23, 9:35, 10:1, 11:8; Luke 7:25.

6. Loader, *Sexuality in the New Testament*, 30.

7. Martin, *Sex and the Single Savior*, 45–47; Nissinen, *Homoeroticism in the Biblical World*, 113–16; Gagnon, *The Bible and Homosexual Practice*, 308; DeFranza, "From the Bible to Christian Ethics," 75–78.

example, the musician Zenobius, who sought to please the ladies by his use of makeup and fancy clothes, garners the nickname Malakos.[8]

Men could be accused of being *malakos* if they ate too much rich food, wore clothing of fine fabric, had too much sex (homosexual or heterosexual), fled from battle, or lacked body hair![9] In and of itself, the word carries no necessary sexual (let alone homosexual) connotation, a fact that is starkly reflected in the wide variety of historic interpretations of the *malakoi* mentioned in 1 Corinthians. Indeed, as Yale theologian Dale Martin recognizes, from the sixteenth to the twentieth centuries, by far the most common translation was "effeminate."[10] It wasn't until well into the twentieth century that the term took a predominately homosexual turn.[11]

All of this comes into sharp clarity when we grasp the ancient view of the masculine and the feminine. In the dusty streets of the world Paul inhabited, social ranking and behavioral scripts were distinctly gendered, with delineated norms and ideals governing both private and public life. Maleness was characterized by rationality, physical strength, sexual aggression, courage, and honor. Protection of the home and ownership of property were the celebrated norms of men who were seen as socially superior in all spheres. Women on the other hand embodied the socially inferior realm of the feminine—emotional (rather than rational), weak (both morally and physically), sexually penetrable, soft, and subordinate.[12] This delineation of the masculine and the feminine was pervasive and informed all social interactions from the courtroom to the bedroom. In the courtroom, a man's testimony carried infinitely more weight than a woman's. In the bedroom, the man was expected to dominate over the submissive woman.

---

8. Papyrus Hibeh I 54, 11 quoted in Nissinen, *Homoeroticism in the Biblical World*, 117.

9. DeFranza, *From the Bible to Christian Ethics*, 77; Martin, *Sex and the Single Savior*, 45; Elliot, "No Kingdom of God for the Softies?," 9.

10. Indeed, Martin argues that this is the most unambiguous (and therefore best) translation of the term. Martin shows that in literature of the time, *malakos* could be used to describe equally men who had sex with men *or* women. Martin, *Sex and the Single Savior*, 43–45.

11. Perhaps it is no coincidence that this timing coincides with the wider societal trend of the gay liberation movement. While I understand the church's desire to combat this, it hardly makes for a scrupulous interpretational method.

12. Elliot, "No Kingdom of God for the Softies?," 9.

With this hyper-masculinized cultural rhetoric, it should come as no surprise then that the elasticity of the term *malakos* enabled it to function as a pejorative label for men who took the feminine role in any sphere of society. In the streets, this might have meant donning makeup. In the bedroom, this could mean anything from failing to wash one's penis of vaginal fluid,[13] to taking the penetrated role in anal sex. It is this last definition that has grabbed the imaginations of commentators and translators to make its way into our modern Bibles and teaching.

Does this understanding of *malakos* have merit? Yes. It most certainly does. Does it have limitations? Yes. It most certainly does.

At this point, we have to ask ourselves why we would assume a sexualized translation over the more common, generic "effeminate" translation. For starters, understanding the word as simply "effeminate" introduces more questions than it does answers. Why would feminine males be denied the kingdom of God? What is particularly horrendous about being effeminate? And how are we to a) identify and b) disapprove of such behavior today? Being more feminine than a given society's ideal hardly feels like the type of moral category that Scripture needs to condemn. Advocates of this position point to 1 Corinthians 11, where Paul draws strict lines around gendered hairstyles (as we've seen),[14] but this hardly closes the case.

Given the feminine nature of the term *malakoi*, many would argue that the word as used here forms a compound with *arsenakoitai*, a term that almost definitely has overt sexual connotations, with the two words taken together to form a whole (*malakoi/arsenakoitai*: passive/active). While this seems to hold more weight, it certainly isn't a foregone conclusion. As we've seen, the word *malakoi* can stand on its own without any modifiers, and the same can be said of *arsenakoitai*.[15] In fact, placing the two words together is exceptionally rare, and assuming that they must form one concept here often appears as somewhat of an arbitrary interpretive decision.

However, that is not the most pressing issue. Even if we assume that the two words go together, and thus *malakoi* is sexualized in nature, we still have to ascertain what it was that defined a male, feminized sex act. Remember that in the context of a vice list, we are looking at an easily

13. As in *Pseudo-Lucianic "Affairs of the Heart"* quoted in Martin, *Sex and the Single Savior*, 47

14. For example, Martin, *Sex and the Single Savior*, 45–47.

15. It is noteworthy that the term *malakoi* does not appear at all in 1 Timothy 1:10.

recognizable, universally condemned behavior. As such, we have to cautiously ask ourselves what such phenomenon existed in the perceivable world of the Corinthian church.

When we ask this question, two institutions that are incontrovertibly prevalent in Paul's Corinthian context present themselves for examination. First, and most pressingly, we see in literature of the time the application of the term *malakoi* to the role of pederasty in society. As we have already discussed, the practice of pederasty was prevalent right throughout the Greco-Roman world of the first century. Whilst differing in its exact nature depending on location and time, the practice involved (usually wealthy) adult men taking young males in a mentor/mentee relationship.[16] Though this often took the guise of a formal educational process, the documented reality is that these relationships usually took on a sexualized nature, with the younger male (the *malakoi* or *erōmenos)* "servicing" the older male.[17] As Nissinen notes, while many of these relationships were documented to last as friendships into the young man's adulthood, these were never the sole or primary relationship that the older male had. The pederast relationship was *in addition* to the man's marital status.[18]

Vitally, this institution reflected the hyper-masculine milieu that we have already explored. Just as the husband-wife relationship was dictated by power differences, so to the pederast relationship took place between a superior male and an inferior youth.[19] The youth sought to make himself more attractive to the man by feminizing himself in ways that we have already explored.[20]

Gagnon, in seeking to broaden the term *malakoi* to incorporate any receptive homosexual sex act, relies solely on the writings of Philo, quoting his instructions regarding homosexuality in *Spec. Laws* 3:37–42.[21] Ga-

16. For a contrast between Greek and Roman practices of pederasty see Olyan, "Meaning and Significance of Leviticus," 190–92.

17. This is significantly explored in Elliot, "No Kingdom of God for the Softies?" This is one of the most thorough exegetical analyses of 1 Corinthians 6:9 to date.

18. Nissinen, *Homoeroticism in the Biblical World*, 64–66.

19. Nissinen, *Homoeroticism in the Biblical World*, 65.

20. Perhaps this is most strikingly presented in the mythological stories of Zeus and Ganymede, in which the Greek God takes the "dandy" boy as a lover. The term *catamite* is the Latinized name of Ganymede. While it is unlikely that the average Corinthian believer would have known these stories, the educated elite (potentially including Paul) would have been versed in them.

21. Gagnon, *The Bible and Homosexual Practice*, 309.

gnon is quite right to assert that Philo's primary focus is on the seemingly abhorrent cultivation of the feminine and he is also right to point out there are some amongst them who are adults. But he fails to note that the entire framing of this discussion is in the context of *paidarastein* (pederasty). The tutor role is harshly condemned for its abusive practices of de-masculinizing the younger males. Those few adults he addresses are those who have grown up as sex partners of older men, and who have sought to retain their youthful beauty in order to *stay* young and therefore attractive. Far from countering the argument, the adults of *Spec. Laws 3:37–42* are the exception that prove the general rule.

The second institution that was societally prevalent in Corinth was male prostitution, a translation of *malakoi* that has continued to enjoy significant airtime (for example in the NRSV and NAB translations). Robin Scroggs contends with some substance that the presence of *pornoi* (most often translated in Greek literature as prostitutes) and *moichoi* (adulterers) alongside *malakoi* in 1 Corinthians 6:9 favors this translation. Loader notes that this use of the term is certainly attested to in ancient literature as one of the many vices that could come under the *malakoi* umbrella.[22] Without context, the term could denote male prostitutes who have entered prostitution by choice, or by force, and could refer to those who service both male and female clients.[23] Philo's *Spec. Laws 3* may give credibility to this translation, recognizing that the *malakoi* are often seen to be leading the processions of religious festivals, a position often reserved for cultic practices.

While some have sought to merge pederasty and prostitution together, this is culturally unwarranted, given that the pederast relationship was not necessarily for financial gain, and was exclusively between an older man and younger mentee/lover. The inhabitants of the ancient world saw the two as distinct institutions and so to place them together is entirely anachronistic. The point of raising them both in this chapter is not to tell you how to define *malakoi*, but rather to point out the variety of ways that the term was used in ancient literature.

22. Loader, *Sexuality in the New Testament*, 30.

23. Gordon Fee, who holds a non-affirming theology, states in his highly respected commentary that they should most likely be translated "male prostitute" or "effeminate call-boy," but hastens to add that these are his best guesses. Fee, *The First Epistle to the Corinthians*, 268.

Arsenakoitai: In Need of Clarification

If the difficulty of translating *malakoi* is seen as an overabundance of varied usage, the difficulty of translating *arsenakoitai* is almost the direct opposite. Its two appearances in the New Testament are the first time that the term is used in any ancient literature that we currently have access to,[24] and by and large it seems to have been promptly dropped from common parlance. As such, much like *malakoi*, history has thrown us an abundance of translations to sift through:

In 1522, the great Protestant Reformer Martin Luther translated the term *arsenakoitai* in both 1 Corinthians 6:9 and in 1 Timothy 1:10 as "men who rape (or ravish) boys".[25] The Clementine Vulgate (1592) translates it as those who keep or use male concubines.[26] As we've seen, the current trend in translation is to place the term in conjunction with *malakoi* to render it as "dominant homosexual partners" (The Lexham English Bible), or just simply "homosexuals" (NASB).[27]

The word itself is a compound word of "man" (*arseno*) and "bed" (*koitē*), with the *koitē* stem commonly used as a euphemism for sexual activity (in much the same manner as current English).[28] The uniqueness of the word leads many theologians to think that the early Christian and Hellenistic Jewish communities had adopted a neologism (a new word), based on the widely circulated Greek translation of the Old Testament (the Septuagint). In this text, Leviticus 20:13 reads: *"kai hos an koimē thē meta arsenos koitēn gynaikos."* The theory goes that the placement of the

24. That's certainly not to say that Paul made it up—a rather strange theory given that it is placed in a vice list without any form of qualification. It is abundantly clear that the recipients of the letter knew exactly what Paul was referring to.

25. Well, technically he translated it to the German word *knabenschänder*. To be clear, Martin Luther most certainly was not affirming of gay unions. In fact he was vehemently opposed to them, which makes his translation of *arsenakoitai* all the more intriguing. Switzer, *Pastoral Care*, 53.

26. Hart, *The New Testament*, 416.

27. An unfortunate outcome of translating the term in conjunction with *malakoi* is the fact that subsequent usage in 1 Timothy 1:10 (where *malakoi* is not present) becomes drastically harder, hence a number of these translations somehow suggest two different meanings of the same word.

28. There has been some debate as to whether *arsen* is the object (those who have sex *with* men) or the subject (*men* who have sex with others) of the compound term here. While we can't be entirely certain, the evidence favors the former, homoerotic translation. See discussions in Boswell, *Christianity, Social Tolerance, and Homosexuality*, 107, 342; and Wright, "Homosexuals or Prostitutes?"

two words together resulted in the compound word that Paul, Timothy, and the Corinthian church were all familiar with.[29] While this may be true, two cautionary points should be made. Firstly, if Paul is quoting Leviticus here, it is at best an obscure reference (both *arsen* and *koitē* were exceptionally common words), and those who suggest that he is invoking the Levitical law for New Testament believers have far more theological hoops to jump through than linguistics. As we saw in the previous chapter, Paul's relationship with the Old Testament legal code (including its sexual mores) was complex and cannot be applied simply to those under the New Covenant.

Secondly, and more importantly, understanding how the word was formed does not bring us much closer to understanding what Paul meant when he used the term in his two letters. As Dale Martin rightly notes,

> The etymology of a word is its history, not its meaning. The only reliable way to define a word is to analyze its use in as many different contexts as possible. The word "means" according to its function, according to how particular people use the word in different situations.[30]

As such, Martin rightly cautions against suggesting that two words joined together necessarily add up to the linguistic sum of their parts. For example, if I were to tell a non-English speaker that I was on my "honeymoon," the interpreter would be well advised to avoid any notions of "honey" or "moons"; "bulldozers" have very little in common with sleeping bovines, and "understanding" something says nothing about one's position, or posture. Martin concludes that to say that the two parts *arsen* and *koitē* joined together "obviously" refers to men having sex with men is "linguistically invalid."[31] It is, to use Carson's terms, an "exegetical fallacy."[32]

As such, we turn the remainder of our attention to how the term was used in literature of the time. Examples are sparse, but they do shed vital light. As we do this, two themes become strongly apparent. Firstly, we see that the term is *never* used to denote exclusive, long-term, monogamous gay relationships. Secondly, and in stark contrast, we see that

29. While some have adopted this theory without criticism, it has been most strongly contended by Wright, "Homosexuals or Prostitutes?," 124–53, and Gagnon, *The Bible and Homosexual Practice*, 315–16.

30. Martin, *Sex and the Single Savior*, 39.

31. Martin, *Sex and the Single Savior*, 39.

32. Carson, *Exegetical Fallacies*, 30–31.

almost every single usage demonstrates a disparity of power between the two people who are usually, *though not always,* engaged in sexual activity.

Take first for example the ancient *Sibylline Oracles'* injunctions against various forms of social injustice. The author is condemning those who abuse the poor for their own gain, stating:

> Do not steal seeds. Whoever takes for himself is accursed to generations of generations, to the scattering of life. Do not *arsenakoitein,* do not betray information, do not murder. Give one who has labored his wage. Do not oppress a poor man.[33]

In a very similar vein, the *Acts of John* (a second-century text) lays out the following warning to the wealthy men of Ephesus:

> And let the murderer know that the punishment he has earned awaits him in double measure after he leaves this (world). So also the poisoner, sorcerer, robber, swindler and *arsenokoites,* the thief and all of his band.[34]

As countless scholars have noted, both the *Sibylline Oracles* and the *Acts of John* include elsewhere in their works substantial lists of sexual sins that are condemned in the harshest of terms. And yet in these lists the term we are looking at here is distinctly absent.[35] Take a moment to reread the above quotes, and ask yourself what the word *arsenakoites* might mean in these contexts? It is abundantly clear (I tend to think) that in these passages, the author couldn't possibly have in mind faithful, monogamous, self-giving gay relationships. In fact, if we take them on their plain reading it is unlikely that homosexual sex is condemned at all. More than likely, the ancient authors seem to understand that the word implies an action which is inherently tied up with exploitative behavior.

With this nuance of the term noted, a variety of other texts begin to make more sense. For example, in his work "To Autolychus," Theophilus of Antioch offers the following list of thematically grouped vices; "adultery, prostitution, thief, plunderer, defrauder, *arsenokoites,* savagery, abusive behavior, wrath, jealousy, boastfulness and conceit . . ."[36] Note where the term is placed. If it is a sexual sin, one would expect it to be listed with

33. *Sibylline Oracles* 2:70–77. Quoted in Martin, *Sex and the Single Savior,* 40.

34. Schneemelcher, ed., *Acts of John,* 178.

35. Of course, it is impossible to define a word by its lack of presence in any given text, but given the author's obvious familiarity with the term, this does make one wonder why these ancient writers refrained from using it.

36. Martin, *Sex and the Single Savior,* 41–42.

the first couplet. But instead, it is separated by actions which all pertain to the unjust acquiring of property.[37]

Finally, take for example the myth of the evil being Naas who according to Hippolytus deceived the first woman Eve, seduced her and committed adultery with her. Naas then went on to "possess Adam like a boy,"[38] and thus *moicheia* (adultery) and *arsenokoitai* entered the world of humans. In the ancient world, this is one of the few texts that explicitly suggest a (homo)sexual translation of the term, but once again note what the text is speaking about. Naas and Adam were in no ways conceived of as equal beings, with Adam being taken like a boy. Many have interpreted this story to suggest that Adam was indeed raped by the evil being.[39]

If this is indeed the case, then the placement of the term in 1 Timothy 1:10 makes considerably more sense. This text lists, in order, the sexually immoral, *arsenokoitai,* and enslavers. If the list follows a thematic ordering (which most suggest it does),[40] it could well be referring as a whole to the well-documented instances of those who sexually exploit people who have been captured and forced into slavery.[41]

We are left with the question, then, what do the terms *malakoi and arsenakoitai* refer to? Contrary to those who would hold that the terms are "obviously" a reference to any and every instance of male-male penetrative gay sex (let alone lesbian sexual activity, which is entirely outside the scope of definitions), the overwhelming evidence of the early usage suggests that this is far from conclusive. In the world that both Timothy and the Corinthian church inhabited, practices of sexual slavery,

---

37. A second list in the same text also uses the term *arsenakoitai,* but with less clarity as to the list's grouping: "adultery, prostitution, *arsenakoitai,* greed, idolatry." If it is grouped with the first two, it would have sexual connotations. If it is grouped with the following, it would have an economic edge. Martin suggests that it is possible that it involves both (sexual exploitation for money), which makes the term a hinge point between the two concepts. Martin, *Sex and the Single Savior,* 41–42.

38. The term "boy" in this text is in some instances substituted for "slave."

39. Martin, *Sex and the Single Savior,* 42.

40. Some claim that the list follows the proscriptions of the Decalogue (the Ten Commandments), but this suggestion relies on removing certain words and reordering others, which renders this hardly a cogent theory. Gagnon, *The Bible and Homosexual Practice,* 330.

41. The six texts that we have dealt with here are the earliest usage of the term that we have access to. In his attempt to prove that *arsenakoitai* necessarily refers to all homosexual sex acts, Gagnon lists six other, later texts (300 to 600 years after Paul). All of these, bar one, however explicitly include young boys, exploitative practices, or extramarital sexual activity.

prostitution, and exploitative pederasty[42] were undoubtedly the readily perceivable and highly condemned permutations of homosexual activity.

The Ancients and Orientation

There is of course, a glaring omission in what we have covered so far. If the people who were *arsenakoitai* and *malakoi* were prevalent in Paul's world, and if we have no clearly discernable definition for the terms as they are used in his work, how do we *know* that Paul wasn't referring to lifelong, monogamous faithful unions? Ultimately, the nature of historical research demands a posture of humility on this point—without the gift of omnipotence, we can't ever be certain. But there are some strong observations that we can make.

There is a branch of research that has proposed that there were some within antiquity who had a concept of orientation that shows similarities to our modern understandings. It was recognized that there were individuals who exhibited lifelong, unchanging attraction to those of the same sex, and there were others who were unquestionably attracted to both sexes.[43] If it is true that Paul knew about such sexual orientation, then the likelihood that he is referencing faithful homosexual relationships naturally increases somewhat.

Most leading scholars, however, suggest that this is an unlikely scenario, given that the vast majority of references to enduring same-sex orientation are found in Greek love spells, ancient dream interpretations, medical writings, and astrological texts.[44] It is highly unlikely that Paul, Timothy, or the Corinthian church at large had a concept of homosexuality that included a lifelong experience of a gay orientation. It is even more unlikely that any of them had access to a single example of a gay or lesbian relationship that was not characterized primarily by power disparity or financial transaction. It is yet more unlikely still that a faithful permutation of a gay relationship was accessible enough to warrant its inclusion in a vice list without any attempt at definition or modification. It is almost preposterous to conclude that the entire Corinthian church

---

42. The 1917 *Oxford Lexicon of the Greek Language* translates the term simply as "pederast." See Souter, *A Pocket Lexicon*.

43. Brooten, *Love between Women*, 1–9.

44. Brooten, *Love between Women*, 1–9. See also Loader, *Sexuality in the New Testament*, 21.

had such permutations accessible and readily perceivable. Ultimately, to say that Paul is condemning in these verses the kinds of faithful, monogamous gay relationships that are seen in the church today, is to say that he is condemning something that he did not know existed, nor even thought possible.[45]

How Would You Translate These Terms?

Given all of this, I have to ask, how would you choose to translate the term *malakos* and *arsenakoitai* in 1 Corinthians 6:9? Or to put the question slightly differently, if it were in your hands, what would you assume Paul is trying to condemn? I certainly do not envy those given the weighty task of translating Scripture, so let me be clear—I am not saying that I know the definition of either term in this discussion, and I am certainly not offering a definitive option for how they should be translated here. What I am hoping you will see is that *nobody* knows for certain exactly what Paul is referencing. At best, we have educated guesses, and the best educated guesses must take into account the fact that Paul and his divided Corinthian congregation had no concept of a faithful, monogamous gay union.

Perhaps I have jumped the gun, but to be frank I have very little confidence in any claim (scholarly or otherwise) that confidently asserts that there is only one way that 1 Corinthians 6:9 and 1 Timothy 1:10 can be understood and applied to our world today.[46] The fact of the matter is that it is simply far more complex than that. History does not present an uncontested interpretation of these verses, and to claim, as I once did, that the condemnations against all gay unions are clear from these alone is tragically misguided. Of course, you may well conclude that gay unions are still outside the scope of biblical faithfulness, but you will struggle to back up this view with either 1 Corinthians 6 or 1 Timothy 1.

And so, before we conclude, let me point out a sad irony which I hope serves as something of a warning.

As we have seen, the theological burden of 1 Corinthians 6:1–11 is designed to repudiate the public shaming of Christian brothers and sisters. The vice list that Paul employs is meant to serve as a wake-up

45. Loader, *Sexuality in the New Testament*, 21.

46. As Gagnon, "It is self-evident, then, that the combination of terms, *malakoi* and *arsenokoitai*, are correctly understood in our contemporary context when they are applied to every conceivable type of same-sex intercourse." *The Bible and Homosexual Practice*, 330.

call to a divided church, urging them to strive for deep unity and a stunningly attractive self-sacrificial love. And yet it is a disheartening reality that today we find this very passage to be the poster child of passages threatening to tear the church in two. The irony of this tragedy is not lost on me. With both sides of the debate (myself included) equally guilty of caricaturing their opponents and misrepresenting their theology with willful ignorance, I humbly suggest that as you reflect on what you have read in this chapter, you do so with reverence for the unity of the church of Christ.

On the one hand, you may well end up disagreeing with all that I have said here, but for the sake of Christ's church and his glory among the nations, I ask that you take the message of 1 Corinthians seriously, and seek to disagree with grace. On the other hand you may well find words of truth here that you cannot deny, but brothers and sisters take heed, I have not offered you weapons to engage, but rather signposts to share in a path to be journeyed together.

10

The Final Pillar

It's "Unnatural"

Jan and Sue have been together for almost twenty years. Both accomplished academics and talented cooks. Their home is constantly full of deep laughter, earnest conversations, and abundant food. Together they have raised Zack and Lucy, two bright teenagers who are sports enthusiasts and keen musicians. No one quite remembers who suggested it, but a couple of years ago one of the kids asked if they could attend a local youth group that their friends were a part of. Eager to have their kids engaged with a faith community, Jan and Sue were happy to oblige and within a few months all four were attending Sunday services together.

It started off so well. The church was warm and the family became friends with a number of other families in the congregation. They went through an introduction to Christianity course and discovered things about God they'd never known. They heard about a creator who wove beauty into the universe, a sustainer who knew their deepest longings, and a savior who embodied all that it means to be a true, self-sacrificing human. They grew to love this church, and for the first time, their faith journeys flickered into being.

But let's be honest, in hindsight, it was never going to last. It began to unwind when Jan and Sue felt like they needed to give back to the church which was looking after their kids so well. Keen to be of use, they offered their gifts. Jan was a senior lecturer in primary education, but there was no room for her on the Sunday school team (the role of kid's church helper was given to a thirteen-year-old). Sue was a hospitality veteran, but she was barred from being a part of the welcoming crew. Both Jan and Sue were musically proficient, but they quickly learned that they wouldn't be allowed on stage. After long conversations with the pastor and his wife, they found that the only gifts they could bring the church were their baked goods and money. Disheartened and tired by what the couple thought were irrational fears, they gave up trying to serve and just attended the church. The final straw came when the pastor called them one day to inform them that the Sunday coming would be a communion service, and politely asked them not to participate. They sat through that service, watching on as people walked past them to receive the bread and wine. They left before the service ended, cheeks stained with tears of anger and abandonment. They never came back.

In his defense, the pastor was gracious and gentle with them. He was simply adhering to "orthodoxy" according to his denomination. And, of course, they could return at any moment if they wanted to. All they would have to do would be to rip their family apart. Twenty years of faithful, self-sacrificing, life-giving love would have to be sundered in two with their children thrown into the limbo of yet another broken family. All of this because, as their pastor informed them, their relationship is "unnatural."

The Final Passage

That pastor was taking his lead directly from his interpretation of Romans 1, perhaps the most vigorously debated passage of Scripture when it comes to the "gay and Christian" debate. As the only text in all of Scripture that contains what is an apparent reference to lesbianism, and as the Bible's only extended description of homoerotic activity, it has been the final playing field of almost every debate. For me, this chapter was the last pillar to fall in my traditional theology of sexuality, but over time, fall it did. In fact, over the past forty years, the *majority* of scholars who have written theological works exploring the Bible's view of homosexuality have concluded that the Bible as a whole does not condemn faithful, monogamous same-sex unions—their pillars have fallen also.[1]

---

1. I owe this observation to the traditionalist author Preston Sprinkle. Sprinkle, *People to Be Loved*, 17.

We have already seen that all of the other references to homoerotic activity in the Bible are incapable of speaking with clarity into the debate as we see it today. Laden with the cultural baggage of sexual exploitation, patriarchy, pederasty, prostitution, and idolatry, the texts that we have covered so far simply cannot be used to condemn the type of relationship that Sue and Jan have had for twenty years. And, as we are about to see, there is far more going on in Romans 1 than many traditional understandings recognize. As always, the task ahead is not about proffering an affirming view of gay and lesbian relationships and it is certainly not about defending Sue and Jan's family. Rather, it is about faithfully reading the Bible and submitting our sexual ethic to its teachings. With this in mind, here is the passage we will be spending considerable time in now:

> The wrath of God is being revealed from heaven against all the godlessness and wickedness of people, who suppress the truth by their wickedness, since what may be known about God is plain to them, because God has made it plain to them. For since the creation of the world God's invisible qualities—his eternal power and divine nature—have been clearly seen, being understood from what has been made, so that people are without excuse.
>
> For although they knew God, they neither glorified him as God nor gave thanks to him, but their thinking became futile and their foolish hearts were darkened. Although they claimed to be wise, they became fools and exchanged the glory of the immortal God for images made to look like a mortal human being and birds and animals and reptiles.
>
> Therefore God gave them over in the sinful desires of their hearts to sexual impurity for the degrading of their bodies with one another. They exchanged the truth about God for a lie, and worshiped and served created things rather than the Creator—who is forever praised. Amen.
>
> Because of this, God gave them over to shameful lusts. Even their women exchanged natural sexual relations for unnatural ones. In the same way the men also abandoned natural relations with women and were inflamed with lust for one another. Men committed shameful acts with other men, and received in themselves the due penalty for their error.
>
> Furthermore, just as they did not think it worthwhile to retain the knowledge of God, so God gave them over to a depraved mind, so that they do what ought not to be done. They have become filled with every kind of wickedness, evil, greed and depravity. They are full of envy, murder, strife, deceit and

malice. They are gossips, slanderers, God-haters, insolent, ar-
rogant and boastful; they invent ways of doing evil; they disobey
their parents; they have no understanding, no fidelity, no love,
no mercy. Although they know God's righteous decree that
those who do such things deserve death, they not only continue
to do these very things but also approve of those who practice
them.

(Rom 1:18-32)

Before we unpack what is going on in this passage, we must first (as
always) consider the context in which it fits. This is particularly important here because Romans 1—3 is not (despite what it may sometimes
feel) primarily a proof text for Paul's sexual ethic. Rather, it is one of the
most vibrant celebrations of the gospel in all of Scripture, culminating in
Romans 3:23-24, "for all have sinned and fall short of the glory of God,
and are justified by his grace as a gift through the redemption that is in
Jesus Christ."

In order to get to this proclamation of such glorious good news,
Paul begins his letter to the Roman church by creating a sharp distinction between two groups of people—the Gentile people who do not have
the written law of God (Rom 1:18-32), and the Jewish people who do
(2:1-29). As he makes this distinction, Paul is taking his audience (the
church in Rome) on a dramatic ride, embarking on a rhetorical "sting
operation" to prove his point.[2] The second half of Romans 1 (see above)
presents itself as a scathing indictment of a depraved people group, bra-
zenly corrupt and worthy of death (1:32). Imagine a first-century Jewish
person reading the text, nodding in agreement and working up into a
frenzy of judgment over the evil ways of the people "out there." Everyone
agrees that Paul is presenting his audience with a textbook case of human
evil in the Gentile world.[3]

But then, all of a sudden, just as his indictment reaches its crescendo,
the tone changes and the trap shuts. Paul instantly ceases speaking of the
Gentile sinners, and instead vividly turns the spotlight onto the Jews in
his audience. "You, therefore, have no excuse, you who pass judgment on
someone else, for at whatever point you judge another, you are condemning yourself, because you who pass judgment do the same things" (Rom
2:1). In other words, stop thinking you've got the moral high ground over

2. Hays, *The Moral Vision*, 389; Loader, *Sexuality in the New Testament*, 14.
3. See for example DeYoung, *What Does the Bible Really Teach?*, 50.

the Gentiles—the reality is, you're just as bad as them! Whether you are a Jew or a Gentile, you are not saved by your works of the law, but rather by grace, which is freely given to all who would accept it (3:22).

In directing his audience through this rhetorical "trap" (snaring them by their own judgmental attitude), Paul is countering a false belief that had risen amongst the Christians in Rome that a person's Jewish status in some manner rendered them a higher position in the sight of God (3:9–20).[4] Much like in the city of Corinth (from where Paul was most likely writing) the church in Rome was a mixed bag of all sorts, Jews and Gentiles, and was facing racial divisions that Paul was eager to quell before they threatened the congregation's unity.

In this context, we see that the homoerotic activity presented in 1:26–27 is utilized by Paul as the rhetorical epitome of Gentile depravity. Paired with a list of twenty-one other sins of willful rebellion, the people are depicted as debased, debauched, and deluded. But it's important to note that this passage is not simply demonstrating the morality of whatever homoerotic activity Paul was pointing to. Rather, in some manner or other it is pointing to its origins. If we read closely, we notice that the Gentile's evil behavior does not *incur* God's wrath, but rather it is itself the *outcome* of God's wrath as God "hands them over" (1:24, 26, 28) to it as a punishment for their idolatry (1:22, 25, 28).[5] Whatever homoerotic behavior they are engaging in, it is first and foremost their own punishment for having turned away from the worship of Yahweh.

And yet, at the same time, there remains a sense in which the homoerotic activity does result in further punishment as the men (though curiously not the women) received in themselves "due penalty for their error" (1:27). Somehow, Paul sees this penalty as already dished out, as completed and in the past tense.[6] The Gentiles in this passage have received a double punishment from God—once for their idolatry, and once for their sex acts. Of course, in this sense Paul is generalizing. Despite

4. Hays, *The Moral Vision*, 289.

5. This is particularly well spelled out by Hays, *The Moral Vision*, 388.

6. Grammatically, most translations take the penalty spoken of here in the past tense (flowing on from the aorist tense of 1:27a) and thus the punishment has already been completed. This has left scholars divided over its meaning. Some attempt to make it an emphasizing of the "handing over," but this doesn't fit the flow—the people were handed over for idolatry, not homoerotic behavior. Others have taken it literally, suggesting that pain or venereal disease caused by anal intercourse is the penalty. Others suggest that the shame incurred from homoerotic activity is in view. Needless to say, there is no consensus as to its meaning.

what the text actually says, it is highly doubtful that Paul genuinely believed that *all* Gentiles engaged in homoerotic activity, just as it is highly unlikely that he believed all Gentiles were guilty of murder (1:29).

Much as we saw in Paul's letters to Timothy and the Corinthian church, by proffering such a generalized caricature of the Gentile people, Paul is making a theological statement. He is pointing his audience to the most despicable sinners out there, and is turning it in on the reader to remind them that if it weren't for God's grace shown in Christ, they would be falling under the same judgment. With this context noted, it is obvious that Paul is working under the (safe) assumption that in Rome, just as in Corinth, the Christian church had a readily accessible and easily demonstrable model of homoerotic activity. As we'll see later, Paul is not bringing anything culturally or theologically new to the table.[7] His very rhetoric demands that his audience already agrees with him and can see within their city a model of sexual activity that is contemptible to God, but approved of by the Greco-Roman, Gentile society in which they find themselves (1:32). Of course, we know from the vast libraries of ancient literature available to us that there were numerous such models available to them, none of which were faithful, exclusive, or mutually self-sacrificing.

As such, it is our task now to read Romans 1 carefully, with prayer and humility, to determine what it was that God (through the Apostle Paul) saw fit to condemn, and then to make the hermeneutical leap through two millennia and vastly different cultural worlds to explore how we are to apply this passage to gay and lesbian people in the twenty-first century. A friend of mine pastoring at a prominent Sydney church once told me that they could explain away every other "clobber passage" but couldn't get around Romans 1. That same friend is now entirely affirming, having explored this passage with fresh insights. What changed his mind? Let's take a look.

To Burn with Passion

If you have taken the time to read any literature that puts forth a non-affirming theology of gay and lesbian relationships, you will undoubtedly know that much of the discussion of Romans 1 revolves around the Greek

---

7. Indeed his narrative, language, and tone are strikingly similar to numerous other Jewish texts that we know were in circulation at the time of his writing.

term *para physin* ("against nature" or "contrary to nature," 1:26).[8] As an apparent appeal to the created order that we have already discussed, this term feels straightforward and clear-cut, and thus the discussion abruptly ends. This term is indeed important to the discussion as it is laden with rich theology, however it doesn't take too much effort to see that there is far more going on in this passage than just these two words. We will come to discuss *para physin* soon, but before we do there are two other concepts that play vital roles in this passage which are often ignored in non-affirming literature.

The first of these is the defining presence of unbridled lust that characterizes the homoerotic activity that God is condemning. If an idea appears once in Scripture, it is important. If it appears twice in one paragraph, it is a key point. If it appears three times, it constitutes a central idea. As such, we would be foolish to miss the threefold description of the Gentile activity as "lusts of their hearts" (1:24), driven by "dishonorable passions" (1:26), and again "consumed with passion" (1:27). Whatever *para physin* is referring to here, it is unquestionably tied up in this context with the presence of an uncontrolled sexual passion.[9] Of course, there is already dissonance between what Paul is describing here and the twenty years of self-giving love between Jan and Sue, but I want to draw our attention to some vital cultural factors that can help us unpack why Paul ties the two ideas of lust and homoerotic activity so closely together.

In today's Western society, there is a distinction between the concept of an *orientation* of a person's sexual desire (whether they are gay or straight), and the *strength* of a person's sexual desire (we might call this their sex drive). This may seem obvious to us—a person can be heterosexual and not want much sex in much the same way that a person can be homosexual and lack sexual drive. But it most certainly wasn't the obvious mind-set of the Greco-Roman moralists of the first century.[10] In fact, the philosophers and theologians of antiquity, without a notion of enduring homosexual orientation, saw no such distinction. Rather

8. For the most often quoted, non-affirming analysis of this term see Gagnon, *The Bible and Homosexual Practice*, 254–70.

9. Much like the English word *passion*, the Greek term *pathē* can be both positive and negative ("he is passionate about sport" or "he burns with sexual passion"). Some affirming writers have attempted to make much of the neutrality of this term, but the context is unambiguously negative, so I tend to think this is not a convincing argument.

10. Martin, *Sex and the Single Savior*, 56–57.

they believed that when a person engaged in homosexual behavior, it was universally driven by excessive sexual urges that had not been reined in. There were no such categories as "straight" and "gay." Instead, there was "sexually restrained" and "sexually unrestrained."[11] To this end, Dio Chrysostom, a first-century Greek philosopher, summarized the ancient view of homosexuality by saying:

> The man whose appetite is insatiate in such things, when he finds there is no scarcity, no resistance, in this field, will have contempt for the easy conquest and scorn for a woman's love, as a thing too readily given—in fact, too utterly feminine—and will turn his assault against the male quarters, eager to befoul the youth who will very soon be magistrates and judges and generals, believing that in them he will find a kind of pleasure difficult and hard to procure. His state is like that of men who are addicted to drinking and wine-bibbing, who after long and steady drinking of unmixed wine, often lose their taste for it and create artificial thirst by the stimulus of eating salted foods and condiments."[12]

Whenever homoerotic activity is viewed negatively in literature contemporaneous with Paul, it is always portrayed in such a fashion. Consider Philo's (an early Jewish theologian writing just prior to Paul) words when he states:

> The inhabitants (of Sodom and Gomorrah) owed this extreme license to the never-failing lavishness of their sources of wealth, for, deep-soiled and well-watered as it was, the land had every year a prolific harvest of all manner of fruits, and the chief beginning of evils, as one has aptly said, is goods in excess. Incapable of bearing such satiety, plunging like cattle, they threw off from their necks the law of nature and applied themselves to deep drinking of strong liquor and dainty feeding and forbidden forms of intercourse. Not only in their mad lust for women did they violate the marriages of their neighbors, but also men mounted males without respect for the sex nature which the active partner shares with the passive.[13]

In other words, homosexual behavior occurs when the person's desire for sex is so great that he or she eventually finds heterosexual sex

11. Brownson, *Bible, Gender, Sexuality*, 155.

12. *Dio Chrysostom*, 152.

13. *De Abr. 133–135* cited in *Philo*, 6:69.

unfulfilling and seeks greater and greater stimulation. There is truth in the observation that for the ancient thinkers, "the problem had to do not with a disoriented desire, but with inordinate desire. Degree of passion, rather than object choice was the defining factor of desire."[14] Under this understanding, all people were capable of experiencing homosexual desire if they allowed themselves to lose control of their sexual passions (or as Romans 1:24 puts it, they follow the "lusts of their hearts").[15]

Paul was not being particularly inventive when he described *para physin* activity as the logical outworking of lust and passion.[16] Indeed his wording shows that he was very much in step with the theological mores of his day.[17] Was Paul thus condemning heterosexual people who engaged "against their nature" in homosexual behavior? This is what some have concluded, but I don't think it's quite that simple, as it is somewhat anachronistic to claim that Paul understood heterosexuality as a distinct orientation. Rather, it is perhaps safer to say that Paul understood all people to be sexual beings, and saw the models of homosexuality around him as qualitative proof that sexual desire amongst the pagan Gentile world had been allowed to go unrestrained. Thus, when God "gave them up to the lusts of their hearts" in retribution for their idolatrous ways, their endpoint was destructive homoerotic activity (1:24).

Surrounded by a culture that tolerated and even applauded such hyper-sexualized institutions as pederasty, prostitution, and cult worship, it is no surprise that Paul's harshest condemnations fall on the self-seeking, exploitative, and lust-driven realm of homoerotic activity. However this realm is vastly different to the monogamous, faithful gay relationships that I see in so many Christians around me. I struggle to see Jan and Sue's relationship as the result of passions and lusts left unrestrained. Characterized by an abundance of sacrificial care and mutual companionship,

14. Martin, *Sex and the Single Savior*, 57.

15. Brownson, *Bible, Gender, Sexuality*, 170.

16. Nissinen, *Homoeroticism in the Biblical World*, 111. Sprinkle (*People to Be Loved*, 99) attempts to play down the lust that Paul is pointing to by stating that female homoeroticism is present in 1:26 and was not conceived of in antiquity as resulting from too much lust. Brooten's work has proven this theory false, revealing a number of ancient texts that directly link female excessive lust with female homoeroticism. Brooten, *Love between Women*, 154–59.

17. As many have noted, the term *para physin* itself, usually translated "against nature," is elsewhere translated "beyond nature" or "in excess of what is natural." Martin, *Sex and the Single Savior*, 57.

their relationship seems to fall well outside the lust-invoking language of Romans 1.

Idolatry in the Picture

The second major motif that we need to cover before we can examine Paul's use of the term *para physin* is the obvious (though once again, often overlooked) presence of idolatrous worship in Romans 1:18–23. Paul makes it clear in this passage that the idol worship undertaken by the Gentile world was the catalyst for their own downward spiral into sexual licentiousness. We would thus be wise to look closely at the narrative presented in this passage to determine exactly what this catalyst was, and how it came to affect the Gentile peoples in such catastrophic proportions.

Somewhat strangely, many who hold a non-affirming view of gay and lesbian relationships take this passage to be describing the universal fall of humanity as recounted in Genesis 3—the theological and historical moment when God handed the pinnacle of creation, humanity, over to their own sinful desires. As a reiteration of Genesis 3, the idea goes that in the pristine garden of Eden there was a neatly universal heterosexual expression of sexuality. Then, when sin entered the world and the curse of God was uttered, the ordering of creation was shattered, sending shrapnel through every part of a now groaning world (Rom 8:22). As humanity fell so too did humanity's sexuality, resulting in disordered desire as God handed the people over to the foolishness of their hearts.[18] I held to this reading of Romans 1 for a long time, as it fits so neatly with my broader created-order theologies and thus I never thought to question it.

The problem with this interpretation, however, is that this is not what Romans 1 actually says. Nothing in Romans 1 suggests it is recounting a generic, universal fall of creation precipitated by Adam and Eve. The narrative does not start in a garden with two people, but rather begins with a whole hoard of people who have abandoned monotheistic worship of Yahweh and implemented polytheistic religions (something that Adam and Eve are notably never accused of in the Bible). Paul never quotes Genesis 3 or speaks of a universal curse. Rather Paul is outlining the downward spiral of the Gentile people into idolatry and subsequent deranged behavior.

18. Hays, *The Moral Vision*, 386.

Whilst there is no doubt that in Paul's theology sin entered the world through Adam (he will expound this extensively later in Romans 5), this is not what is in view here. The comparison is not being made between a heterosexual pre-fall creation and a disordered creation post-fall. Instead Romans 1 outlines a historical moment (either real, or theologically constructed) at which point God handed a now polytheistic people over, thus giving rise to the homoerotic activity on display.[19] The presence of creation-type language by no means requires us to conclude that Paul is echoing the effects of Genesis 3, but rather highlights the folly of the time when that creation became deified in the minds of humanity.[20] Romans 1 is thus centered around the idolatrous tendencies of the Gentile world.

There are some significant (and unintended) theological implications if we conclude with many non-affirming interpreters that Romans 1 is outlining a universal fall of all humanity (recounting Genesis 3). As we have seen, Paul maintains a stark contrast between the Gentile people and Jewish people in Romans 1—3. If Romans 1:18–32 is indeed speaking about the universal fall of humanity (and not the Gentile introduction of idolatrous polytheism), then what do we do with Romans 2, which addresses the Jewish people as entirely separate, untarnished by the specific sins of chapter 1? Our only option is to conclude that Paul did not believe that the Israelite nation was included in the Genesis 3 curse and thus subsequently exempts them from the need for salvation and undermines the entire gospel he is teaching! Paul indeed considered Jews guilty, and in need of saving, but he is not addressing them in chapter 1.

I was speaking to a friend a while back who was struggling to understand why he was gay. He was unconvinced by any psychological reasons, and felt that science as a whole provided no answers. He had thus

19. Martin, *Sex and the Single Savior*, 52. It should also be noted that if Paul wanted to make the point that the homoerotic activity the Roman church saw was a violation of the created order as recounted in Genesis 1—3, there was a perfectly good word that he could have used for this (*ktisis*, "creation"), which he utilizes elsewhere (see for example Romans 1:20, 8:19-22; 2 Corinthians 5:17; see outside Paul Hebrews 9:11, Revelation 3:14). This word captures the theology of creation that he so often uses to speak about the fall, however here he does not describe homoerotic activity as "against *ktisis*" but rather as *para physin* (against "*nature*"), a distinct concept, as shall be seen later.

20. There are some clear parallels between Romans 1 and Genesis 1—2. There is talk in 1:20 of the "creation of the world" and "the Creator," Paul uses the terms for "male" and "female" that are used in the LXX of Gen 1:27, and there are overlaps with words between Romans 1:23 and Genesis 1:26, such as *image, human,* and three types of animals.

concluded that homosexuality is an otherwise unexplainable part of a "disordered creation," a corollary of living in a post-fall world.[21] Humbly I have to admit that this may well be true. For all we know, there was no possibility of a homosexual orientation in the garden,[22] but to argue this from the narrative in Romans 1 (which is the only place in Scripture it could possibly be derived) is entirely unfaithful to the text. Romans 1:18–32 is not simply painting a post-fall picture, instead it is specifically depicting a post-idolatry picture.

I have already stated that Paul is not bringing anything theologically new to the Hellenistic Jews in this chapter, and this is no exception. Intriguingly, we have numerous documents from significant Jewish theologians and philosophers, writing around the same time as Paul, who trace the origins of lust driven activity to the invention of idolatry, in strikingly the same way that Romans 1 does.[23] Of course, these "decline narratives" are not Scripture, and as such contain no authority, however they do give us vital insights into how Paul's audience would have understood and applied Romans 1. Read, for example, from Wisdom of Solomon, an apocryphal text written not long before Paul:

> For the idea of making idols was the beginning of fornication, and the invention of them was the corruption of life . . . For whether they kill children in their initiations, or celebrate secret mysteries, or hold frenzied revels with strange customs, they no longer keep either their lives or their marriages pure, but they either treacherously kill one another, or grieve one another by adultery, and all is a raging riot of blood and murder, theft and deceit, corruption and faithlessness, tumult, perjury, confusion over what is good, forgetfulness of favors, defiling of souls, sexual perversion, disorder in marriages, adultery, and debauchery. For the worship of idols not to be named is the beginning and cause and end of every evil." (Wisdom 14:12, 23–28, NRSV)

In much the same way, the contemporaneous books of 1 Enoch and Jubilees present the series of events from God's self-revelation, to

---

21. To give it a theological label, this is the post-lapsarian state.

22. Much scholarly literature is devoted to determining whether or not there was a literal garden in which humanity originated. Whether Eden existed as a real place or as a theological construct is an important discussion, but I think unnecessary here, given that Romans 1 is not actually addressing such a time or place.

23. Martin, *Sex and the Single Savior*, 52–55.

the folly of idolatry, to the resultant decline into sexual licentiousness.[24] Like Romans 1, none of these present lustful homoerotic activities as a "disordering of creation" from the Genesis 3 fall, but rather as a result of the idolatrous worship of whole civilizations. This is important, as we shall soon see, because many people wrongly read into Paul's language of "against nature," suggesting that he is actually saying "against the created order." This is not a clear understanding of the text, and it almost certainly isn't what Paul's first-century Jewish audience would have heard.

Specifically Speaking

The undeniable centrality of lust-filled sexual perversion and their obvious connections with idolatrous worship have further led many theologians to consider how the original audience would have interpreted the opening chapter of Paul's letter. Seated as they were in the metropolitan heart of the Roman Empire, the church he is addressing was undoubtedly exposed to some of the most vulgar forms of sexual licentiousness known to the ancient world. This being the case, many have sought to identify the possible models of homoerotic activity that Paul may have been pointing his audience to when he penned Romans 1:26–27. We already know that there were no readily available monogamous, faithful gay unions in the ancients' purview, so we have to ask what else they may have seen.[25]

Some have suggested that the most readily available model of homoerotic behavior was found in the idolatrous temples themselves, either in the form of temple prostitutes or as socially sanctioned sex-on-premises venues where offerings of sexual practices were made to the fertility gods.[26] There is strong evidence that these were prevalent both in Rome and in Corinth at the time of Paul's writing, and would have provided a graphic example for Paul to refer his audience to.

24. Loader, *Sexuality in the New Testament*, 15.

25. Some have attempted to argue that the phrase "consumed with passion for *one another*" (Rom 1:27) is a reference to mutual, consensual relationships and thus Paul cannot be only condemning exploitative same-sex sex acts (Sprinkle, *People to Be Loved*, 91). This anachronistic interpretation is a long stretch considering the socio-cultural climate Paul is writing in, and would far better be understood as men burning with lust for other men, not as a vague reference to faithful, committed relationships.

26. See for example Townsley, "Paul, the Goddess Religions," 130.

Others have sought to narrow this down, focusing on particular cults that were known for their theriomorphic (deified animal being) worship reflected in Romans 1:21–22. For example, the well–documented Isis Cult fits much of the condemnation that Paul offers here, and could easily have been a referent for the church in Rome to examine and condemn as the epitome of Gentile evils.[27]

Alternatively, many who have studied the Roman imperial court recognize striking similarities between the behaviors of the debauched ruling elite, and the vices Paul expounds. If applied to the everyday Roman citizen, Romans 1 constitutes extreme hyperbole (very few everyday Gentiles could be charged with such debauched living), however if the imperial court is in view, the words of the opening chapter of Romans are hauntingly accurate.[28] Their extravagant parties, their public lechery, their murderous vindictiveness, and their unbridled license were in full view of the Roman church, and may well have been an obvious referent point for what Paul is describing.[29]

Read what James Brownson writes about one particular emperor, Gaius Caligula, who strikingly resembles Paul's rhetoric in Romans 1 and reigned just prior to Paul's writing:

> First of all, Gaius is closely linked to the practice of idolatry. The Roman writer Suetonius reports how Gaius "set up a special temple to his own godhead, with priests and victims of the choicest kind." Another Roman writer, Dio Cassius, comments negatively on how Gaius was the only emperor to claim to be divine and to be the recipient of worship during his own lifetime. Gaius also tried at one point to erect a statue of himself in the Temple in Jerusalem; he was dissuaded only by a delegation from Herod Agrippa. Hence the link between Gaius and idolatry would have been well-known indeed, particularly in Jewish circles. But Gaius also serves as "Exhibit A" for out-of-control lust. Suetonius reports how Gaius "lived in perpetual incest with all his sisters and at a large banquet he placed each of them in turn below him, while his wife reclined above." He records gruesome examples of Gaius's arbitrary violence, vindictiveness, and cruelty. Later, Suetonius chronicles Gaius's sexual liaisons with the wives of dinner guests, raping them in an adjoining room and then returning to the banquet room to comment on their

---

27. Gnuse, "Seven Gay Texts," 82.

28. Elliot, *Liberating Paul*, 159.

29. Dodson, "The Fall of Men."

performance. Various same-sex sexual encounters between Gaius and other men are similarly recounted. Finally, a military officer whom he had sexually humiliated joined a conspiracy to murder him, which they did less than four years into his reign. Suetonius records that Gaius was stabbed through the genitals when he was murdered. One wonders whether we can hear an echo of this gruesome story in Paul's comments in Romans 1:27: "Men committed shameless acts with men and received in their own person the due penalty for their error."[30]

The ancient influential writers Dio Chrysostom, Philo, Suetonius, and the apocryphal Wisdom of Solomon all make explicit links between the judgment of God and the licentiousness of Gaius Caligula and the imperial court.[31] It is more than probable that when Paul wrote to the Roman church, he intended to draw these images to mind, categorically condemning their sexual exploitations, their refusal to worship God, their violent dispositions, and the breadth of their corruption.

Whether the referent of the vices in Romans 1 is cultic or imperial in nature, the force of the passage remains—the idolatrous practices of the Gentile world resulted dramatically in a lust-filled frenzy of sexual excess, unrestrained desire burning in self-centered, destructive exploitation. This is the context and content of Romans 1, as Paul leads up to the glorious pronouncement that because of the work of Christ, *even this* can fall under the extravagant grace of God.

Against Nature

And so we come to what many feel is the crux of the non-affirming view in Romans 1. Jan, Sue, myself, and millions in our situation have been told over and over again that our desires and our relationships (potential or real) are "against nature." As such, these relationships can never (and should never) receive the blessing of God or God's people. Derived straight from this passage, this view rightly recognizes the "great exchanges" that took place. Worship of Yahweh was exchanged for worship of elements of the created world (1:18–24), and natural relationships were

30. Brownson, *Bible, Gender, Sexuality*, 156–57.

31. In addition, as Megan DeFranza notes, the indictments could just as easily describe Gaius's successor, Nero, who was reigning as Paul was writing. Nero's tutor, Seneca, concluded that Nero was "another Caligula" thanks to the emperor's sexual excesses with both men and women. DeFranza, *From the Bible to Christian Ethics*, 86.

exchanged for unnatural ones (1:25–27). For some, the term *para physin* is where the story ends. Forgetting the huge amount of context that we have already explored above, they simply cannot move past what appears to be the black and white condemnation that God is putting forth in these two words. I hope it is apparent by now, however, that there is more going on in this passage than many traditionalist views would care to admit. Far from being the end of the road, the presence of the term *para physin* here, when read in its literary and historical context, provides one of the most beautiful affirmations of God honoring sexuality in Scripture. As such, it is safe to say that God detests sexual activity that is *para physin* because sex is beautiful, and its sanctity is to be maintained. The question that obviously needs asking is "what does *physin* (nature) actually mean?" And subsequently "what constitutes activity that is *para physin*?"

As we noted above, some take the term to be synonymous with "creation." Paul is harking back to the garden of Eden in a pre-fall era where homosexuality did not exist. Thus when Paul says that homoerotic activity is against nature he is actually saying it is against the created order and therefore is inherently sinful. However, we also noted that the Romans 1 narrative (idolatry) is very distinct from the Genesis 1—3 narrative (fall), and while there is some overlap in language, this is not intended to suggest that Adam and Eve's sin is in view, but rather to highlight the folly of the idolatrous actions of the Gentiles. Further, as we are about to see, *physin* (nature) is not *ktisis* (creation) in Paul's theology. The two words are used for distinct concepts.[32]

With this, we are going to dive into one final round of word studies. Firstly we'll unpack how Paul uses the term *physin,* and then we'll examine how it is utilized in the world around him in order to determine what he is actually intending to communicate to his audience.

Have a read of how Paul invokes the concept of *physin* in 1 Corinthians 11:13–16:

> Judge for yourselves: is it proper for a wife to pray to God with her head uncovered? Does not nature (*physis*)[33] itself teach you that if a man wears long hair it is a disgrace for him, but if a woman has long hair, it is her glory? For her hair is given to her

---

32. Nissinen, *Homoeroticism in the Biblical World*, 107.

33. For the sake of clarity, the slight change in spelling between the *physis* and *physin* is just a difference in case (similar to "he *threw* a ball" and "the ball was *thrown* by him") from the nominative to the accusative.

for a covering. If anyone is inclined to be contentious, we have
no such practice, nor do the churches of God.

I don't think there can be any question about what Paul is saying here—
he is stating that *physin* demands that men have short hair and women
have long hair, and any alternative practice is not welcome in the church.
The argument could be made (I think implausibly) that Paul is stating
that in the garden of Eden Eve had long hair and Adam had short hair,
and any other grooming would be thus inappropriate. However, this is
not how we interpret the term *physin* in 1 Corinthians 11. Why should
we do so then in Romans 1? Even here there seems a gross hypocrisy in
any long-haired, male pastors who deny gay and lesbian people a place
in God's kingdom.

But, interestingly, in Paul's theology, it is not only humans who can
act "contrary to nature." In Romans 11:11–24, Paul marvels at the way
in which God has now brought the Gentile people into the fold of the
church. Like a branch that was cut off from a wild olive tree, the Gentiles
were "grafted, *para physin,* into a cultivated olive tree" (Rom 11:24). Look
at who is acting "against nature" here—none other than God! Is Paul arguing that God is acting against the divinely embedded created order?
Surely not! Rather, he is arguing that God acted in a way that was so
contrary to what would be expected that it feels as though it is somehow
against a deeply embedded way of doing things.

This brings us closer to an understanding of what the term *physin* is referring to. As we have noted several times, Paul is not bringing
anything philosophically or theologically new to his Roman audience.[34]
For Romans 1 to fulfill its rhetorical function, it was necessary that his
language and assumptions were well attested in Hellenized synagogues,
and as such he utilizes what is essentially popular philosophical language
about nature.[35] To be clear, "nature" as seen in the above texts is not a particularly Jewish concept.[36] The term itself is never found in the Old Testament (LXX) and it is absent from Jewish writings prior to Greco-Roman
rule. It is recognized by both affirming and non-affirming scholars that
Paul is drawing on Stoic philosophy to make his case.[37] Rich and diverse,
Stoicism was the predominate philosophy of the Roman world (we see

---

34. Nissinen, *Homoeroticism in the Biblical World*, 105.

35. Loader, *Sexuality in the New Testament*, 15.

36. Nissinen, *Homoeroticism in the Biblical World*, 104.

37. See for example Hays, *The Moral Vision*, 387.

Paul debating Stoics in Acts 17), and would have been part of everyday language for the Roman Christians. Particularly relevant to our passage in Romans 1, it's important to understand that Stoicism's primary pillar was the regulation of emotions and sexual desire or "passions."[38]

Across the board in first-century Jewish, Roman and Greek literature, *physin* referred to a cultural behavior which was seen to be what was expected by convention or character.[39] If something broke the *physin* norm, it was obscenely contrary to how one should behave. Thus at its broadest, things that were contrary to nature could include hot baths, plants that remained in pots, and banquets after sunset![40] Specifically in regards to sex, the term was employed to describe sex acts that violated the strictly delineated gender boundaries in which men performed the dominant (penetrating) role, and women were submissive (penetrated). We are, in almost every sense, reading a historical document that is steeped in the patriarchal values of its day. When it comes to discussion of what is "natural" about sex in the first century, male honor is the singular most vital factor we must consider. Thus one prominent historian makes the following sobering statement about what constituted a "natural" sex act:

> The shapers of Paul's culture saw any type of vaginal intercourse, whether consensual or coerced, as natural, such as between an adult man and woman married to each other, an adult woman and a slave woman or slave girl, an adult man and his daughter, or an adult woman and her son . . . The "natural relations" that women gave up include a wide variety of heterosexual relations, such as marital relations, adultery, rape, incest, prostitution, and sexual relations between and adult male and a minor girl.[41]

38. Sellars, *Stoicism*, 34.

39. Nissinen, *Homoeroticism in the Biblical World*, 105.

40. Nissinen, *Homoeroticism in the Biblical World*, 105, quoting Seneca (122:7–8).

41. Brooten, *Love between Women*, 251–52. It should be noted that there is significant, ongoing debate as to whether Romans 1:26 is referring to female-female sexual activity, or if it is referring to more general sexual behavior that could be deemed *para physin*. The text itself does not explicitly state that homoerotic sex is in view here, but rather that the women simply "exchanged natural relations for those that were contrary to nature." The connection to homoeroticism is based on the linkage to 1:27 with the word *likewise* (*homoiōs*). It is highly significant that the early church (which clearly understood Greek language and culture with far more nuance than we do today), did not take 1:26 to refer to homoeroticism but rather to heterosexual, non-vaginal sex. Further, analysis of the term *homoiōs* does not conclude that the concepts of the two sentences are working in parallel, but rather are likely related by their thematic

This male-honor notion wove its way into the cultural understanding of male-male homoerotic activity. Grounded firmly in a patriarchal, shame-based culture, the term *para physin* was used to describe behavior that "feminized" the penetrated male.[42] The horror of such an act was the stripping away of honor that was due to that person in the humiliation of being made to play the part of a woman. It is easy to see then how the homoerotic activity that was prevalent in the ancient world was labeled by Paul and his contemporaries as *para physin*. The Hellenistic Jews picked up on this Stoic term, and utilized it to describe the models of gay and lesbian sex that they saw in the world around them, and rightly so. The violent sexual exhibits of the imperial courts, the exploitative molestation practices of the pederastic institution, the degrading rape of slave men and prisoners of war, and the humiliation of both temple and brothel prostitution were condemned as vile intruders into a world that ought not accept such practices. Even in those instances where the individual consented to the intercourse, the patriarchal structuring of society ensured that it still resulted in a deep shaming of the penetrated man. This is simply the world that Paul inhabited, as did the audience to which he wrote.

Paul, speaking into the Stoic milieu of his day naturally adopted Greco-Roman norms and principles. The question that we have to wrestle with is whether or not this term, laden with patriarchal value, is thus valid today as a description of monogamous, faithful gay unions that so many Christian men and women display. Do these relationships instill shame upon their participants? On some level, we are asking what the ongoing role of male domination is within society. If you conclude that God's design is for men and women to coexist equally within humanity, then you have directly challenged the logic that Paul was assuming his first-century audience would hold.

I have no doubt that you, like most in the church, have reconsidered Paul's driving principles around long hair on men and short hair on women—recognizing them to be bound in cultural practices and assumptions that pertained to patriarchal values. Our task is finally thus

---

links—in other words, the women and men are alike in that they are acting "contrary to nature" not in that that they are engaging in homoerotic activity. If this is the case (which is likely), then the Bible is resolutely silent on female homoerotic activity. For extended discussions on this, see Brownson, *Bible, Gender, Sexuality*, 208; Banister, "*Homoiōs* and the Use of Parallelism"; and Miller, "The Practices of Romans 1:26."

42. Brownson, *Bible, Gender, Sexuality*, 208.

to consider if such a cultural understanding is warranted with the Stoic notion of *para physin* to our lives today.

What Then Shall We Condemn?

Paul uses the opening chapter of his letter to the Roman church to decry the evils of the Gentile world. We have seen that he does this in the context of a fiercely patriarchal society, driven by insatiable lust and uncontrolled passion, falling prey to their idolatrous hearts and succumbing to all forms of degrading and self-debasing behavior. Guided by these underlying driving ethical principles, the great evil of this passage is not homoerotic activity per se, but rather the downward spiral of delusion and depravity built on lust and ego, as those who turned against the moral virtues of Yahweh received in themselves precisely the punishment that they deserved. Their humiliation was of their own making.

Where do Jan and Sue fit into this? As a Christian, where do I fit into this? Where do thousands of others in our position fit into this? To take a faithful, gay Christian relationship from the twenty-first century and superimpose it onto the text of Romans 1:26–27 not only ignores the context of the letter, but also serves to undermine the driving theological principles on which it stands. When people do this, they (often unwittingly) read back into the text ideas and condemnations that Paul never intended to include. We can say this with confidence because the models of homoerotic activity that both Paul and the Roman church had available to them were categorically different to those that we are here discussing. When context is accounted for, claiming that faithful gay unions are inherently sinful based upon Romans 1 is akin to claiming that faithful heterosexual unions are inherently sinful because the Bible condemns the rape of women.

Of course, once again, I admit that it may well be that Paul, if transported to the twenty-first century could indeed find such loving, faithful unions outside the scope of God's will,[43] however I do not take as my highest authority hypothetical assumptions about what a mythical, modern Paul may or may not say. I take as my authority Scripture, gloriously written in time and space by God's chosen authors. Our task in exegesis is to ask how these words would have been heard and understood by their

---

43. As Gagnon suggests when he posits such a hypothetical. *The Bible and Homosexual Practice*, 328–29.

audience, to ascertain the principles that must stand across all times and cultures, and to faithfully submit our lives to their teachings.

At the end of the day, Romans 1–3 stands not as the scathing condemnation of gay and lesbian people that it is so often taken for. Rather, it is a magnificent pronouncement of the fact that all people, Jews and Gentiles, can now participate in the feast of the kingdom of God through faith in Christ. Though tainted by the wretched mark of sin, I, like you, can approach the throne of God with boldness because I stand not in my own righteousness, but robed in Christ's.

Summing Up

We've made it through the texts that have so often been used to bar the way for lesbian and gay Christians to have a seat at the table. Tragically, these isolated verses have for so long been taken out of context, misrepresented, and utilized to perpetuate a marginalization that I was part of for so long. As we have seen, it takes a little bit of time, some openness to new voices, and a willingness to question long-held assumptions, but when all is said and done, I find myself overwhelmingly saying to my LGB brothers and sisters, "You are so welcome here." Whether it be the Genesis accounts of creation and fall, the narrative of Sodom and Gomorrah, the holiness codes of Leviticus, the vice lists of the New Testament, or the idolatrous decline narrative of Romans, all of these passages spoke, and continue to speak, into the vital need to maintain the sanctity of sexuality as a powerful force within creation. They do not, however, as some claim, provide a united or unanimous voice against committed, faithful, and God-honoring same-sex unions. At the end of the day, the Bible simply does not provide us with such a voice, and so we turn our attention now to what the Bible *does* say. Marvelous in its precepts and enthralling in its vision, the Bible speaks both powerfully and poignantly into a world that is sex-obsessed and intimacy starved. Into this vision we now venture.

11

Losing Our Theology

"The worst possible thing that can happen to a gay Christian would be to fall in love."

I distinctly remember hearing these words as a teenager, having discovered to my horror that I was a textbook case. The person who said them was nonchalant, making a comical remark to mock what they saw as the regressive teachings of an institution they despised. But it didn't matter who said it. These words shattered me. Like a dagger driven into the chest, they are undeniably sharp. I was a fifteen-year-old, awkward adolescent bracing myself for a life of celibacy. I held my breath, and attempted to pray away the loneliness that I felt descending like ominous clouds.

From then on, there were glimmers of light when the sun broke the thick layer of darkness, and I dare say I fared the journey better than most. But the darkness was never far from sight and so with marriage off the table I embraced with gusto a theology of celibacy that centered on the knowledge that nothing was too great a sacrifice for the sake of God's kingdom.

That central premise is something I continue to stand upon unashamedly. Like treasure found in a field, the kingdom of God is worth giving up everything for (Matt 13:44–46). After all, what does it benefit a man if he gains the whole world, but loses his soul (Mark 8:36)? But what I didn't realize at the time was that in pursuing, and later teaching, the theology of celibacy that I had been handed, I was sacrificing other theologies that the church has held for millennia.

And so it is for the sake of clarity that I offer this warning: if the church is to continue condemning faithful, God-honoring gay unions, it can only do so by relinquishing parts of Scripture that have played vital roles in shaping our traditions. That's what we are exploring in this chapter.

Celibacy

As we saw in earlier chapters, the church's theology around both gender and homosexuality arose entirely in reaction to societal shifts that took place around it. Obviously, this reactionary method of appropriating Scripture for a newly engaged phenomenon demanded quick thinking on the part of (often ill-equipped but well-intentioned) theologians and pastors, and as such, the church as a whole received (and continues to receive) a cacophony of confused and uncertain voices that have very little tradition to draw upon in this area. The ex-gay movement betrays this dynamic perfectly, with almost every evangelical institution promoting a theology of sanctification that promised heterosexuality by the power of the Spirit.

At the somewhat embarrassing failure of ex-gay ministries, the church was forced to reconsider its theology and so came the rise of the "gay celibate" movement. This branch of sexual theology is still exceedingly young (largely unheard of in Christian literature prior to 2005), but claims to stand upon the tradition of thousands of years of theology around celibacy. As I said, this was a movement that I was deeply engaged in, because I believed (and still believe) that celibacy can be a beautiful thing. After all, Jesus was celibate, as were John the Baptist and Paul (at least at the writing of 1 Corinthians).

Further, history is replete with monastic orders and intentional communities that have embraced the celibate life and gone on to achieve great things for the kingdom of God.[1] There is a profound truth in the fact that those who abstain from the gifts of marriage and sex have the ability to focus their time and energy in ways that the majority of people don't, with resources necessarily being divided amongst familial duties (1 Cor 7:32–33).

1. Indeed, the Protestant tradition has much to learn from the Catholic tradition in this area, and much of the literature developed by gay, celibate Christians takes its lead from Catholic priests.

I find all of this both beautiful and enriching. As a church, we are indebted to a countless number of men and women who have gone before us, forgoing marriage, and in doing so furthering the kingdom in unique and glorious ways. And yet when it comes to the gay celibate movement, I am extremely uncomfortable. I am uncomfortable because what is being talked about in this movement is something fundamentally different to what the Bible speaks about and history has handed down to us.

In order to see this, let's turn to Jesus' own words about marriage and celibacy. In Matthew 19 Jesus castigates a group of Pharisees who are pushing the boundaries of God's words in the Old Testament in order to promote divorce. Culturally, the man of the household was permitted to divorce his wife should she not meet his expectations, but Jesus (far from buying into their ploys) heightens the bar, stating that "whoever divorces his wife, except for sexual immorality, and marries another, commits adultery" (Matt 19:9).

Jesus' own disciples, shocked at the strict requirements that their Rabbi has laid down, exclaim, "If such is the case of a man with his wife, it is better not to marry!" And Jesus takes this opportunity to teach them a truth that would lay the foundation for monastic movements for millennia to come:

> Not everyone can accept this word, but only those to whom it has been given. For there are eunuchs who were born that way, and there are eunuchs who have been made eunuchs by others—and there are those who choose to live like eunuchs for the sake of the kingdom of heaven. The one who can accept this should accept it. (Matt 19:11–12)

If we look beyond the somewhat foreign concept of eunuchs,[2] Jesus is stating that in the kingdom of God, there is no one singular path of service—some are called to marriage, just as some are called to celibacy.[3] Those who are called to a path of marriage will be able to receive the words he has spoken about the strength of its union. Those who are called to abstain from marriage for the sake of the kingdom, they too will be able to receive their relevant teaching. These are the ones who have

2. Almost without exception, a eunuch was a man who had been castrated for the purpose of filling an official function in society (such as care of a harem). There are some who have sought to suggest that the definition can extend here to those who did not experience heterosexual desires, but most agree that this is an unnecessary stretching of the term. Dallas, *The Complete Christian Guide*, 126.

3. Morris, *The Gospel According to Matthew*, 486.

"made themselves eunuchs," voluntarily giving up sexual relationships to focus on other kingdom work.

The two different paths that Jesus lays out—marriage and celibacy—are both understood as high callings, neither better nor worse. And likewise, they are both understood as callings to be "received" and voluntarily entered into.

This same notion of the "gifting" of celibacy is a central focus in Paul's principles for marriage found in 1 Corinthians 7. Here the apostle gives a series of commands for both single people and married people, and instructs them in light of the fact that they are living in the last days (1 Cor 7:29). Read what he has to say about those who are deciding whether or not to remain voluntarily single:

> I say this as a concession, not as a command. I wish that all of you were as I am. But each of you has your own gift from God; one has this gift, another has that.
>
> Now to the unmarried and the widows I say: It is good for them to stay unmarried, as I do. But if they cannot control themselves, they should marry, for it is better to marry than to burn with passion. (1 Cor 7:6–9)

For Paul, as with Jesus, there are two groups of people. There are those who are gifted with celibacy, and those who are not. How does one know if they have the gift of celibacy? Well, they are those who in some measure have a personal quality and disposition that enables them to not "burn with passion." In Paul's logic, it is undeniably clear that should a person find themselves burning with passion, then they should pursue marriage. In this sense, Paul is going out of his way to ensure his readers understand that he is making a concession, not establishing a requisite for any given person. By no means is he stating that a person should, or must pursue celibacy, but rather if one is suitably gifted, then they should see this as an equal calling to marriage.[4]

These two passages, from Jesus and Paul, form the basis of all theologies of celibacy. Often predicated on the notion that "it is not good for man to be alone" (Gen 2:18, which we will explore further below), 2,000 years of historical church teaching has held that celibacy is made

---

4. It should be said that this teaching is a blessing of the New Covenant. Contrast the Old Testament where celibacy is never spoken about, and the blessings of God are strongly equated with offspring (see for example Exod 32:13; Deut 4:20; 1 Kings 21:3; 1 Chr 21:8).

up of two components: firstly, it is abstinence from sexual relations, and secondly it is voluntarily entered into.[5]

This is where utilizing the church's historical teachings on celibacy becomes untenable in the gay celibate movement. Those who maintain a traditional, non-affirming view of same-sex unions have no answer for the exclusively and enduringly gay Christian, other than to say that they must remain single for life.[6] Under the pretext that their sexuality is disordered and their ability for intimacy is unnatural, these men and women (including myself) are told that we have no option other than to forgo sexual and monogamous intimacy and embrace the celibate life. Any which way you frame this message, this is, in its simplest form "enforced celibacy" upon an entire group of Christians who have no control over their situation—a concept which has been entirely absent from orthodox Christianity until extraordinarily recent days.[7]

Ambrose, the early church father, had a high view of celibacy, but stated that that "virginity [in the form of celibacy] cannot be commanded but must be wished for."[8] Since then, the testimony of the church has universally followed Jesus and Paul's lead in claiming that celibacy can only be voluntarily entered into. Fast forward to the Reformation era and Calvin, rebuking the elevation of celibacy that was taking place amongst the clergy, declares "each individual must know what his particular gift is; and in this connection must not try to do something he has not got the ability to do; for everybody is not called to the same state."[9]

Given this rich understanding of the nature of celibacy, the current answer that traditionalist theologians are offering the church—that those who experience exclusive and enduring same-sex attraction have no option but to enter into lifelong avoidance of intimate relationship—is dangerously in opposition to Scripture.

---

5. Stickler, *The Case for Clerical Celibacy*, 13.

6. There are few mainstream evangelical, Catholic, or Pentecostal theologians that would advocate the idea of "mixed orientation" marriages. Rather this is seen as unwise and often harmful to both parties. For helpful discourse on this see Brownson, *Bible, Gender, Sexuality*, 143.

7. Of course, some may argue that the celibate requirement of priesthood in the Catholic Church constitutes "enforced celibacy," but it must be remembered that no Catholic person is forced to enter the priesthood, and the vow that is taken goes to great lengths to ensure that the candidate does so of their own volition.

8. St. Ambrose, *Sacred Writings*, 2017.

9. Calvin, *The First Epistle*, 11–12.

And to be sure, I do not use the term *dangerously* lightly, nor do I think it is an overstatement. I have spoken to countless LGBTQI people who have pursued or are pursuing this "enforced celibacy" and the picture is marred with a destructive culture of secret sexual rendezvous and disastrously poor mental health. Loneliness is rife, and symptoms of depression are almost universal. Across the board, rather than finding themselves free from the idolatry of sexuality, this enforced celibacy serves as a crucible for crippling isolation, decrepit intimacy, and a thwarted concept of what healthy relationship can look like. For these people, Paul's unambiguous advice that those who "cannot exercise self-control should marry" is, according to traditionalist interpretations, inapplicable, despite the exact same existential nature of their struggle.

Of course, there are exceptions. There are those such as Wesley Hill,[10] Vaughn Roberts,[11] and Ed Shaw[12] who grasp the gospel and who appear to live satisfying, grace-filled lives. But surely these are the exceptions that simply prove the rule that both Paul and Jesus offer—there are some to whom celibacy is gifted. To assume that their experience is capable of being appropriated into another person's vastly different temperament and character goes further than Scripture itself goes, and to that end, I no longer hold to such a theology.

All of this is said with the very strong caveat that I wholeheartedly believe that no sacrifice for the kingdom of God is too much, and if God calls a person to forego marriage for the sake of the kingdom, they will be provided for along the journey. The sacrifices they make will be richly rewarded. To extend this sacrifice beyond that which God requires, however, is not the prerogative of humanity. Be very, very cautious.

Marriage

As we saw in chapter 6, the creation accounts of Genesis 1 and 2 paint a spectacular cosmic picture of that moment when God spoke and the universe came into existence. In doing so, they serve as the foundational building blocks of a Christian anthropology—our understanding of what it means to be part of creation. Throughout the spectacular process, God

---

10. Hill, *Washed and Waiting.*

11. Roberts, *Battles Christians Face.*

12. Shaw, *The Plausibility Problem.*

consistently "sees that it is good."[13] Over and over again, goodness flows forth as God blesses it with divine accolades. But then this repetition reverses and God recognizes something within creation that is "not good." This "not goodness" is the "aloneness" of the man, Adam.

And so, as we have seen, God weaves into the stunning creation the concept of family—unions that would offer companionship, support, and mutual care as humans go forth into the garden. Adam's exclamation of joy upon discovering Eve resonates so beautifully throughout history. Void of sexual and erotic connotations, the union is based upon the fact that the two are compatible because they share the same flesh and bones (2:23). Situated as it is, this passage launches us into an exploration of marriage, the cure that God offers to the aloneness of the man.

Up front then, it must be stated that marriage is a beautiful gift from God. As the school of life marches on, those who enter it know that marriage teaches us sacrifice, commitment, patience, and courage. On a level elsewhere unattainable it reveals to us our flaws and our faults, and it simultaneously provides a place in which, by God's grace, they can be healed. While many Christians hold that faithful, committed unions are exclusively reserved for the male-female prototypical relationship established in the garden, the case for this begins to break down when we look broadly at the purposes for which God created marriage in the first place.

Our task now is to examine the purposes that God directly gives for marriage, and to establish a framework for discerning whether or not gay and lesbian unions can fulfill these purposes. Traditionally the church has broken these down into three areas, which we will address in order.[14]

Sex . . . and Babies

Firstly, the Bible speaks about marriage as the appropriate boundary for the expression of sex. On a strangely primal level, 1 Corinthians 7:6–9 (as we have seen) treats marriage as a "remedy against sin" or as the 1662 *Book of Common Prayer* puts it, a "remedy agaynste synne."[15] Thus, rather than leaving us to journey through life with "burning lust," marriage is designed to supply an avenue for desire to express itself.

13. Gen 1:4, 12, 14, 18, 21, 25, 31, 2:9.

14. This trifold purpose of marriage dates as far back as Augustine with his *De Bono Coniugali*.

15. *The Book of Common Prayer*, 157.

Song of Songs grandly celebrates this, emotively paying tribute to the physical beauty of two bodies in the act of intimate pleasure. Thus we see that sex, on one level, is designed to enhance and enrich the experience of unity between the two married partners.

But of course, this is not the only purpose of sex. To claim such would be overtly reductionistic. The Bible also asserts that marriage (and therefore sex) is also given for the task of procreation and the raising of children. Primarily this theology is established from the commandment in Genesis 1:28, "Be fruitful and multiply, fill the earth and subdue it." Multiplication requires sex between a man and a woman, and nobody is under any illusion that gay or lesbian relationships can obtain this, and thus, at this point, many Christians simply stop thinking, assuming that the case is closed and the path for gay unions is barred.

But we should be hesitant to close the case too soon, because doing so ignores (and perhaps even jeopardizes) scores of other beautiful ideas. It is clear from Scripture that God designed sex with this dual purpose—both unitive and reproductive. What has intrigued Christians for centuries is not so much what the Bible says here so much as what the Bible remains silent on. Tantalizingly, Scripture *never* insists that any sex or relationship act must fulfill both purposes simultaneously. There is never the requirement in Scripture that every act of sex translates into reproductive potential, or indeed that any marriage be barred should it fail to do so.[16]

Practically speaking, for Protestants (and many within the Catholic Church), this has translated into the acceptance of contraceptives. Based on this dual purpose of sex, Protestant theology recognizes that within marriage, there is great value in the partners pursuing sexual intimacy, without necessarily working toward having a baby. For both Protestants and Catholic traditions, it has also translated into the church blessing the marriages of those who enter matrimony knowing that they are biologically incapable of producing offspring (either due to age or medical complications).[17] The church is able, with good conscience and within the

16. Outside the scope of this chapter is the trajectory of Scripture, which initially sees the blessings of God as intrinsically tied up with offspring (Exod 32:13; Deut 4:20; 1 Kgs 21:3; 1 Chr 21:8) to the New Testament emphasis that these blessings are now enjoyed in Christ through "spiritual offspring" and "the children of the promise" not through Abraham but through faith (Gal 3; Rom 9:6–8, Eph 1:14, 18; 1 Pet 1:3–4). For an extended examination of this see Köstenberger and Jones, *God, Marriage, and Family.*

17. As outlined in St Thomas Aquinas's theological tome, largely considered the

bounds of sound doctrine, to do both of these things precisely because the Bible does not provide one singular, exclusive reason for why marriage (or more precisely, sex within marriage) exists.[18]

And so we have to ask the question, can lifelong, monogamous gay or lesbian unions fulfill this first purpose of marriage? Within sound doctrine, the answer is an unequivocal yes. These unions may not have the same procreative potential as a young, fertile couple, but they do have the ability to fulfill the unifying sex role that the Bible speaks about quite apart from such procreation.

Mutual Support and Companionship

Ecclesiastes, within the depths of its wisdom makes the observation that "two are better than one" (4:9–12). Whilst not necessarily speaking about a marriage union in this section, the idea is quite simple—life in this world is notoriously hard, and having a companion to travel with provides much needed support and relief along the journey.

There are very few who would doubt the fact that gay and lesbian unions are capable of fulfilling this task of kinship unions, and I have found very few theologians or scholars who would argue such.

Perhaps (as we have seen) somebody might argue that the nature and temperament of maleness and femaleness underscore concepts of functional co-existence in family. However the reality that we see in the church every day is that there are men who strongly exhibit traditionally "feminine" qualities such as care, compassion, and gentleness and we conversely see women who exhibit traditionally "masculine" qualities such as leadership, courage, and strength. The Bible (once again) is silent on what constitutes a masculine or feminine quality, and as such this argument seems more based on modern Western cultural concepts of gendered norms than on what God actually has to say on the matter.

A Reflection of the Greatest Marriage

Revelation 19—22 contains some of the most dramatic scenes in all of Scripture, indeed in all of literature. Peering through the veil of time into

---

clearest summary of official Catholic Church doctrine to this day. Saint Thomas Aquinas, *Summa Theologica*, Volume 5, 2767.

18. Geisler, *Christian Ethics*, 396.

the cataclysmic last days, we see Christ, the lamb that was slain, coming forth to claim his bride, the church, who is beautifully dressed, prepared to meet her groom (21:2). This vividly portrayed wedding ceremony provides the hauntingly beautiful bookend to the salvation narrative that began so many, many years before in a garden, with another marriage between a different man and woman.

Paul, in his instructions to husbands and wives, deliberately ties the idea of Christ's marriage to the church with the institution of human marriage. Ephesians 5:28–32 states:

> In this same way, husbands ought to love their wives as their own bodies. He who loves his wife loves himself. After all, no one ever hated their own body, but they feed and care for their body, just as Christ does the church—for we are members of his body. "For this reason a man will leave his father and mother and be united to his wife, and the two will become one flesh." This is a profound mystery—but I am talking about Christ and the church.

Gloriously, this passage paints a picture of marriage as a faithful covenant, modeling its love paradigm after the greatest act of sacrifice that Paul could conceive—that of Christ's sacrifice for the church. In Ephesians 5 we see that Christ is the head of the church (5:23), loves the church (5:25), gave himself up for the church (5:25), cleansed the church (5:27), and nourishes and cherishes the church (5:29). As we have previously seen, Paul grounds all of this in his quotation from Genesis 2:24, demanding that the two have "become one flesh," and are thus inseparable as a kinship unit.[19]

What greater show of commitment could Paul call the church to aspire toward? What tenderness and concern, passion and strength? Where else could Paul have drawn his audiences' eyes but to Christ? Those who would enter marriage must first recognize that it is not an institution in which they can seek gain, but rather, a relationship in which they must pour themselves out.

In this sense, when enacted with obedience and mutuality, marriage on earth reflects a far greater reality—the reality that Christ is drawing to himself a people from every tribe, tongue, and nation (Rev 7:9). This is the great mystery that Paul is speaking about, and about which we are to get excited!

19. Foulkes, *Ephesians,* 164.

When it comes to the discussion around LGBT people, the conclusions reached by both affirming and non-affirming stances are extremely polarized, yet both rather simple. After surveying the passages above, Ed Shaw (non-affirming) draws the following conclusion:

> Marriage between a man and a woman—that complementary union of sexual difference—is central to the very wiring of God's plan for the universe, from its beginning and into eternity. So, change its constituent parts (a man and a woman) and you are interfering with where God has said his world is heading—the unity in difference of the heavenly marriage of the divine and human.[20]

In other words, in order for the gospel to work, Jesus (the savior) had to be *different* from the church (the one who needed saving), and thus, in order for marriage to reflect the gospel, the two parties must be *sexually different* from one another.

There are two major logical inconsistencies with this way of interpreting the gendered depiction of the salvation narrative. The first goes back to our question (cast your mind way back when to we looked at Genesis) around the applicability of norms into legislative practices. That is, when the Bible presents any given relationship or situation, what rubric do we use to determine that this is to be *normative* for all people, at all times, and in all places? There is no denying that Paul is speaking about a husband and wife relationship here when he calls people to model their relationships off Christ. Given his situation in first-century Judaism, this is precisely what we would expect. As we have seen, there were no faithful gay relationships from which he could have drawn any other narrative, because in a patriarchal society the very idea of a faithful, mutually respectful gay relationship was not even considered a possibility.

At its core, the argument states that because Jesus is a man, and the church is a woman, gay unions are not permitted. Laying aside the literary observation that the church makes for a very strange "woman," the logic in this statement is simply not in the passage, and nor is it anywhere else in Scripture. Paul is drawing from his experience of the world, and, inspired by the Holy Spirit, is offering practical applications for how the glory of the gospel impacts the marriage relationships that his audience were in. Drawing conclusions about the legitimacy or illegitimacy of gay

20. Shaw, *The Plausibility Problem*, 146–47.

or lesbian unions from this passage goes far further than is warranted or appropriate.

Building on this, the second inconsistency is in the assumption that *sexual difference* is the exclusive prerequisite for reflecting Christ. In what ways is Christ different from the church? Surely in a million different ways! In what ways are women different to men? Surely in a million different ways! And in what ways are two men different from one another? Surely in a million different ways! The beauty of the passage is not in two "biologically compatible" bodies coming together (there is no mention of physical difference here), but rather, in two people reflecting the total, self-giving, sacrificial love that Christ displayed on the cross. In this sense, there is the very real need for some in the church to stop wielding Ephesians 5 as a treatise on gender, and to recognize it as a call to covenantal, faithful unions that take their lead from the glorious work of Jesus.

At the end of the day, the picture that we get of marriage in the Bible is enthralling, and, having worked through how it is depicted, I find it impossible to deny gay and lesbian people the covenantal union that Christ offers them. I began this chapter with a sentence that shook me to the core as a teenager. "The worst possible thing that can happen to a gay Christian would be to fall in love." There is some truth in this statement—the opportunity to form a family unit of mutual companionship is so close to the core of what it means to live as a human in this world. However, as I have journeyed through the years, I have revisited these words and modified them to fit what I now see as the reality that I wish to uphold with every breath I take: "the worst possible thing that can happen to a gay Christian would be to fall out of love with Jesus."

I long for the day when LGBTQI people are welcomed into our churches and given the full embrace that Christ offers them. But even more than that, I long for the day when every person (whatever their sexuality) who calls Christ their king, gets to stand before him and finally meet him face to face in the most glorious wedding ceremony of all the ages.

12

Changing Biblical Interpretations—A New Thing?

What we have laid out so far in this book is a journey of theological conviction, examining the pillars of a traditional, conservative sexual ethic,
and how in my mind they came toppling down. Through countless conversations and endless dialogue, it is increasingly clear that these pillars
are likewise coming down in the minds of so many within our churches,
and the destabilizing call is ringing out for winds of change.

I understand more than many that what we are calling for here is
a theological shift that feels unprecedented and altogether daunting.
But what I want to examine in this chapter is the reality that the path of
theological change is a well-worn track, and we stand on the shoulders
of giants who have gone before. When we look at history we see that the
church in every generation has a duty to read and defend the words of
God. As part of this, we also see that many generations, faced with new
and (often exciting) shifts in global history, have carried the dubious hon-
or of interpreting the Bible for these new worlds—not changing Scripture, but humbly seeking to apply it to vastly unfamiliar contexts. There
is no doubt that we live in just such a generation. The tides of change and
societal advancements in the areas of sexuality and gender are moving
far further than any person could have predicted fifty years ago, and, in
looking forward, I want to draw your attention to the past. It is there that
we find the church in much the (seemingly) same precarious place over
and over again, on the edge of a precipice and ready for something different. This is by no means a new thing, but it is rightly intimidating, and it

is at these times, more than any other, that we require caution, prayerful guidance, and rigorous attention to the Bible.

In this chapter, I want to take us through three different changes that have taken place in prevailing church theology. This is not an exercise in drawing parallels between LGBTQI discussions and what follows, but rather an opportunity to explore not just *what* changed, but *how* these changes took place. We begin with what is perhaps the most controversial institution that the church has ever been intimately involved with—the world of slavery.

Slaves and Their Christian Masters

The abolitionist movement of the nineteenth century was led, in the most part, by a group of passionate evangelical Christians who took the Bible to heart. Convicted by the dignity that God's word instilled within humanity, this group successfully championed the charge that would eventually overthrow one of the most pervasive of global institutions.[1] Rightly so, the church today celebrates the work of these men and women, but it would be historically remiss of us to think that the battle they fought was between the church (anti-slavery) and the world (pro-slavery). Far more often than not, the battle that this movement faced was Christians trying to convince other Christians that slavery was not only immoral, but was antithetical to a biblically informed theology. As such, the abolitionist movement can be historically construed as less of a demand for social justice, and more of a theological crisis that was gripping the global church.[2]

Somewhat astoundingly, from the earliest days of the church right through to the 1800s, there were no sustained challenges to a Christian theology that asserted that slavery was an institution divinely instilled by God into the created order. Indeed, quite the opposite is true. Across the world, (and towards the latter days, most notably in the Southern states of North America), sermons were regularly preached, extolling the virtues of slavery. In response to the change of theology being presented in the 1800s, Henry Van Dyke, a prominent Northern Presbyterian minister exclaimed "the tree of abolitionism is evil, and only evil—root and

---

1. For a dramatic retelling of the story, see Tomkins, *The Clapham Sect.*
2. Noll, *The Civil War as a Theological Crisis*, 52.

branch, flower and leaf, and fruit."[3] So closely held was the connection between good theology and pro-slavery movements, that the chairman of the Texas Baptist Association could claim that the Lord had ordained slavery just as he had ordained marriage. Should slaveholders lose their slaves, they risked losing their religion.[4]

The beauty of the pro-slavery argument lay in its simplicity—read the Bible for yourself, and you will see that *nowhere* does the Bible condemn slavery. In fact, you will see that Scripture is replete with examples of slavery that God appears to at the very least condone (1 Cor 7:21; Col 3:22, 4:1), sometimes bless (Gen 9:25–27, 17:12; Eph 6:5), and, on occasions, even command (Lev 25:45–46; Deut 20:10–11). To the biblically literate, the case was closed, and to those who would question the theology, the call was clear—if the Bible blesses it, then only the godless would condemn it.

"That the relation betwixt the slave and his master is not inconsistent with the word of God, we have long since settled," proclaimed James Henley Thornwell, one of America's leading theologians. "We cherish the institution not from avarice, but from principle."[5] This line of argument had been assumed for centuries, and while it's rightly argued that the slave trade of the sixteenth to the nineteenth centuries was substantially more degrading than previous permutations, concepts such as humans as property, slavery from birth, the master's right to govern a slave's every move, and a divinely sanctioned class system were part and parcel with every iteration of a theology of slavery since the early church.[6]

With such a rich historical theology, doubt about the biblical defense of slavery was equated with doubt about the authority of the Bible itself.[7] While many were willing to admit that abuses of the slave trade had taken place, they saw the abolitionist movement as throwing the baby out with the bathwater, and in doing so, a capitulation to human ethics over the divinely sanctioned word of God. Thus, Henry Van Dyke passionately held that:

3. Noll, *The Civil War as a Theological Crisis*, 3.

4. Rable, *God's Almost Chosen Peoples*, 279.

5. Thornwell, *Collected Writings*, 539.

6. For historical clarity, the fact that the slave trade was deeply racial at the time is best seen as a separate, though by this stage intricately linked theological issue. For an examination of the changing theology of racial subordination, see Whitford, "Curse of Ham."

7. Dupont, *Mississippi Praying*, 40.

> Abolitionism leads, in multitudes of cases, and by a logical pro-
> cess, to utter infidelity . . . One of its avowed principles is, that it
> does not try slavery by the Bible; but . . . it tries the Bible by the
> principles of freedom . . . This assumption, that men are capable
> of judging beforehand what is to be expected of Divine revela-
> tion, is the cockatrice's egg, from which, in all ages, heresies have
> hatched.[8]

With the theological stakes so high, it's no wonder that schisms began forming within denominations. Disillusioned by the godless aboli- tionists, huge divisions broke off, and thus the Southern Baptist Confer- ence was formed, as were the Methodist Episcopal Church, South, and the Presbyterian Church, US.[9] Passionate about their biblical theology, these denominations fought for the God-ordained right to own slaves. While these views maintained their vehemence most strongly in Protes- tant America (and most noticeably in the South), there was a time when a pro-slavery interpretation of the Bible was widespread across the globe, across all denominations (even the most vocal abolitionists, the Quakers, began with a call only for good treatment of slaves).[10]

In Britain and the Commonwealth Colonies, 1807 saw parliament banning the slave trade. This was a watershed victory for the band of Brit- ish evangelicals who, spurred on by the broader human rights ethics of the day, had turned to Scripture and appealed to such theological themes as the dignity and worth of all people made in the image of God. As one historian has summarized, "biblical humanitarianism was trumping biblical traditionalism."[11] However it wasn't until 1865, after more than a century of vicious theological debate that the constitution of the United States was amended to ban the practice of slavery.

How did it change? Tragically we know that there are more slaves today than ever before. Slavery is very much alive and well, but what is readily apparent is that there are no churches, pastors, or theologians that would even think to suggest that the Bible sanctions or blesses the ownership and servitude of any person to another. While we can't draw too strong correlations between the emancipation of slaves and current debates about the status of LGBTQI people, there are certainly things we can learn about how theology is shaped.

8. Noll, *The Civil War as a Theological Crisis*, 30.

9. Dupont, *Mississippi Praying*, 41.

10. Noll, *The Civil War as a Theological Crisis*, 31.

11. Noll, *The Civil War as a Theological Crisis*, 35.

Firstly, we are forced to humbly recognize that the church has not always had it right. A belief that historical theology is inherently superior cannot be our *a priori* assumption. The church has made mistakes, and it has taken other people in the church (and outside of the church) to point out those mistakes, guided by the Holy Spirit into new applications of ancient words.

Secondly, the charge laid upon the abolitionists was that they were abandoning the authority of Scripture. While there were some who did, history shows us that by and large, this was patently a false accusation. When traditionalists condemn affirming theologians as "abandoning the authority of Scripture," this charge largely falls on deaf ears, as many affirming theologians have wrestled faithfully with Scripture and have not come to their position lightly.

Thirdly, the pro-slavery movement had simplicity in their favor. They were able to rely on a plain reading of Scripture (remember addressing that in chapter 9?). On the other hand, the abolitionists had to appeal to a somewhat more complex line of argument that relied not on proof texts but on the driving theological principles that Scripture provides. What I find striking about the slave movement is not so much its arc toward justice as the vehemence of the theological debates upon which it both rose and fell. Utterly convinced that their reading of Scripture was not only correct, but also the *only* correct interpretation, people defended their convictions right up unto the last.

This leads us to a sound principle that should be noted—*history can be passionately certain, and still wrong.* Recognizing this demands humility and a willingness to not rely overly heavily on the past, but rather a willingness to engage Scripture as we have it before us. Because, sure enough, a groundswell of thinking Christians saw the oppression that was synonymous with the dominant paradigm of the time, and God used them to lead people to freedom.

This brings us then to another group of people who, for almost the entire history of the church, were marginalized, vilified, and systematically persecuted by people who claimed to be acting in the name of God.

Child-Skewering, Bloodthirsty Kidnappers

When Martin Luther, the great Reformer of the Protestant faith, wrote with disdain about the Jews in the early sixteenth century, he was not

writing anything particularly controversial or, in fact, new. In the introduction to his book *On the Jews and Their Lies,* he wrote:

> I had made up my mind to write no more either about the Jews
> or against them. But since I learned that those miserable and ac-
> cursed people do not cease to lure to themselves even us, that is,
> the Christians, I have published this little book, so that I might
> be found among those who opposed such poisonous activities
> of the Jews . . .[12]

After caricaturing Jews as well-poisoning, child-skewering, blood-
thirsty kidnappers (as was common practice of the day), Luther proclaimed, "So we are even at fault in not avenging all this innocent blood
of our Lord and of the Christians which they shed for three hundred
years after the destruction of Jerusalem, and the blood of the children
they have shed since then (which still shines forth from their eyes and
their skin). We are at fault in not slaying them."[13]

Guiding his theology was the sure fact that this was justice playing
itself out, "for the Jews have cursed and harmed themselves more than
enough by cursing the Man Jesus of Nazareth."[14] While there were times
in his life when he softened his stance somewhat, Luther's last series of
four sermons before his death urged any civil leader who had held a
position of power to expel the Jews from their land, lest they be caught
"partners in another's sins."[15]

There are many Christians today who find Luther's remarks regarding Jews both perplexing and embarrassing, but in reality, we have to see
that Luther, in this area, was a product of his times. Despite his sweeping
reforms and status as a heretic for his views on doctrines of salvation
and papal power, in this matter he remained entirely orthodox with the
prevailing church. And this was not simple racism at play. It was deeply
informed by the church's understanding of Scripture—this was believed
to be sound theology through and through.

The Israel of the Old Testament was seen as the epitome of a failed
nation, with God abandoning the Jewish people for a new people, this
time in Christ. This new kingdom superseded the old (how else could
you account for the destruction of the temple and the loss of Israelite

---

12. Luther, *On the Jews and Their Lies,* 1.
13. Luther, *On the Jews and Their Lies,* 126.
14. Luther, *On the Jews and Their Lies,* 133.
15. Kaufmann, *Luther's Jews,* 3.

ownership of the land?). If God had abandoned (and even cursed) the Jewish people, what right did any Christian have to bless them? Doing so would contradict the will of God himself! Since the earliest days of the church, this thinking had been grounded in the belief that the Jews were guilty of the blood of the Messiah—a sin for which every generation of Jewish person must be held to account. As early as the fourth century, the polemical language associated with the Jews was that Satan dwelt among them as their partner.

And so we see that Luther was not contradicting his understanding of the Bible when he spoke with such vehemence against the Jewish people. Indeed, he was backed up by almost 1,500 years of theological unanimity. Summing up this theology succinctly, Erasmus (1466–1536) concluded, "If it is part of the good Christian to detest the Jews, then we are all good Christians."[16]

Whilst every region had its own narrative, and many Christian pastors began to soften their anti-Semitic rhetoric, over the next several hundred years the general trajectory rarely swung in a positive direction. Moments of reprieve were met with suspicion, and suspicion with outright, church-sanctioned hostility. What is striking through all of this is not so much the articulated doctrine of the church (no major denomination had an official public stance), but rather the silence which rung deafening notes of complicity.

So what changed? Never in my lifetime have I heard a church leader or theologian espouse any such vehemence against the Jews. It's simply unheard of in today's theological terrain. It's difficult to put any major theological shift down to any one cause, but the glaringly obvious horrors of the twentieth century warrant special attention in this case. Tragedy struck when the historical theology of the church was allowed to play itself out:

> I have been attacked because of my handling of the Jewish question. The Catholic Church considered the Jews pestilent for fifteen hundred years, put them in ghettos, etc., because it recognized the Jews for what they were. In the epoch of liberalism the danger was no longer recognized. I am moving back toward the time in which a fifteen-hundred-year-long tradition was implemented. I do not set race over religion, but I recognize the representatives of this race as pestilent for the state and for

16. Poliakov, *History of Anti-Semitism*, 226–27.

the church, and perhaps I am thereby doing Christianity a great
service by pushing them out of schools and public functions.

History records that when Hitler spoke these words in the presence of
the Vatican leadership, his words were met with a warm handshake.[17] But
finally, for the church, the horrors of the death camps crossed a line from
which there was no going back.

Piles of decaying bodies made their way onto the newspapers in
people's lounge rooms. Emaciated figures, gaunt eyes, and tattooed wrists
scorched the psyche of the global church, and the pangs of complicity
finally seared the psyches of an all-too-silent majority. Jews moved from a
caricatured enemy to being radically humanized in a new wave of popular
media. They could no longer be seen as a distant money-hungry threat.
Thanks to the global access to moving images and graphic stories, people
saw for the first time their suffering, up close and personal.

In the secular world, this episode launched a human rights ethic en-
shrined in international creed that stated "All human beings are born free
and equal in dignity and rights. They are endowed with reason and conscience and should act towards one another in a spirit of brotherhood."[18]
In the realm of the church, no such apology was forthcoming, but over-
night, centuries of anti-Jewish theology simply evaporated.

This leads us to a second principle that warrants articulating: *any
theology which breeds death and perpetuates division deserves radical
scrutiny.*

Hear me closely. This does not mean that we blindly assume that any
such theology is necessarily unbiblical or wrong—although a good case
could be made for this—but rather it is to assert that no line of theology
is above reasoned discussion, especially when lives are at stake. I have
no doubt that the early church fathers along with Luther, Erasmus, and a
long succession of theologians were thoroughly convinced that they were
teaching sound doctrine. But whilst ever the implications of that doctrine
were one step removed, unable to be felt by its instigators, the doctrine
was never held up for review.

It is an unassailable truth that current church doctrine about LG-
BTQI people leads to profound exclusion, endemic depression, and

17. The extent to which the church is complicit in the unfolding history of the Nazi
party is a source of much literature and far outside the scope of this chapter. Suffice it
to say with confidence, the historical theology of the church did nothing to assist the
cause of Jews during this time.

18. *Universal Declaration of Human Rights*, Article 1.

soaring suicide rates. Of course, this does not directly equate to poor theology—there may be other areas (such as poor community support or lack of pastoral care) that may contribute to such an environment. But surely we can agree this is the starting point for inviting a review.

And so, with this in mind, we turn our attention to one final area of theology that has undergone momentous changes throughout the life of the church, one that has profound implications for, at the very least, half of us.

In the Image of God . . . Almost

Augustine, one of the great founders of the early church (of "original sin" fame), made the somewhat startling claim that women are human, but not made in the image of God.[19] Lest anyone take offense at such a statement, we would do well to hear his reasoning: women have a lower intellect ("directed to the cognition of lower things") while men on the other hand have been blessed with a "spiritual brain."[20]

For Augustine, it's almost safe to say that women were purely the instrument of procreation—what other purpose could they serve in the world? Even in the realm of companionship, "yet for company and conversation, how much more agreeable it is for two male friends to dwell together than for a man and a woman."[21]

For Tertullian, whose legacies include coining the term *Trinity*, the picture was much the same, if not more bleak. Speaking to a gathering of women, he connected the guilt of Eve to every subsequent woman who ever lived:

> This sex of yours lives in this age: the guilt must of necessity live too: *You* are the devil's gateway: *you* are the unsealer of that (forbidden) tree: *you* are the first deserter of the divine law: *you* are she who persuaded him whom the devil was not valiant enough to attack: *you* destroyed so easily God's image, man. On account of *your* desert—that is, death—even the Son of God had to die.[22]

19. Augustine, "On the Trinity," 158.

20. Sumner, *Men and Women in the Church*, 60.

21. Augustine, as quoted in Sumner, *Men and Women in the Church*, 41.

22. Tertullian, "On the Dress of Women," 4:14.

Or, finally, take Ambrose (337–397 AD), whose theology has permeated almost every area of church life right up to the present day. Without any qualifying remarks, Ambrose stated that "even though the man was created outside Paradise (i.e., in an inferior place), he is found to be superior, while woman, though created in a better place (i.e., inside Paradise) is found inferior."[23] The lack of qualifications to such a statement demonstrates the pervasiveness of such theological understandings of women. Women, as reflections of men, were inferior to men, incapable of fulfilling the task of imaging God in creation.

If we fast forward almost a millennia to St. Thomas Aquinas (1225–1274 AD,) we discover that things really haven't changed at all. The theology of the church has remained resolutely steadfast in the assumption that women are the inferior counterparts to men. With very little adjustment, Aquinas (whose treaties stand to this day as some of the most complete systematized theologies of the Catholic Church) followed the footsteps of Augustine, Tertullian, and Ambrose in understanding that biblically, men were made in the image of God in a superior way to women.

> Subjection is twofold. One is servile, by virtue of which a superior makes use of a subject for his own benefit; and this kind of subjection came after sin. There is another kind of subjection, which is called economic or civil, whereby the superior makes use of his subjects for their own benefit and good; and this kind of subjection existed even before sin. For good order would have been wanting in the human family if some were not governed by others wiser than themselves. So, by such a kind of subjection woman is naturally subject to man, because in man, the discretion of reason predominates.[24]

Given the fact that reason is of the utmost virtue, Aquinas makes the following casual observation:

> Strictly speaking, however, the father should be loved more than the mother. For father and mother are loved as principles of our natural origin. Now the father is principle in a more excellent way than the mother, because he is the active principle (*reason*), while the mother is a passive and material principle. Consequently, strictly speaking, the father is to be loved more.[25]

23. Ambrose, *On Paradise*, quoted in Sumner, *Men and Women in the Church*, 43.

24. Aquinas, *Summa Theologica, vol. 1*, 466.

25. Aquinas, *Summa Theologica, vol. 3*, 1296.

Throughout the Reformation period and well on into the modern era, much the same theology permeated the global church. With very few exceptions, women were seen as inferior to men, not quite made in the image of God, and duly subservient because of their inability to partake in higher level reasoning. This was driven by their selective prototypical readings of the Genesis narratives, coupled with a few New Testament references (most notably 1 Corinthians 11:7–12).

Contrast this theology to that of Wayne Grudem, who represents some of the most conservative of major evangelical voices in current Christian thinking:

> Therefore, we should treat men and women with equal dignity, and we should think of men and women as having equal value. We are *both* in the image of God, and we have been so since the very first day that God created us. "In the image of God he created him; *male and female he created them*" (Genesis 1:27). Nowhere does the Bible say that men are more in God's image than women.[26] (his emphasis)

Notice the dramatic change in the theological rhetoric—women are not subservient, they are not inept at reason, they are equal within creation and most notably, men and women are *both* in the image of God. To his credit, Grudem recognizes that in coming to these conclusions, he is standing against the tide of millennia of orthodox church teaching:

> I personally think that one reason God has allowed this whole controversy on manhood and womanhood to come into the church at this time is so that we could correct some mistakes, change some wrongful traditions, and become more faithful to Scripture in treating our wives and all women with dignity and respect.[27]

Further, it should be noted that Grudem by no means holds the only (or even majority) view in regards to a theology of womanhood. The egalitarian movement (which sees women as equally gifted by God and capable of administering such gifts) is summed up by Gordon Fee:

---

26. Grudem, "Key Issues," 20.

27. Grudem, "Key Issues" 23. It should be stated as a side note that it strikes me as paradoxical that Grudem can be so adamantly confident that after millennia of people claiming to be adhering to biblical standards of manhood and womanhood, that he should now be the one to offer the definitive definition, without considering that he may, still, have things to learn about the Bible.

It seems a sad commentary on the church and on its understanding of the Holy Spirit that "official" leadership and ministry is allowed to come from only one half of the community
of faith. The New Testament evidence is that the Holy Spirit is
gender inclusive, gifting both men and women, and thus potentially setting the whole body free for all the parts to minister and
in various ways to give leadership to the others. Thus my issue
in the end is not a feminist agenda—an advocacy of women in
ministry. Rather, it is a Spirit agenda, a plea for the releasing of
the Spirit from our strictures and structures so that the church
might minister to itself and to the world more effectively.[28]

It's difficult to exaggerate the immensity of theological transformation that has taken place in regards to the status of women before God
and their place in the church. For Fee, this goes beyond the rectifying of
an inherently sexist anthropology, and into the realm of correct pneumatology (the theology of the Holy Spirit). If we get this one wrong, says Fee,
we lose who God is!

Once again, we must ask the question, "What changed?" And once
again, we must conclude that numerous factors drove people back to
Scripture to reassess what they had seen in the texts and to examine
whether or not there was another, more faithful way of reading the Bible.

Undoubtedly, the suffragette movement played a crucial role, insti-
gating a changing cultural milieu which not only permitted, but encouraged women to pursue higher education. This naturally led to women
receiving prominent roles within society and subsequent recognition of
their capacity to reason being equal to men.

As this took place, women were received into theological schools
(once the exclusive domain of men) and began doing theology for themselves. This vital turning point saw women leading Christian groups,
teaching, bearing faithful fruit, and sharpening the body of Christ. Scripture didn't change. People's respect for Scripture didn't change. Rather,
we have come to understand new insights about what it means to be man
and woman.

This leads us to our final principle in how theology can adhere to
Scripture during times of dispute and simultaneously, cautiously approach change: *Listening to voices from the margins can lead to new, more
faithful understandings of how God is working in the world.* All of the momentous changes we have examined in this chapter were the product of

28. Fee, *Discovering Biblical Equality,* 254.

hard work, faithful exegesis, and humble listening to what the Spirit has taught through believers around the world.

Of course, history has shown that there are untold challenges to church theology that have not resulted in significant theological change, many for good reason. But this does not give any person license to claim that their theology is not open to review. Without the humility of faithful men and women who were willing to rethink the way they approached slaves, Jews, and women, the church would look like a vastly different entity today. Guided by the three principles that we have outlined here (*history can be passionately certain, and still wrong; any theology which breeds death and perpetuates division deserves scrutiny; and listening to voices from the margins can lead to new, more faithful understandings of how God is working in the world*), is it possible that just such a change is immanent on the horizon of the church?

With all of the above in mind, I humbly submit that I may be wrong in the way I have exegeted Scripture throughout this book. If the greatest theologians of history could be so disastrously entrenched in poor readings of the Bible, who am I to assume that I have attained the pinnacle of correction? However, gifted with the ability to reason and guided by the Spirit, I have to conclude that I am right. As such, I am part of the resounding call to the church to abandon theology that condemns faithful and God-honoring lesbian and gay unions, to listen to the voices from the margins, and to welcome to the table those whom God himself, in Christ, delights in.

Thus, dear reader, we have come to the end of the second part of our journey—examining the Scriptures for a faithful understanding of homosexuality. We finally turn our attention now to what this looks like on the ground, as messy churches seek a messy path forward into the tumultuous terrain ahead.

PART THREE

Looking Forward

13

If the Bible Is Not Against It...

Welcome to Part Three, and congratulations on making it this far! We've done the hard yards of working our way through large portions of Scripture, and now we have the chance to draw some threads together. As we move into this section, the hope is that we would be able to paint a picture of what it means to have gay and lesbian people fully included in the life of the church. The more I have pondered this, the more I have naturally become enthralled by the beauty of God's people working together, pointing as one to Jesus. When outcasts become family, something truly powerful happens. But before we get to the hope that is ahead for the church in this area, we need to ground this final part in some honest reflections. I'd like to tell you about an encounter I had in a coffee shop.

William's usual smile and cheerful manner were clouded that day. A capable preacher and gifted writer, this budding pastor's career was advancing rapidly in church circles, but as we sat in chic couches with untouched coffee, I watched this confident young man's façade dissipate.

Will would describe himself as a conservative evangelical, first by osmosis as a child, then by conviction as an adult. This was his world, and he felt at home here. But Will told me that ever since before he was a teenager, he knew at a foundational level that he did not fit in. Despite feeling compelled to serve God in ministry, Will's same-sex attraction had for so many years been the catalyst for an ever-increasing rift in his relationship with God.

Will struggled to keep his voice steady as he recounted countless nights spent weeping, crying out to God for relief from the pain of carrying this burden. Lonely to the point of exhaustion, he saw his future before him, and couldn't escape the fact that it was unwaveringly black. He had a strong community around him that he shared with regularly, but, he lamented, at the end of the day they would all go home to their lives and he would be left stranded once again. Will so desperately wanted to serve God, yet as we spoke, it was clear that the faith that had once brought him so much joy was now the source of insurmountable grief. The very well from which he had once found life was now the force filling his mind with thoughts of suicide.

Will wanted to love God, but, if the truth be told, he found it hard not to resent God. In his words, "It just hurts so much, all the time."

We're tired. That's the truth. There are millions of us, and we're tired. Weary pilgrims in foreign lands, seeking to follow Jesus. I look around at my LGBTQI brothers and sisters and I see strength, yes, but I also see wounds. Wounds from battles we never wished to enter. I see survivors, yes, but I also see casualties. Unwilling soldiers whose strength has been sapped. They too were tired once, but now they have been defeated.

Once upon a time they sat at this table beside you. They laughed and ate and sang and worshiped and prayed and served, beside you. But somewhere along the line, somebody, maybe even you, decided that there was no room at this table for people like them. There was no room at this table for any form of love that didn't fit a mold, a class, a type. The love they sought, this somebody thought, was second-rate, destructive, and perverse. But longing to be held, they were torn in two—born into an orientation they could not change and drawn into a kingdom they could not deny. And so, bruised and shamed, they hid in the shadows of the feast, biding their time and longing for kindred spirits to greet them with a smile. But the smiles that came hid scorn and shot blame. And so one day, while nobody was watching, they quietly slid out the door. They too were tired once, but now they have been defeated. These are the casualties that I see.

Dear reader, the stakes in this game are tragically high. I have no doubt that you can see that much. And if you have made it this far, I have no doubt that you can see that the condemnations that are launched by non-affirming theology can no longer hide behind a guise of "for the Bible tells me so."

This is why we're tired. But we're also hopeful. I have lost count of the number of conversations I have had in which people have been open to exploring affirming theology. I am astounded by how many individuals, both straight and gay, have taken initiative in researching this area for themselves. I am humbled by the diligence of so many faithful brothers and sisters who are fighting for an open posture to LGBTQI people. And when I survey the terrain, I can't help but be amazed at the rapidity with which churches and people are rethinking long-held beliefs.

Slowly but surely, it would seem that tides are turning, and the trajectory of their course is now toward a more nuanced biblical understanding of sexuality. Where twenty-five years ago, there was silence, there is now movement. Where there was once unanimity of condemnation, there is now openness. Even the fact that many theological institutions have closed their doors harder is providing me with hope, because their doubling down is an admission of the fact that they are facing a pushback that never before existed.

The question that is driving all of this change is simple in some senses, but in other ways is complicated. If the Bible does not condemn faithful, monogamous same-sex unions, where does that leave us?

That Which the Bible Does Not Condemn

At its core, we are all trying to "join the dots"[1] of what God has revealed to us, and for many in the church today, the traditional way of joining the dots is becoming an increasingly less convincing picture. We see how the church used Sodom and Gomorrah as a source of condemnation for so many years, and with integrity we rejoin the dots to see that it is not a tale of God's judgment against loving, faithful same-sex relationships, but a story of retribution against cities who flaunted their power and privilege, raping even those who would seek shelter in their midst.

We take Leviticus, and rejoining the dots, see that it speaks powerfully of a God who is intimately involved in the lives of humanity, but is inapplicable to the situations that we find ourselves in today. We turn to the New Testament, and see that where once the dots were joined in a way that condemned every gay and lesbian relationship, a faithful reading of the texts speaks poignantly against exploitation and abuse, sexual licentiousness and depravity. And, of course, we are guided by a rich understanding of the creation accounts in which we see a God who declares that "it is not good for man to be alone." Where once we joined the dots to

1. I have found David Gushee's metaphor of "joining the dots" a particularly helpful one. Gushee, *Changing Our Mind*, 54.

declare that this can only and always be a gendered prototype, we rather see that the theological weight of this stunning narrative establishes "one-flesh" kinship units in which companionship, mutuality, and the sharing of life can take place.

But, some may still counter, if God does not explicitly condemn faithful gay and lesbian relationships in the Bible, does that necessarily give us an unconditional ability to state irrefutably that he blesses them? In matters that the Bible remains apparently silent on, are we not still in need of a moral compass? And if the Scriptures don't directly provide our North, where then do we turn? The church for millennia has adjudicated this ethical quandary on any number of different topics, and these are questions that we as a Christians must ask ourselves over and over again. After all, for something that feels so important in the life of the church, could God not have given us more information? Surely if homosexual relationships fall in the realm of kingdom living, could God not have provided us with a model to follow—at least one recorded instance in Scripture where such a blessing is given?

In many cases, the "safest" course of action is to retain historical theological positions. Standing on the shoulders of those who have gone before us and have developed theology over the years ensures that the boat is not rocked, and provides a buttress by which we can watch our lives and doctrines closely (1 Tim 4:16). But at some point in every theological journey, we have to ask what cost we are willing to pay for retaining traditional beliefs. On one level, there is the observation that sound theology (one would hope) leads a person closer to God, while poor theology is expected to yield a very different crop.[2] It is an indisputable fact that non-affirming sexual ethics have for decades reaped a harvest of despair in millions of people's lives and driven countless hoards away from Jesus. In so many circles that I move in, depression, self-loathing, and suicide are synonymous with the traditional church's teachings here. We cannot simply say that "churches" or "people" alone have caused this damage, but rather it is the theology itself that has undergirded the deleterious impact on people's lives.

And then on a very different level, outside the realm of the effects of theology, by simply holding on to traditional teachings we run the risk of misunderstanding Scripture and holding on to that which is not necessarily true or faithful. From the Copernican revolution (in which the

---

2. For a thoughtful exploration of this dynamic, see Achtemeier, *The Bible's Yes*.

church adamantly taught that the universe revolved around the earth), through to our understanding of women as made in the image of God, it is abundantly clear that the safest (traditional) course of action has on occasions historically resulted in a trajectory away from truth itself. Is it possible that this is one of these moments? These are the costs that we must weigh.

But even if we count up these costs, study Scripture, and come to the conclusion that the Bible is not inherently against faithful, monogamous gay and lesbian unions, there are still questions that are left hanging. What rubric do we use at this point to navigate those things that are seemingly left open? When there is no black and white, how do we determine God's will? Two key themes present themselves throughout Scripture to help us in just such times as these.

Godly wisdom: Firstly, we have to recognize that there are situations in life in which we are called upon to exercise wisdom that is governed by the parameters of Scripture. By design, we have intellect, and by union with Christ we have the power of the Holy Spirit. If the Bible does not condemn a specific course of action, then we have moved out of the realms of sin and holiness and into the realm of wisdom, free to exercise our volition in myriad iterations that bring glory to God.

Covenantal relationship: Secondly, throughout this book we have sought repeatedly to look for the driving theological principles that undergird any given text. In the specific context of our task here, we have been particularly interested in what drives God's intentions for one-flesh unions, or, in other words, what permutation of marriage is in line with God's will. Traditionally, this has been conceived of as only fulfilled by gender difference, but as we have seen, this doesn't form an adequate framework in which to hold both Scripture and the undeniable reality of gay and lesbian people in our world. As such, we have seen that the overwhelming witness of Scripture is that one-flesh unions are covenantal relationships. We will explore this terrain in the next chapter, but for now we can conclude that relationships are "covenantal" when they are characterized by solemn vows of self-sacrifice to another person, to the exclusion of all others and to the glory of God.

Combining these two observations, the next logical step is to ask, if the Bible does not condemn same-sex relationships, is it *wise* to embrace such unions as honoring to God and in line with God's creative purposes for *covenantal relationships?* I (along with many others) have come to the conclusion that yes, it is eminently wise to do so, but in order to flesh out some sort of conclusion on this question, I want to look at the alternative—what does it look like when people say "no"? I've found that a good way to do this is to examine our eating habits.

"Welcoming but Not Affirming . . ." An Impossible Paradox?

Who you choose to eat with says an awful lot about who you are as a person. Who you welcome into your home reflects so much of the way that you view the world. Across cultures spanning millennia, there has always been something powerful about the act of sharing a meal, something which says to the other "I see you, and I accept you." If we rewind 2,000 years, we see that for the first-century Jew, who you ate with was far more than just an indicator of your class or civil standing—it was a social boundary marker of utmost importance. There were strict cultural guidelines about who you could be seen eating with, and where.

It was into this world that Jesus inaugurated the "upside down kingdom" setting the trend for who we as his followers are to welcome into our homes. These included tax collectors and sinners (Luke 5:27–32), lepers and weeping women (Matt 26:6–13) short people and thieves (Luke 19:1–1), crowds of thousands (John 6; Mark 6:30–44; Matt 14:13–21), and wayward disciples (Luke 24:46–33). Jesus, the radically inclusive deity, didn't just eat with them. He welcomed them. And, in turn, they were drawn to him. Of all the people the sovereign creator of the universe could have dined with, the marginalized and outcasts were his company of choice. But of course, he didn't just dine with them—he changed them. An encounter with Jesus left more than a few transformed as they came to identify themselves as followers of the Messiah.

As those who hold a traditional sexual ethic scramble for pastoral solutions to the situation they find themselves in, an influential tag line has captured the position of many churches. "We welcome you, but we do not affirm your sexuality" is the catch-cry of these congregations. One prominent commentary sums it up like this:

> The gospel of grace is inclusive; it is open to everyone, men and women, Jew and Greek, black or white, Arab or American, gay or straight, bisexual or transsexual, and people may come as they are. But, and this is important, no one is allowed to stay as they are. God does his transforming work in us to change our

values, our character, our conduct, and even our sexuality into conformity to the image of his Son.[3]

In an effort to be inclusive (which I applaud), and uphold Jesus' call to holiness ("go and sin no more," John 8:11) the author of this statement shows himself to be radically misguided. There is much that I uphold in this statement, but notice what he does here. Without clarification, he places together two categorically different groups of people. I concur wholeheartedly that the gospel of grace does indeed transform us, and I could not agree more that by being brought into the fold of Christ we are fundamentally changed. But what is the "transforming work" that God does? Surely the gospel doesn't change us from being Arab to American. Nor does God require that black Christians act like white people in order to be more aligned with his values and character. When a black person proclaims Christ as Lord, they aren't called upon to renounce their identification as a black person. Their fundamental allegiance has changed, but the transformation that the gospel requires does not demand that they sacrifice their identity as a man or woman of color. This is why it is entirely possible to be a black Christian, or a Greek believer, or an Arabic follower of Christ.

Yet categorically, this is exactly what the analysis above is asking gay people to do. They are welcomed into the family, but then they must change, because (working under this concept) a "gay identity" is fundamentally at odds with God's kingdom.

At this point we need to be abundantly clear that a Christian person's sexuality (either straight or gay) is not, and must never be their *core* identity. First and foremost they are children of God (Eph 5:1) adopted into a global family and co-heirs to the eternal riches of the kingdom (Rom 8:17). These are the glorious realities of being a Christian. But a glorious reality of being a creature in God's creation is that we are sexual beings, and as such, a person's sexuality is a significant and irreducible *part* of their identity. It is impossible for a person to completely separate their sexuality from their identity because by God's creation their sexuality forms an integral part of the lens through which they see the world.

According to the "welcoming but not affirming" movement (which I adhered to for so long), the gay or lesbian part of a person's identity is viewed as something that needs to be done away with. Handled with care, but ultimately discarded. Obviously, some would call this "coming

3. Bird, *Romans*, 110.

in line with God's values." Others would call it an impossible task. Still others would call this "repressive." For the small group of people who are genuinely blessed with the gift of celibacy (as we outlined earlier), this stance truly can be liberating—they are able to enter a church and feel a sense of peace. But it is a stretch too far to claim that this model of thinking works for all people.

And so, as it stands, here is where the theological rubber hits the personal road. When a church welcomes a gay or lesbian person, but cannot (because of their interpretation of Scripture) affirm a key part of who they are, that church will very rarely be experienced as a welcoming place. A pastor may intend for this to be a loving stance, but at the end of the day, we cannot expect LGB people to pretend that they see it this way. The subtitles of such a church will inevitably read something along the lines of "you are welcome here, but the most significant human relationship in your life is not." Or perhaps "you are welcome here, but you will always be inferior." What astounds me greatly is that even with such a harsh experience of church, LGB people still rock up to services every Sunday. Facing the sideway glances of congregations and barred by pastors from using their gifts, these men and women still come. They are given the scraps of the table, and still they attend, waiting, hoping that one day somebody will invite them—truly invite them—to the feast.

It strikes me then that perhaps lesbian and gay people are not the ones in need of transformation. Their patience is inspiring. Their ability to forgive is astounding. Their persistence is admirable. Long-suffering and faithful, these men and women have borne the burden of unquestioned traditionalist stances for so long. They have demonstrated, more times than we could count, true Christ-likeness. Maybe the radical, "upside down kingdom" of Jesus is indeed demanding a change. Not from our LGB family, but from those who would seek to change them.

In some ways, historically speaking, the onus of proof has now shifted. There was once a time when sexuality was deeply misunderstood and misrepresented in our society, and therefore in our churches. When this was the case, it was easy to pick out a few verses from Scripture and claim that God is adamantly opposed to all LGB unions, and that these people needed transformation. But the reality is that times have changed. People have access to the cultural data of the ancient world, they have deeper knowledge of what the Scriptures condemn, they have scientific understandings of the power of same-sex orientations, and they are bringing all of this knowledge into a fresh reading of the Bible. The task of this book has never been to simply affirm gay and lesbian relationships, nor has it been to project a preferred theological conclusion. The task of this book has always been to understand the Bible (and therefore God's heart) more clearly.

At the end of the day, if the Bible is not against faithful covenanted relationships, then we as God's people have no prerogative to condemn them. That is not our decision to make. What we can do, however, is, like Jesus, rally around the outcasts, draw them in, and together carry them home. That is where our final chapters are heading.

14

Christian and Gay—A Path Forward

One is a gardener. Another is a school teacher. Yet another is a carpenter. A musician; a pastor; a social worker; a scientist; a documentary maker; a PhD student; a financial planner. Some of them are "out and proud," others are gently, gently attempting to make their way forward in the world. All of them call Jesus their Lord and Savior, and all of them are seeking to honor God with their sexuality. These are the people around me whom I have grown to love and care for deeply. I wish that you could meet them too. They inspire me and challenge me, encourage me and point me to Jesus.

As we explore a path forward for LGB Christians and their communities, we would once again do well to keep people like these in the forefront of our minds. They are those who are treading new paths, revitalizing old ways, and shining the hope of Christ into dark places. In this chapter, I want to draw on their faithful witness to paint a picture of what being gay and being Christian might look like. Having laid the theological foundations in Scripture, we have the chance now to discuss how this plays out practically in real people's lives. By no means is this the authoritative model for all sexual minorities, but it is one that I personally find both satisfying and compelling.

A Beautiful Picture of Sexuality

Let's start with sex. As my married friends are quick to remind me, being in a relationship is not just about sex. Needless to say, there are a million and one other things that make a relationship beautiful, but the Bible has a lot to say about sex, and so I think it will do us well to draw our attention to some key ideas.

It may sound strange, but I love the way the Bible speaks about sex. In fact, in my humble opinion, the Bible's view of sex is one of the most enthralling things that Christians can offer a sex-obsessed world. It is both dignifying and humbling. It is intriguing and theologically satisfying. Of course, the Bible is not a self-help book for the bedroom, but in divine grace, God has offered us parameters in which people can thrive. And when these are heeded, this ancient wisdom offers a profound critique of the world that we find ourselves in. This wisdom is often spoken about in a heterosexual context, but, as we will see, the principles are equally vital for LGBTQI people in our congregations.

Historically, the sexual revolution of the sixties and seventies saw an unprecedented revelry in the sexualization of our culture. The Western world is still reeling from the roller coaster that has envisaged itself as "freedom," coming to terms with the cost of cheapening sex in the name of "free love." In stark contrast to a world that sees sex as cheap and free, the Bible elevates sex with an unapologetic reverence—it is something to be treasured for intimacy. The Bible holds that sex is the ultimate act of vulnerability as you physically expose yourself to another human being. Our bodies are sacred (1 Cor 6:19–20), and what we do with our bodies is to reflect what we do with the rest of our lives. The book of Song of Songs celebrates this with striking beauty, capturing the intimate moments of youthful, uninhibited sexuality. At its core, sex is imbued with a power that is diluted to our own detriment when casually cast aside.

Conversely (and somewhat paradoxically) the world we inhabit heightens the act of sex to say that in some manner you aren't living unless you are having it. Whereas our post-sexual revolution society condemns the "forty-year-old virgin," and the contented celibate as a repressed oddity, God dignifies them and their sexuality by reminding us that who we are intimate with is not what defines us (1 Cor 7:6–8). The Bible liberates us by claiming that nothing, not even our sexuality, has the capability of defining who we are, because sex is not the reason for our existence.

Against a world that says that sex is a commodity, to be used for gain, the Bible teaches that sex is a gift, given by a good God who delights in the intimacy that faithfulness brings. Thus, against a world that paints you as the consumer (it's all about you), and sex as a product to be taken for your pleasure, the Bible tells us that sex, like all things in a Christian's

life, is an act of self-sacrifice, in which you give of yourself fully to another person.

And finally, in a society where past failures and sexual brokenness
are destined to haunt relationships for years to come, the gospel offers
freedom from the bondage to hyper-sexualized histories that so many are
running from. 1 Corinthians 5:17–18 celebrates the new creation that a
Christian becomes when they offer themselves over to the cleansing work
of the Spirit:

> Therefore, if anyone is in Christ, he is a new creation. The old
> has passed away; behold, the new has come. All this is from
> God, who through Christ reconciled us to himself and gave us
> the ministry of reconciliation.

To those who have lived pasts of sexual licentiousness that they now
regret, the gospel freely proclaims a fresh start. They are no longer defined by their past mistakes, but rather are found in Christ, filled with his
righteousness.

When we look at this beautiful picture of human sexuality, we see
that the focus of Scripture is unashamedly on covenantal one-flesh unions,
monogamous, faithful, exclusive, joined together by God himself. This is
the picture I find altogether enthralling. I want this type of self-giving,
God-honoring relationship for myself, and for those I love, because I am
entirely convinced that it is within this context that relationships are able
to thrive. When understood as such, God's regulations around sexuality
aren't burdensome or repressive, but are dignifying and liberating.

But at the same time, I hasten to add, I am under no illusion that
such covenantal self-sacrifice is an easy task. Years of seeing marriages
play out before me have demonstrated with stark clarity that this covenantal, self-sacrificing marriage union is no walk in the park. For all its
dizzying heights and momentous joys, there are times in all relationships
in which one or both parties struggle to see the value of either the other
person, or the partnership itself. We long for this type of intimacy, but
what many people (both heterosexual and homosexual) fail to comprehend is that like all good things in life, intimacy requires work.

In some ways, this observation boils down to the very nature of what
it means to be human in relation to the "other." Our natural tendency as
fallen men and women is to orient ourselves at the center of our own
relational solar system, the star around which everything else is in orbit.
Born into the selfishness of humanity, our colleagues, our friends, our

family, and even our most emotionally invested relationships all too often fall into the category of planets that pander to our desires and are bound to our will, following the set path that we mentally project onto them.

But inevitably at some point, another person (partner or otherwise) comes into that orbit who also self-identifies as the central force around which everything must rotate. This is when collisions become a certainty. In a one-flesh union in which two people are vying for the role of central force, orbits will necessarily compete, because they have bought into the worldview that this relationship is designed for their own happiness, satisfaction, and fulfillment.

In contrast to this, the gospel of grace demands a perspective shift that recognizes that I am not the center of my world. Christ is. The gospel of grace shows us that the greatest good and most profound satisfaction we can achieve in life is not the consumption of intimacy, but rather the continual act of self-giving (Phil 4:1–11). In so many LGBTQI communities (as mirrored in the heterosexual realm) self-seeking, consumerist, and deprecating relationships are, sadly, the norm. The Bible's insistence on the centrality of Christ, around which all of our covenantal relationships are to revolve, provides a stunning antidote to this self-perpetuating cycle. Far from being the repressive dogma it is so often painted to be, it is in this picture that people can find freedom, confident in the fact that they are supported and loved by somebody who unconditionally accepts them and sacrificially seeks to see them thrive.

A Beautiful Picture of Identity

Adding all of this together, we discover once again that while our sexuality is an irreducible part of who we are as humans, God never allows us to be defined purely by our sexuality. Our identity is not to be confined to or founded upon either our orientation or relationship status. First and foremost, we are children of God, co-heirs to the eternal riches of God's grace (Rom 8:17–18). In Christ, we are new creations—this is who we are. In a strange way, this task of identifying first and foremost with Christ comes with a unique aspect for sexual minorities.

Sociologists tell us that the experience of any minority group entails uniting around a common narrative of being, in some manner or another, on the outside. These narratives fundamentally shape our worldviews, and, in turn, these worldviews play a crucial role in our identity formation. Thus, if somebody is getting to know me, I feel obliged at some point as the friendship unfolds to inform them that I am a gay person. Without that key part of data, I can't be fully known. Because I break the social norm at this point, I am forced to constantly think about my sexuality in a way that many others aren't. Most heterosexual people have never felt this tension, because their identity as a straight person is naturally assumed.

It would be a mistake then to conclude that simply because I identify as a gay person, my identity in Christ is therefore jeopardized. It is a strange reality that gay and lesbian Christians (unless they are celibate) are often accused of finding their identity in their sexuality, rather than in Christ. Whilst this may be true for some (in much the same way that many heterosexual people find their core identity in their marriages rather than Christ), it certainly cannot be assumed *a priori*. As we have seen over and over again throughout this book, there are countless examples of faithful, covenanted lesbian and gay relationships that hold at their core the glorious gospel of Christ, and who seek within their power to center their lives around him.

To show all my cards, I believe wholeheartedly that all gay and lesbian people are sinners who need Jesus. Sin permeates every aspect of their lives, but neither their homosexuality nor their faithful expressions of it are their sin. Rather, as they embrace that part of their identity in which they call themself a gay man or woman, they have the profound freedom to enter a life-giving relationship that points them to Christ, centered around his glory and held accountable to his stunning picture of identity and sexuality.

Preparing for the Road Ahead

Realistically however, for those who are gay and Christian, the road ahead is long, and following Christ as a faithful steward of his gift of sexuality is not without its sacrifices. All people who come into God's kingdom are called to take up their cross and follow Christ (Luke 9:23), but for those who are on the margins of church life, these sacrifices are somewhat unique, and we would do well to spend some time exploring them, because the path that we are treading may in many instances be something of a lonely road.

Given the current political state of the church, I suspect that even those who seek with their whole heart to honor God will come across snide remarks and questioning glances. The nature of our current divisive climate is such that some LGBTQI-affirming people will be asked to step down from leadership roles in church (I have). Some of us will be asked not to share our views (I have). Silence will feel like our only option (it isn't). Some will continue to be shown the door. Some of us will lose our jobs, and still some of us will lose our families (I know too many who have). The reality is that we won't make sense in the church for a long time to come. We will be a confusing anomaly whilst ever we are helping people to join the dots to see that faithfulness to God's word is playing itself out in our lives.

In recognizing this dynamic, we need to be honest that an already difficult journey is compounded by lack of support. Any person who has weathered the storms of marriage for some time will tell you that there have been periods when they have relied on the support of Christian brothers and sisters. They have, during turbulent times, sought counsel and comfort from pastors, elders, and community leaders. This is often not a luxury that faithful gay and lesbian Christians have. I sadly know of some pastors who have candidly shared with me that they would sooner sabotage than support a gay relationship, leaving many people wanting to live lives of holiness, but attempting to do so against the very tide that should be spurring them on to love and good deeds (Heb 10:24).

And as this dynamic works its way throughout our church life, we also have to recognize the fact that those who pursue monogamous, faithful marriage unions will also be an anomaly in the broader society in which we live. In a tragic way, there is an almost universal expectation that covenantal relationships (both heterosexual and homosexual) are outmoded, superseded by the "freedom" to express one's sexuality. Those who withhold from sexual expression until marriage, and those who pursue one partner for life, receive very little support from our cultural milieu. In a minority that has received so little support for such a long time, this dynamic is intensified such that there is sadly a strong correlation in many people's minds between being gay and being promiscuous.

Decades of marginalization have left far too many gay communities around the world scarred and seeking shelter in all the wrong places. Casual hookups (whether in bars or on apps) are often the norm and without the support of mentors, community, and pillars of faith, relationships are often sporadic and disjointed. Unlike any other group of people, gay Christians have the chance to be light in these disorienting places, showing people the beauty of Christ. However, the gay Christian is also likely to receive very limited support from both secular and church circles, despite attempting to navigate a notoriously difficult terrain.

Doing Discomfort Well

Have I painted a bleak enough picture yet of the road ahead? There is hope coming—trust me—but there is another layer that we need to acknowledge before we arrive there. There is a strong chance that even those who have well-informed and pastorally nuanced Christian supports around them will, at times, feel as though they are somewhat isolated in their journey. We are, and probably always will be, a minority (gay) within a minority (Christian), and as no doubt many of us are aware, those who are not a part of the majority almost invariably experience a level of internalized discomfort caused by their status. This has certainly been my journey.

I experience this stress every time I enter church, unsure of who will be there and how they will respond to me. I feel this every time I attend extended family functions. I expect this whenever the topic of gay marriage is raised. It's just there, always present. This discomfort, played on repeat over and over, inevitably leads to a measure of stress. And this stress, an accumulation of strained interactions, over the long haul has significant impacts. People who do not fit the married, heterosexual norm in our churches so often experience the volatile state of mind that comes with being "other." In the realm of social work, this has a name— we refer to it as "minority stress."

"Minority stress" is a well-documented phenomenon, and occurs when a person or people feel somehow on the outside of a community because of situations beyond their control.[1] In particular, this stress is centered around themes of perceived burdensomeness, failure to belong and ongoing expectation of rejection.[2] The relentless nature of adhering to an LGBT-affirming theology renders each of these experiences a regular phenomenon for people of sexual minorities in our churches.

With all of this in mind, we recognize that for sexual minorities, there is a process that must take place, both corporately and individually, by which LGBT people can work through the discomfort and pain they have endured, and will continue to live within. This pain and discomfort

1. Iniewicz et al., *Minority Stress*.
2. Plöderl et al., *Explaining the Suicide Risk*.

is most naturally understood as a significant loss—the loss of belonging, the loss of close relationships, the loss of comfort within their congregations, the loss of status, and the list goes on. The natural and appropriate response to any loss is to go through a process in which we grieve that which has been taken from us.

This grief may take us through seasons of anger and frustration. We may become disillusioned with the church as we are burned over and over again. Grief can cause us to isolate ourselves or hide from reality, denying the fact that we are hurt. Grief may lead some to place masks on in order to present a façade of capability. Grief may play itself out in our own perceptions of our own self-worth, leading us down the path of hyper-awareness of the opinions of others. Grief in all of its ugly reality *will* come, and we must be prepared for it.

In a beautiful way, the Bible teaches us how to grieve well. The book of Psalms for example is replete with the anguished crying of people who call out to God in their pain. For me, praying through the Psalms during times of loneliness and isolation has been a powerfully healing experience. These lament Psalms take us on a journey as we read them, from a place of pain and bitterness to a deeper understanding of the character of God, and finally into a place of worship. Take for example Psalm 142. David, forced into refuge by Saul pens these words whilst hiding from the violent king in a cave:

The Psalm begins with an address to Yahweh (the LORD), and a cry that introduces his pain:

> With my voice I cry out to the Lord;
> > with my voice I plead for mercy to the Lord.
> I pour out my complaint before him;
> > I tell my trouble before him.
> When my spirit faints within me,
> > you know my way!

Next, David brings his lament before God, explaining in tormented words the loneliness of his situation:

> In the path where I walk
> > they have hidden a trap for me.
> Look to the right and see:
> > there is none who takes notice of me;
> no refuge remains to me;

>   no one cares for my soul.

But notice that it doesn't end here (it never does). The Psalm then goes on to express the psalmist's trust in the character of God:

>   I cry to you, O LORD;
>   I say, "You are my refuge,
>   my portion in the land of the living."

This character of God (in this case, his status as refuge and portion) informs a prayer of deliverance that we cry out to God for:

>   Attend to my cry,
>   for I am brought very low!
>   Deliver me from my persecutors . . .

And this deliverance leads in the end to a renewed future state, imbued with trust and overflowing with thanksgiving. This hopeful end to the lament Psalm reminds us that we have a God who is a mighty deliverer, who holds us in our every need, and has a future planned for us that is beyond our comprehension:

>   Bring me out of prison,
>   that I may give thanks to your name!
>   The righteous will surround me,
>   for you will deal bountifully with me.

>   Psalm 142 (ESV)

This is the pattern which so many Psalms take. In essence, they provide us with a model of grief that is faith articulating itself through pain and into worship. The pain of this world is unmasked and the façade of comfort is wiped away. These psalms are written into the canon of Scripture so that we might have a divinely inspired avenue by which to bring our distress before the creator. Grief that grumbles against God inevitably festers and slowly eats away at faith. But when we approach God with our deepest cries and call out to him from isolation and pain, we are acting in faith, trusting that he holds us and will guide us through faithfully.

Those who are allies in this journey have the power to help LGBT people to grieve well. To keep pointing LGBT people to Jesus and proclaiming that our trust in God is not in vain. When we face discouragement from the church and confusion from within the world, allies have the vital task of reminding us to come before God in faith, calling us to remember God's character, and praying beside us for a future state in which all pain is wiped away. We, along with you, long for the new creation, the kingdom of God established in all of its glory.

There are no doubts in my mind that the journey ahead for people who are gay and affirming in their theology is going to lead us through difficult times. But at the same time, I am so full of hope that change is taking place, and will continue to do so wherever dialogue is granted. As such, we turn briefly now to the hope that we have in this journey.

Being Hopeful for Change

With all of the above preparations in place for the journey ahead, I want now to give an encouragement to those who are allies in this path, and to those who are faithfully LGBT people in our churches. There is movement. There are people who are engaging deeply with Scripture and are coming to places where they can honestly say that they welcome and affirm LGBT people in the life of the church.

At an astounding pace, the Christian conversation is changing. I know that it may feel slow, but let me remind you that twenty-five years ago it was unheard of that prominent Bible-believing Christian leaders would affirm same-sex unions. Yet today, the list of those who do so is rapidly expanding.

Within my lifetime I have seen the church go from a place where homosexuality was unanimously condemned, to a place where there are burgeoning pockets of faithful Christians seeking to embrace gay and lesbian populations. Not only are individual churches coming to this point, but entire denominations are taking the risky stance, opposing the status quo and venturing with integrity into what they see is Jesus' plan for his people. Even within those denominations that remain staunchly traditionalist, there are dissenting congregations in almost every region.

Simultaneously, there are grassroots organizations springing up across the world that retain the authority of Scripture and call for full acceptance of lesbian and gay people at every level of church participation. Resources are being developed and conversations are being had at an ever increasing pace.

But perhaps most importantly, a paradigm shift has taken place. This paradigm shift may feel subtle, but I believe that it is the single most powerful transition that could have occurred, and it has happened whilst most people were looking the other way. Here it is: The church is, by and large, no longer speaking about the LGBTQI *issue*, rather, it is speaking about LGBTQI *people*. The discussion has moved from the abstract into the human. It is no longer about ideas, it is now about lives. And it can no longer hide behind shallow theology because when something becomes personal, it necessarily becomes deep.

The next generation of church leaders is being raised in a world where discussion is taking place at an unprecedented level. This is far better than the world of silence in which I was raised. Many wise and godly people are discerning that the Spirit is moving amongst the church for change, and so, having prepared ourselves for the journey ahead, we turn to our final chapter, exploring what this change is and how it is coming about.

15

What Might Change in the Church Look Like?

Friends, we are coming towards the end. We have cast our minds into the deep webs of theology and sexuality; we have sought careful insight into the Bible's witness on faithful covenantal marriage, and have captured something of the waters that our church is currently sailing through.

Importantly, as we have journeyed through this book, we have met a host of people. These are people whose existence is lived out in the constant tension between their Christian faith and their sexuality. Like me, these people never chose this life, and I dare say that if it were up to them, they may well have opted for an easier path. There are certainly many days when I wish I could just fit in without standing out. But for us, that's not an option, and so we strive now with what we have been given.

For these people, and so many more, I picture a world in which a child can come out to their parents, knowing that they will find a warm embrace and a faithful hand as they navigate the treacherous landscape into adulthood. I long for a day when LGBT brothers and sisters can walk into a congregation and eagerly expect to encounter Jesus, rather than brace themselves in order to defend who they are. As the years roll on, I for one will be eagerly watching the statistical paths of LGBT suicide rates, and praying for the safety of my brothers and sisters. And, of course, I will be watching the church to see how it embraces, or excludes, those who so keenly desire acceptance. I will be keeping a keen eye on sexual minorities moving in and out of our faith communities, and my prayer is that with time the church would become a safe haven for those seeking God's work in their lives.

I hope and pray for all of this because I believe firmly that when the Bible is read faithfully and his people are obedient, then the name of Jesus is lifted high. Remarkably, the church is God's chosen banner to display the Trinity's manifold wisdom (Eph 3:10), and in a world that is sex-obsessed and bent on the self, we have more need than ever for just such wisdom. That's what this final chapter is about—a future state of the church, and how you and I can safely arrive there.

Zooming Out

As we have seen over and over again, the reality is that there are LGBT "refugees" everywhere. These are the people who have either been forced to leave their churches, or who have experienced so much pain that their places of worship are now no longer places of safety. In many instances, this is the fruit of the traditional theologies that so many of us have been raised on.

As such, whether we like it or not, gay and lesbian people *are* the hot button topics that are currently defining the church of the Western world. If we zoom out to a whole-of-church level, we see that huge changes are taking place. Some of the global church's foremost Christian thinkers are reconsidering this issue and as they are doing so momentous shifts are occurring. It seems that the church, as has so often happened before, is bordering on a kind of schism.

At this point, on a denominational and even larger interdenominational level, we must take the time to listen to all voices in this discussion. This is a long and often arduous process that requires a great deal of patience and willingness to walk in another person's shoes. Thankfully, we are reminded once again that we are not the first generation of church thinkers to face theological disagreement.

In Acts 15 we discover in fact that theological disagreement has a history as old as the church itself. Confounded by the outpouring of the Holy Spirit into the lives of Gentile people, the early church called the gathering of a council. Converging on Jerusalem, this council drew together the leaders of the church. These were deep thinkers and theologians who were struggling to make sense of what God was doing in the world. What took place was a momentous theological shift in which the "people of God" was expanded to encompass not just the Jews, but also all people who called themselves followers of the Jewish Messiah, Jesus.

While obviously not wanting to draw too close a parallel between this turning point in salvation history and the current discussion taking place regarding LGBT inclusion, we do get a glimpse of how dialogue took place in the early church, and perhaps how it can continue to take place today.

The stubborn reality that presented itself to the council was that the Gentile people were showing all the hallmarks of the Christian faith. The Holy Spirit had been poured out on them, their lives were being transformed, and they were declaring Christ as Lord. Those who had a high view of the role of national Israel were pitted against those who had witnessed the gospel going forth into all the world. The result was that they had "no small dissension and debate" (Acts 15:2) or as the New Living Translation puts it, they "argued vehemently" (NLT).

At one point in the proceedings, the book of Acts recounts the dramatic moment when Peter stood up among the assembly and testified that God:

> Who knows the heart, bore witness to them, by giving them the Holy Spirit just as he did to us, and he made no distinction between us and them, having cleansed their hearts by faith. Now, therefore, why are you putting God to the test by placing a yoke on the neck of the disciples that neither our fathers nor we have been able to bear? But we believe that we will be saved through the grace of the Lord Jesus, just as they will. (Acts 15:8–11, ESV)

By God's grace, the leaders of the early church were willing to hear a radical new proposal. They were open to listening, and in time became convinced by the evidence which was put before them. The Gentiles were bearing fruit. The result was an extraordinary re-theologizing not only in regards to who had the right to sit in the church pews, but further, what laws and regulations they were to follow. This all happened because a group of people gathered together to *listen*, to *hear* how God was moving and to *engage* with God's word (in their case, the Torah and Writings).

At a large, denominational and global church level, church leaders can no longer hide behind the guise that gay and lesbian people do not exist in their congregations. Church leaders can no longer maintain the position that gay people are inherently promiscuous and debauched. Nor can church leaders claim that affirming theological positions are unfaithful to Scripture or treat the Bible with careless regard. All of these positions now fall so far short of reality that they cannot be retained with the integrity that church leadership demands.

To this end, it is no longer a radical statement to suggest that such discussions must be had. These discussions cannot simply take place between homogenous voices that are unified around a common, traditional sexual ethic, because this does not constitute discussion at all. Rather, if church leaders are serious about faithfully handling God's word in the world around us, they should welcome voices from all experiences to engage in "healthy debate." My fear is that those churches that fail to engage in deep conversation are, it would seem, setting themselves up for failure as they present themselves to a watching world as willfully ignorant at best, and callously indifferent at worst.

With this in mind, we need to take heed of three dangers that encroach upon the human mind when it comes to rigorous dialogue. Firstly, to those who hold an affirming view of gay and lesbian relationships, you mustn't allow yourself to become jaded or self-righteous in your assessment of those with whom you engage. Complexes that promote themselves (either internally or explicitly) as somehow "more enlightened" are inevitably going to transform themselves into doctrinal pride that sits over other people in judgment. Believe me when I say that I am so aware that you, like many others, will be tempted to speak out of a place of pain and the temptation here is to lash out at anybody who sits to the theological "right" of your position. If we are to engage in rich discussion, then the call is upon us to listen also, and listen well. We engage out of love, graciously offering insights where God would have us speak. I know that for many of you, you feel as though you have been listening to damaging words for far too many years, but by God's strength, the task ahead will require more listening still and—of course—a willingness to confess that you may in fact be wrong in some areas. This is the humbling work of doing theology in community.

Conversely, to those who hold a traditional sexual ethic, the warning must be given to not write off your affirming brothers and sisters as having nothing from which you can learn. You stand within the majority on this topic, and the very real temptation whilst in this position is to take on a groupthink mentality in which you become uncritical or idle in your theological pursuits. Many of us have spent enough time in church circles to know that when a homogenized group reaches a majority status, they often become self-congratulatory in their theological correctness. As we have seen throughout this book, this cannot be an assumed position.

In countless examples this correctness has undergone radical shifts as people realized once again that the majority does not necessarily adhere to the only, or even the best, biblical interpretation.

Thirdly, both for those who hold an affirming view and for those whose sexual ethic is more traditional, the radical nature of the gospel calls for us to be quick to apologize, and ready to forgive. Both sides of this discussion are guilty of demonizing the other, flagrantly ignoring and deriding their "opponents" as subversive and ill-fated. I am comfortable in stating that my LGBT brothers and sisters have been incalculably hurt by much of the church's rhetoric and actions, but I will also be the first to admit that there are times when I am more than tempted to decry the church and slight its leaders. For this I know that I need to repent and ask for forgiveness; likewise I must be ready to work towards reconciliation with those who have hurt me by their words and actions. This is the nature of conversation within the body of Christ—it is rigorous, but it must be characterized by grace and repentance.

To be sure, whilst engaging this conversation we must always be careful to come back to Scripture, to the purposes of God in the salvation of humanity. God calls us to be careful in both our lives and our doctrine, guarding them carefully (1 Tim 4:16). God is passionate about the church taking the Bible seriously and as such we must be careful to ensure that our leadership is dedicated first and foremost to understanding and sitting under God's word. This is particularly true for those who take on a teaching position within the church (Jas 3:1).

Having covered all of the above, we should simultaneously (and perhaps counterintuitively) be under no illusion that unity within the church directly equates to total agreement on all facets of church life. Acts 15 is remarkable because it begins with one theological disagreement that leads to consensus, but astoundingly it closes with a second disagreement that is so sharp that it sees the apostles go separate ways, leaving the dispute apparently unresolved (Acts 15:36–41). There is the very real possibility that not all people within the church will come to a theological position of acceptance of lesbian and gay covenantal unions and I am convinced that this does not render one or the other outside the bounds of Christ's keep. This is a humble place to be, because it reminds us that we as a body are made up of many parts that cannot discard any other part (1 Cor 12:21–27). With such a reminder in place, we must be quick to assert that there is so much that we can agree on, and it is necessary for the unity of the faith that we allow our core gospel witness to be central, with Jesus at the helm of everything that we do.

Perhaps many of you who are reading this book aren't in a place where you can directly influence denominational discussion with any immediate effect. You can perhaps engage in channels of communication with people in such positions, but the immediate impact of theological discussion for you is closer to home. As such, we would do well now to zoom in, moving from the systemic, structural level, and into the personal, everyday encounters that we experience. Here, a very different story is being told.

Transforming Encounters

With a highly conservative estimate suggesting that 2 in every 100 people identify as part of a sexual minority group, virtually every person in today's Western society is in regular, amicable contact with a gay or lesbian person. Daily, they eat with them, work with them, train with them, and serve with them. They are our brothers, colleagues, aunties, coaches, bosses, daughters, students, and bus drivers. We laugh with them and drink coffee with them; we eat meals that they have prepared and discuss the latest movies that we have enjoyed. All in all, the novelty value of the existence of gay and lesbian people has been slowly wiped away, and we are left with the altogether mundane existence of profoundly deep friendships. When we zoom in to this level we see people, families, and friends, working through the discomfort of theological disagreement together, and so often coming out the other end having drawn closer to Christ.

These are what David Gushee calls "transformative encounters."[1] When you meet a person who holds firmly to God's word and is committed to the faithful stewarding of their sexuality in a gay or lesbian relationship, you need to create a new category for them in your mind. They are not heretics, and they are not debauched. They are not distant concepts or theological debates. Instead they are real people, living real lives of real service to a very real God.

It is through these transformative encounters that deep, worldview changes so often take place. As we have said over and over again, these encounters don't hold authority over the Bible, but they do draw us back to the text to ask once again if we have interpreted the Scriptures rightly.

1. Gushee, *Changing Our Mind*, 106.

This time, we come with fresh questions and new insights. With all honesty I admit that if I was not a person who was forced against my will to engage with the topic of homosexuality, then there is every chance that I would have a wife and two kids and a nice home in the suburbs, blissfully unaware of the debate raging around me. To my shame, I know that as a busy pastoral worker, it isn't until somebody places a topic overwhelmingly within my line of sight that I can stop making excuses in order to actually give it the time of day that it deserves. This is what transformative encounters do, and as I have witnessed them time and time again in the people around me. I have been astounded by the profound power that relationships have in driving us to think deeply about the God we serve.

The Task Ahead

And so it is that we reach the pointy end of our journey together—the part where I pass on the baton and call upon you to take up your role in this wild adventure. If you have come this far with me, and are convinced that God loves, embraces, and has a place for lesbian and gay people at the table, then in every way you have the deep responsibility to walk with Jesus into the task of standing up for those who find themselves on the margins of our churches. It has oft been recognized that history is most dramatically shaped by those who remain silent, and this is in some ways simply a call for you, if you truly are my ally, to raise your voice.

What follows hereafter is a series of practical ways that you can achieve this. Some of these are daunting, and some may prove impossible. But others will be within your reach and by God's grace you may see transformation in the lives of the people around you.

Share your story

Share your story, because you have one. You have a story of transformation in which you have journeyed from one perspective into another. There have been paths traversed and prayers uttered. You have met people and ideas and they have changed you. Your story doesn't have to be eloquent or particularly profound. It doesn't have to capture every aspect of your theological expeditions or every conversation that you had.

But it does need to be honest, and it does need to be told. Perhaps it will start when somebody laments the fact that his or her nephew has entered into a gay relationship, and you can humbly begin by saying, "I used to be so sure that your nephew was sinning, but to be truthful, I've been on quite a journey with that . . ."

Tell the story of how you came to read a book like this (and, I hope, many others). Perhaps it is that "my church had a seminar on sexuality and I picked up some literature that I'd never considered . . ." Or maybe "my daughter's friend who is gay recommended reading this, and out of respect for her I did . . ." Or for you it might have been "I am gay myself and for years (maybe even decades) I thought that the only option for me was celibacy. I avoided theological discussions for so long, but one day a friend recommended that I read . . ."

And finally, end your story with an offer to engage further—"I am constantly learning so much, but now I have reached a point where I simply can't use the Bible to condemn faithful, God-honoring gay and lesbian marriages. I know it might sound strange, but I'm more than willing to discuss it over coffee some time . . ."

I've shared some of my story with you throughout this book, and I hope that you have come to see something of the journey that it has been. There is something powerful about sharing how God is moving in our lives, and it is an honor when we get to use our stories to bring people back to the Bible.

Share resources

There are so many phenomenal resources that delve deep into theology and sexuality, and the list keeps growing. For the sake of brevity, let me recommend three that I have seen have profound impacts on people's lives.

Changing Our Mind, by David Gushee, is an easily accessible, deeply thoughtful retelling of how the author (a prominent evangelical ethicist) embraced an affirming theology. Poignant, humble, and challenging, this book provides a good overview of passages related to the topic, and calls upon the church to welcome LGB people in.

God and the Gay Christian, by Matthew Vines, is another easier read. Similar to myself, Vines is a gay evangelical who once believed that celibacy was his only option. But on further reading and a long, prayerful journey he came to embrace faithful, monogamous lesbian and gay unions. This book provides a biblical defense of these unions and is a good place to start for those who are new to the world of theology.

Finally, James Brownson's book *Bible, Gender, Sexuality* offers a more in-depth examination of theological themes that inform discussion around LGBT people and the church. Brownson's work is rigorous in its exposition, deeply informed by rich historical analysis and broad in its scope. This is one essential book for those who want more "meaty" reading!

Speak to your church leadership

I understand that this is daunting. Trust me, I get it. But it is also incredibly valuable. As a church leader myself, I know the propensity toward blindness that comes with pastoral work. It is so easy to assume that everybody in your flock is on the same page, safely working within one's own version of what is "right." It isn't until a member of the congregation voices another opinion that church workers are forced to sit up and take notice.

You, friend, have the right to be honest and open with your pastors. It is a sad but true reality that many leaders would much rather hide from this topic than address it, and many will not give it their valuable time without somebody ensuring that this happens. For the sake of the sexual minorities who are struggling within your congregation, I certainly hope that you would be courageous enough to gently broach this with them and ask that they might read another view.

Don't leave your church (yet)

There is a very real temptation for people who are affirming in their theology to band together, leaving their more traditional churches behind and gathering in like-minded, safer spaces. For some, this will be necessary because the pain of existing in places of undeserved judgment is perilously threatening. But for many, perhaps we should consider the notion that these are the very places where you are needed most.

Transformational encounters can only take place when we share our lives with those who we do not see eye to eye with. If we seclude ourselves, unwilling to open dialogue with our churches, then change will not take place.

If it comes to the point that you feel that you are no longer safe or welcome within your church, then let me encourage you to speak to your leadership about this because they must be made aware of the damage of their actions. Of course, we do this with gentleness and respect, honoring their position but also being willing to faithfully critique their views. It is far better for them to feel the weight of your leaving than to simply see your name disappear from the schedule.

Make your support known

It is almost impossible for me to exaggerate the encouragement I have found in non-LGBT people who have sought to meet me where I am at and journey with me in both my faith and my sexuality. Sadly however, for many years I lived under the assumption that I had nobody that I could turn to for support. I felt isolated and alone as I sought to integrate a contested theology and a deeply entrenched, shame-filled sexuality. I desperately wanted people to speak to, but I found very few whom I was safe to explore affirming theology with.

It wasn't until after I "came out" as affirming that I discovered the sheer number of supportive Christians in my life. By then of course, so much of my journey had been written in silence—a silence that could so easily have been avoided if affirming Christians in my life had made their stance more publicly known. I fear that in our congregations, our youth groups and our communities this story is being played on repeat. Silence breeds shame and shame breeds silence—the cycle can only be broken when that silence does not have the final word.

If you want to help your struggling brother or sister, let them know that you support them, and will journey with them wherever the river may wind.

Start some movement

Imagine gathering some people around you to read one of the books mentioned above. Perhaps you tap some people on the shoulder and suggest that this is a topic that you think your congregation should consider and maybe this is a good place to start. You meet together for a meal and discuss chapters that you have read. You see people's minds widen and their views challenged. You pray with them for wisdom and discernment.

You open the Bible and read passages over and over again. Some think you are insane, but others can't help but agree with what you are talking about.

Movement begins when people gather. People gather when somebody challenges the status quo. We live in a time when more and more gatherings of people are feeling the rift between what they have traditionally been taught, and what the Bible teaches. At times like this in history, groundswells of people standing up for what they believe have a potency that can rarely be ignored.

You may feel that you are too small to make waves. But the truth is that waves are already in motion. You don't need to make sweeping reforms—you are simply called to be faithful with what you have been given, and maybe—just maybe—this is one of those times when making ripples is scary, but it is also enough. Perhaps it is the (admittedly rather benign) revolutionary within me, but I have always felt that people in churches must be ready and willing to challenge the status quo. If we are to work towards biblical truth, then we mustn't allow tradition to set the incontrovertible trajectory. At the end of the day, I must give an account to God as to what I did with my time in this world, and how I treated the least of these. That is a far more fearsome prospect than what any church leader or disapproving congregation member might do to me.

Drawing to a Close

I began this book by stating that what lay ahead was not going to simply be a treatise on homosexuality. It has not been a rallying call for affirming theology, or a soapbox by which to demonize traditional theologies. My hope all along is that this book would primarily be centered around Jesus, and the radical gospel of grace that has gone out to all nations.

I say this because I am so convinced that the sexual minorities of this world do not need another self-help book. They don't need an inspirational leader to unite them or a majority vote to validate them. Certainly these things may be good, but they do not constitute the deepest cry of the human heart. What LGBT people of this world need more than anything else is the transformational message of Christ and the hope that he offers them—hope of an eternal life spent in the holy presence of a God who bestows good gifts for all of eternity.

Right now, I fear that this glorious message has taken second place in the witness of the church. A huge portion of God's people have idolized a traditional interpretation of sexual ethics and have utilized this to draw a line designating those who are "in" and those who are "out." Friends, more than anything, this breaks my heart. It breaks my heart because every day I see the devastating damage that such a theology brings. It breaks my heart because I want so dearly for my brothers and sisters to look at me and see Jesus rather than only seeing my sexuality. And it breaks my heart because I know too many people who want nothing to do with Jesus because they have been taught unquestioningly that the very God who formed them despises a beautiful part of their existence.

But, friends, I also close this book with hope. I have this hope because I see how things are changing. I see how God is shaping the church and moving amongst the people who call Jesus their king. The gospel is being preached to sexual minorities, and by grace, God is drawing them into the fold. I am full of hope because I see leaders being raised up who handle this topic with the care and sensitivity that it deserves. I see young people and old people drawing closer to God's heart for their LGBT brothers and sisters, and I see whole churches excited to rise to the occasion and proclaim God's message of good news to the lost.

The feast is being prepared. The kingdom of God awaits us. Gathering from every tribe, tongue, and nation is a people who will take their seats at the banquet and forever bask in the glory of their creator. To my gay and lesbian brothers and sisters I end with this affirmation—there is a place here for you. You are welcome at this table.

Bibliography

Achtemeier, Mark. *The Bible's Yes to Same-Sex Marriage: An Evangelical's Change of Heart.* Louisville: Westminster John Knox, 2014.

Allberry, Sam. *Is God Anti-Gay? And Other Questions About Homosexuality, the Bible and Same-Sex Attraction.* Questions Christians Ask. Croydon, UK: The Good Book Company, 2013.

Ambrose. *The Sacred Writings of St. Ambrose.* North Charleston, SC: CreateSpace, 2017.

Aquinas, Saint Thomas. *Summa Theologica, Volume 1.* New York: Cosimo Classics, 2013.

———. *Summa Theologica, Volume 3 (Part II, Second Section).* New York: Cosimo Classics, 2013.

———. *Summa Theologica, Volume 5 (Part III, Second Section & Supplement).* New York: Cosimo Classics, 2013.

Ashford, José B., Craig Winston LeCroy, and Kathy L. Lortie. *Human Behavior in the Social Environment: A Multidimensional Perspective.* Belmont, CA: Cengage Learning, 2009.

Augustine. *De Bono Coiugali and De Sancta Viginitate.* Translated by P. G. Walsh. Oxford: Clarendon, 2001.

———. "On the Trinity." Translated by A. W. Haddan. In *On the Holy Trinity, Doctrinal Treatises, Moral Treatises,* edited by Philip Schaff, 3–199. Buffalo, NY: Christian Literature, 1887.

Bailey, J. Michael, and Richard C. Pillard. "A Genetic Study of Male Sexual Orientation." *Archives of General Psychiatry* 48, no. 12 (1992) 1089–96.

Bailey, Jacqueline M., Mary Dunne, and N. G. Martin. "Genetic and Environmental Influences on Sexual Orientation and Its Correlates in an Australian Twin Sample." *Journal of Personality and Social Psychology* 78, no. 3 (2000) 524–36.

Banister, Jamie A. "*Homoiōs* and the Use of Parallelism in Romans 1:26–27." *Journal of Biblical Literature* 128, no. 3 (2009) 569–90.

Barker, Paul. *Deuteronomy: The God Who Keeps Promises.* London: Langham Partnership International, 2017.

Bauckham, Richard. *Jude and the Relatives of Jesus in the Early Church.* London: Bloomsbury, 2015.

Bayer, Ronald. *Homosexuality and American Psychiatry: The Politics of Diagnosis.* Princeton, NJ: Princeton University Press, 1981.

Bayes, Jonathan F. *The Threefold Division of the Law*. Newcastle upon Tyne: The Christian Institute, 2012.

Bieber, Irving, and Cornelia B. Wilbur. *Homosexuality: A Psychoanalytic Study of Male Homosexuals*. New York: Baker, 1962.

Bigger, Stephen. "The Family Laws of Leviticus 18 in Their Setting." *Journal of Biblical Literature*, 98, no. 2 (1979) 187–203.

Bird, Michael F. *Romans*. Grand Rapids: Zondervan, 2016.

Bird, Phyllis A. "The Bible in Christian Ethical Deliberation Concerning Homosexuality: Old Testament Contributions." In *Homosexuality, Science and the 'Plain Sense' of Scripture*, edited by David L. Blach, 142–76. Grand Rapids: Eerdmans, 2000.

Blanchard, Ray. "Review of Theory and Handedness, Birth Order and Homosexuality in Men." *Laterality* 13 (2008) 51–57.

The Book of Common Prayer: The Texts of 1549, 1559, and 1662. Edited by Brian Cummings. Oxford: Oxford University Press, 2011.

Boswell, John. *Christianity, Social Tolerance, and Homosexuality: Gay People in Western Europe from the Beginning of the Christian Era to the Fourteenth Century*. Chicago: The University of Chicago Press, 1981.

Brooten, Bernadette J. *Love between Women: Early Christian Responses to Female Homoeroticism*. Chicago: The University of Chicago Press, 2009.

Brown, Francis, Samuel Rolles Driver, and Charles Augustus Briggs. *Enhanced Brown-Driver-Briggs Hebrew and English Lexicon*. Oxford: Clarendon, 1977.

Brownson, James V. *Bible, Gender, Sexuality: Reframing the Church's Debate on Same-Sex Relationships*. Grand Rapids: Eerdmans, 2013.

Calvin, John. *The First Epistle of Paul the Apostle to the Corinthians*. Grand Rapids: Eerdmans, 1960.

Carden, Michael. *Sodomy: A History of a Christian Biblical Myth*. New York: Equinox, 2004.

Carson, D. A. *Exegetical Fallacies*. Grand Rapids: Baker, 1996.

Chrysostom, Dio. *Dio Chrysostom*. Translated by J. W. Cohoon and H. Lamar Crosby. London: G. P. Putnam's Sons, 1932.

Clines, David J. A. "The Image of God in Man." *Tyndale Bulletin* (1968) 53–103.

Cross, Frank Moore. *From Epic to Canon: History and Literature in Ancient Israel*. Baltimore: Johns Hopkins University Press, 2000.

Cymet, David. *History Vs. Apologetics: The Holocaust, the Third Reich, and the Catholic Church*. New York: Lexington, 2012.

Dallas, Joe. *The Complete Christian Guide to Understanding Homosexuality: A Biblical and Compassionate Response to Same-Sex Attraction*. Sisters, OR: Harvest House, 2010.

———. *The Gay Gospel?* Sisters, OR: Harvest House, 2007.

Davids, Peter. *The Letters of 2 Peter and Jude*. Grand Rapids: Eerdmans, 2006.

De Bono Coniugali: De Sancta Virginitate. Translated by P. G. Walsh. Oxford: Clarendon, 2001.

DeFranza, Megan K. "Journeying from the Bible to Christian Ethics in Search of Common Ground." In *Two Views on Homosexuality, the Bible, and the Church*, edited by Preston Sprinkle, 69–101. Grand Rapids: Zondervan, 2016.

DeYoung, Kevin. *What Does the Bible Really Teach About Homosexuality?* Wheaton, IL: Crossway, 2015.

Dodson, Joseph R. "The Fall of Men and the Lust of Women in Seneca's Epistle 95 and Paul's Letter to the Romans." *Novum Testamentum* 59, no. 3 (2017) 355–65.

Dupont, Carolyn Renee. *Mississippi Praying: Southern White Evangelicals and the Civil Rights Movement, 1945–1975.* New York: New York University Press, 2015.

Elliot, John Hall. "No Kingdom of God for the Softies? Or, What Was Paul Really Saying?; 1 Corinthians 6:9–10 in Context." *Biblical Theology Bulletin* 34 no. 1 (2004) 17–40

Elliot, Neil. *Liberating Paul.* Maryknoll, NY: Orbis, 1994.

Fee, Gordon D. *Discovering Biblical Equality: Complementarity without Hierarchy.* edited by R. W. Pierce, R. M. Groothuis, and G. D. Fee. Downers Grove, IL: InterVarsity, 2005.

———. *The First Epistle to the Corinthians.* Rev. ed. Grand Rapids: Eerdmans, 2014.

Foulkes, Francis. *Ephesians: An Introduction and Commentary.* Downers Grove, IL: InterVarsity, 1989.

Gagnon, Robert A. J. *The Bible and Homosexual Practice: Texts and Hermeneutics.* Nashville: Abingdon, 2001.

Garcia-Falguieras, A., and D. F. Swaab. "Sexual Hormones and the Brain: An Essential Alliance for Sexual Identity and Sexual Orientation." *Pediatric Neuroendocrinology* 17 (2010) 22–35.

Geisler, Norman L. *Christian Ethics: Contemporary Issues and Options.* Grand Rapids: Baker, 2010.

Glassgold, Judith M., Lee Beckstead, Jack Drescher, Beverly Greene, Robin Lin Miller, Roger L. Worthington, and Clinton W. Anderson. *Report of the American Psychological Association Task Force on Appropriate Therapeutic Responses to Sexual Orientation.* Washington, DC: American Psychological Association, 2009.

Gnuse, Robert K. "Seven Gay Texts: Biblical Passages Used to Condemn Homosexuality." *Biblical Theological Bulletin* 45, no. 2 (2015) 68–87.

Grudem, Wayne. "The Key Issues in the Manhood-Womanhood Controversy, and the Way Forward." In *Biblical Foundations for Manhood and Womanhood,* edited by W. Grudem, 16–68. Wheaton, IL: Crossway, 2002.

Gushee, David P. *Changing Our Mind.* 2d ed. Canton, MI: David Crumm Media, 2015.

Haller, Tobias S. *Reasonable and Holy: Engaging Same-Sexuality.* New York: Seabury, 2009.

Hamer, Dean H., Stella Hu, Victoria L. Magnuson, Nan Hu, and Angela M. L. Pattatucci. "A Linkage between DNA Markers on the X Chromosome and Male Sexual Orientation." *Science* 261, no. 5119 (1993) 321–27.

Hart, David Bentley. *The New Testament: A Translation.* London: Yale University Press, 2017.

Hays, Richard B. *The Moral Vision of the New Testament: Community, Cross, New Creation: A Contemporary Introduction to New Testament Ethics.* San Francisco: HarperCollins, 2013.

Heil, Reinhard, Stefanie B. Seitz, Harald König, and Jürgen Robienski. *Epigenetics: Ethical, Legal and Social Aspects.* Weisbaden: Springer Fachmedien Wiesbaden, 2017.

Hill, Wesley. *Washed and Waiting: Reflections on Christian Faithfulness and Homosexuality.* Grand Rapids: Zondervan, 2010.

Hillier, Lynne. "'I Couldn't Do Both at the Same Time': Same Sex Attracted Youth and the Negotiation of Religious Discourse." *Gay and Lesbian Issues and Psychology Review* 4, no. 2 (2008) 80–93.

Iniewicz, Grzengorz, Kinga Salap, Malgorzat Wrona, and Natalia Marek. "Minority Stress among Homosexual and Bisexual Individuals—from Theoretical Concepts to Research Tools: The Sexual Minority Stress Scale." *Psychiatry and Psychotherapy* 3 (2017) 69–80.

Johnson, Gregg. "The Biological Basis for Gender-Specific Behavior." In *Recovering Biblical Manhood and Womanhood*, edited by John Piper and Wayne Grudem, 280–93. Wheaton, IL: Crossway, 2006.

Jones, Stanton L., and Mark Yarhouse. *Ex-Gays? A Longitudinal Study of Religiously Mediated Change in Sexual Orientation*. Downers Grove, IL: InterVarsity, 2007.

Jordan, Mark D. *Authorizing Marriage?: Canon, Tradition, and Critique in the Blessing of Same-Sex Unions*. Princeton, NJ. Princeton University Press, 2009.

———. *The Invention of Sodomy in Christian Theology*. Chicago: The University of Chicago Press, 1997.

Josephus, Flavius. *The Works of Josephus: Complete and Unabridged*. Translated by William Whiston. Peabody, MA: Hendrickson, 1987.

Kaufmann, Thomas. *Luther's Jews: A Journey into Anti-Semitism*. Oxford: Oxford University Press, 2017.

Keane, Christopher. *What Some of You Were: Stories About Christians and Homosexuality*. Kingsford, NSW: Matthias Media, 2001.

Kinnaman, David, and Gabe Lyons. *Unchristian: What a New Generation Really Thinks About Christianity . . . And Why It Matters*. Grand Rapids: Baker, 2007.

Klar, Amar J. "Excess of Counterclockwise Scalp Hair-Whorl Rotation in Homosexual Men." *Journal of Genetics* 83, no. 3 (2004) 251–55.

Köstenberger, Andreas J., and David W. Jones. *God, Marriage, and Family: Rebuilding the Biblical Foundation*. Wheaton, IL: Crossway, 2004.

Köstenberger, Andreas J., and Margaret Elizabeth Köstenberger. *God's Design for Man and Woman: A Biblical-Theological Survey*. Wheaton, IL: Crossway, 2014.

Lee, Justin. *Torn*. New York: Jericho, 2012

Loader, William. *Sexuality in the New Testament: Understanding the Key Texts*. Louisville: Westminster John Knox, 2010.

Luther, Martin. *On the Jews and Their Lies*. Translated by Domenico d'Abrruzo. Princeton, NJ: Eulenspiegel, 2015.

Martin, Colby. *Unclobber: Rethinking Our Misuse of the Bible on Homosexuality*. Louisville: Westminster John Knox, 2016.

Martin, Dale B. *Sex and the Single Savior: Gender and Sexuality in Biblical Interpretation*. Louisville: Westminster John Knox, 2006.

Melcher, Sarah. "The Holiness Code and Human Sexuality: Listening to Scripture." In *Biblical Ethics and Homosexuality*, edited by Robert Lawson Brawley, 87–102. Louisville: Westminster John Knox, 1996.

Milgrom, Jacob. *Leviticus 17–22: A New Translation with Introduction and Commentary*. New York: Doubleday, 2000.

Miller, James E. "The Practices of Romans 1:26: Homosexual or Heterosexual?" *Novum Testamentum* 37, no. 1 (1995) 1–11.

Morris, Leon. *The Gospel According to Matthew*. Grand Rapids: Eerdmans, 1992.

Morrison, Steve. *Born This Way: Making Sense of Science, the Bible & Same Sex Attraction*. Kingsford, NSW: Matthias Media, 2015.

Nissinen, Marti. *Homoeroticism in the Biblical World: A Historical Perspective*. Minneapolis: Fortress, 2004.

Noll, Mark A. *The Civil War as a Theological Crisis*. Chapel Hill, NC: The University of North Carolina Press, 2006.

Olyan, Saul M. "'And with a Male You Shall Not Lie the Lying Down of a Woman': On the Meaning and Significance of Leviticus 18:22 and 20:13." *Journal of the History of Sexuality* 5, no. 2 (1994) 179–206.

Petro, Anthony M. *After the Wrath of God*. Oxford: Oxford University Press, 2015.

Philo. *Philo*. Translated by F. H. Colson. Loeb Classical Library. Cambridge: Cambridge University Press, 1935.

———. *Works*. 11 vols. Translated by F. H. Colson, G. H. Whitaker, and J. W. Earp. London: Harvard University Press, 1929–1962.

Plöderl, Martin, Maximilian Sellmeier, Clemens Fartacek, Eva-Maria Pichler, Reinhold Fartacek, and Karl Kralovec. "Explaining the Suicide Risk of Sexual Minority Individuals by Contrasting the Minority Stress Model with the Suicide Model." *Archives of Sexual Behaviour* 43, no. 8 (2014) 1559–70.

Poliakov, Leon. *The History of Anti-Semitism, Volume 1: From the Time of Christ to the Court Jews*. Translated by Richard Howard. Philadelphia: University of Pennsylvania Press, 2003.

Pruitt, M. "Size Matters: A Comparison of Anti- and Pro-Gay Organisations' Estimates of the Size of the Gay Population." *Journal of Homosexuality* 42, no. 3 (2002) 21–29.

Rable, George. *God's Almost Chosen Peoples: A Religious History of the American Civil War*. Chapel Hill, NC: The University of North Carolina Press, 2010.

Regele, Michael B. *Science, Scripture, and Same-Sex Love*. Nashville: Abingdon, 2014.

Roberts, Vaughan. *Battles Christians Face: We Feebly Struggle, They in Glory Shine*. Milton Keynes: Authentic, 2007.

Rosenstreich, Gabi. "LGBTI People, Mental Health, and Suicide: Revised 2nd Edition." Sydney: National LGBTI Health Alliance, 2013.

Savin-Williams, Rich C. "Who's Gay? Does It Matter?" *Current Directions in Psychological Science* 15, no. 1 (2006) 40–44.

Schneemelcher, Wilhelm, ed. *Acts of John*. In *New Testament Apocryha*, translated by R. McL. Wilson. Louisville: Westminster John Knox, 2003.

Schreiner, Thomas R. *40 Questions About Christians and Biblical Law*. Grand Rapids: Kregel Academic, 2010.

Sellars, John. *Stoicism*. Berkeley, CA: University of California Press, 2014.

Shaw, Ed. *The Plausibility Problem: The Church and Same-Sex Attraction*. Nottingham: Inter-Varsity, 2015.

Sklar, Jay. *Leviticus: An Introduction and Commentary*. Downers Grove, IL: InterVarsity, 2014.

Souter, Alexander. *A Pocket Lexicon to the Greek New Testament*. London: Oxford University Press, 2017.

Sprinkle, Preston. *People to Be Loved: Why Homosexuality Is Not Just an Issue*. Grand Rapids: Zondervan, 2015.

Stickler, Alfonso M. *The Case for Clerical Celibacy: Its Historical Development and Theological Foundations*. Translated by Father Brian Ferme. San Francisco: Ignatius, 1995.

Sumner, Sarah. *Men and Women in the Church: Building Consensus on Christian Leadership*. Downers Grove: InterVarsity, 2009.

Switzer, David. *Pastoral Care of Gays, Lesbians and Their Families*. Minneapolis: Fortress, 1999.

Tertullian. "On the Dress of Women." Translated by S. Thelwall. In *Ante-Nicene Fathers*, edited by Alexander Roberts, 14–26. Peabody, MA: Hendrickson, 1994.

Thornwell, James H. *The Collected Writings of James Thornwell*. Bedford, MA: Applewood, 2009.

Tomkins, Stephen. *The Clapham Sect: How Wilberforce's Circle Transformed Britain*. Oxford: Lion, 2012.

Townsley, Jeramy. "Paul, the Goddess Religions, and Queer Sects: Romans 1:23–28." *Journal of Biblical Literature* 130, no. 1 (2011) 707–27.

Universal Declaration of Human Rights. United Nations General Assembly, 1948.

Vines, Matthew. *God and the Gay Christian: The Biblical Case in Support of Same-Sex Relationships*. New York: Crown, 2014.

Ware, Bruce A. "Male and Female Complementarity and the Image of God." In *Biblical Foundations for Manhood and Womanhood*, edited by W. Grudem, 71–92. Wheaton, IL: Crossway, 2002.

Wenham, Gordon. *Genesis*. Word Biblical Commentary. Dallas, TX: Dallas Word, 1987.

———. *Genesis 1–15*. Waco, TX: Word, 1986.

Westermann, Claus. *Genesis 1–11: A Commentary*. Translated by John J. Scullion. Minneapolis: Augsburg, 1984.

Whitaker, Richard E. "Creation and Human Sexuality." In *Homosexuality and the Christian Community*, edited by C. L. Seow, 3–13. Louisville: Westminster John Knox, 1996.

Whitford, David. "A Calvinist Heritage to the 'Curse of Ham': Assessing the Accuracy of a Claim About Racial Subordination." *Church History and Religious Culture* 90, no. 1 (2010) 24–45.

Wilson, Helen, and Cathy Spatz-Widom. "Does Physical Abuse, Sexual Abuse, or Neglect in Childhood Increase the Likelihood of Same-Sex Sexual Relationships and Cohabitation? A Prospective 30-Year Follow-Up." *Archives of Sexual Behaviour* 39, no. 1 (2009) 63–74.

Wright, David. "Homosexuals or Prostitutes? The Meaning of *Arsenokoitai* (1 Cor 6:9, 1 Tim 1:10)." *Vigiliae Christinae* 38 (1984) 125–53.

Yarhouse, Mark. *Homosexuality and the Christian: A Guide for Parents, Pastors, and Friends*. Grand Rapids: Baker, 2010.

A Series of Open Letters

This series of "open letters" is designed to address four categories of people who are in unique positions within LGBT dialogue in the church. I have written each letter over much prayer and thought, seeking to capture more personally the task that has been outlined in the book above. There are many other groups of people who could have been addressed in this series. I have chosen these people because I feel that at this point in my journey, I am most comfortable addressing them. I humbly offer them to you for your consideration.

An Open Letter to Christian Parents
of Young LGBT people

I am not a parent. I don't know what it's like to raise a child. In my experience, this world can be a dark and fearful place, and I can only imagine what it is like to bear the responsibility of preparing a son or daughter to face it with courage and conviction. You have a weighty task and I would be lying if I said that there is nothing to fear. If you are reading this, then I assume that you are seeking wisdom for how you can best equip your child for the future that lies ahead of them, and for that I commend you. It is you, not I, that must walk this journey, and while I cannot grasp the uncertainties you feel, I hope I can help in bearing some of the weight that you carry.

No doubt, when you first learned that your son or daughter is LGBT, your mind raced with the huge complexities that this naturally entails. No parent wants to see their child suffer, and the reality is that in our current social and political climate, it is hard to pass through life in a sexual minority unscathed. Further, if you are anything like my parents, then your heart hopes in its deepest crevices that your child will grow up to follow Jesus, never knowing a day when they don't walk with him as king. LGBT people so often experience such a sharp disconnect between their faith and their sexuality that many, sadly, feel forced to resign themselves to the margins and slowly drift away from the church. This fear is real, and it is tangible.

As you navigate this space, my prayer is that this fear will translate into action. We cannot know what the future holds, but I for one do not think that we yet have reason to despair. Jesus is still on his throne, and while ever this is true, there is hope. Right now, hope is growing stronger every day, but it will take God's people putting in hard work to realize this hope's potential. I may not be a parent, but I am a son, and I'd like to share with you what wisdom I have gleaned from having two remarkable parents.

One of the most profound things that my parents have done in my journey is to take on a posture of learning. Together we have read books and shared articles. We have compared notes and clarified thoughts. We have read theological masterpieces and tacky blogs. Most of the time they have sharpened me. Occasionally, there were times when it was appropriate for me to sharpen them, and they humbly engaged with my thoughts.

They did not sit over me as moral enforcers, but rather acted as navigators, older and wiser. Like most parents, they had not walked this specific path before, but they knew how to read the signs, and together we shared the journey.

The power of this posture was in its relational force. They did not simply limit themselves to reading from the conservative theological tradition that they cherished, but, together with me, broadened their perspectives. As they did this, I realized something powerful had happened. I saw my parents in a new light, as fellow pilgrims seeking truth, and as such my respect for them has continued to rise exponentially. Their diligent reading and deep insights proved that out of love for me, their first priority was the truth and, boldly, they weren't afraid to contest long-held traditions. I came to trust my parents in ways that I had never before.

Not all family dynamics are comparable, but I take it that a child who trusts their parents is in a remarkably different position to one who is forced to tolerate their parents' advice. A posture of learning embodies trust and communicates a powerful willingness to meet a child where they are.

Alongside of this trust, we would do well to explore what love looks like in this situation. Love takes many forms. There is a time for tough love. Correction, rebuke, and stern words. It is, doubtless, a parent's role to be willing and able to administer such love. But in order to be effective, this type of love takes great wisdom, careful nuance, and deep respect.

Another type of love, equally as powerful and transformative, is love which enters into the confused, disoriented world of a young LGBT person and reminds them gently that no matter what happens, you will always be a safe person to run to. I can say with some confidence that your child is most likely scared (what teenager isn't?). The unknowns in their world are insurmountable right now, and they will cling to whatever stabilizing source they can find. This will take openness, a willingness to broach hard topics, time spent in the kitchen and time walking the dog. Gentleness can only come from a place of strength, and right now, there is a task for you in simply being present with your child.

I should warn you, though, that there are things that will sap your strength and steal your time. Scared people are prone to behaviors that seem irrational. There is the likelihood that your child, out of a place of fear, will attempt to fill a void of sorts with decisions that we all know will not fare them well in the future. I do not presume to be in a place to offer disciplinary advice, but I would ask that you consider the impetus for their actions as you gently handle their confused behavior.

And to be clear, it will not only be your child's experiences that will sap your energy. There will be some within the church who will question your parenting. With or without your consent, they will pick apart your cherished home life and critique your every move. I am so sorry that you will have to endure this. They will face God one day to give an account for their actions, but until then, might I remind you that you are doing the best you can, and that is all anybody can expect of you. Perhaps you can learn from this experience what it is like to walk into church and feel somehow tainted. Remember that feeling and let it shape you, because your child will be feeling that for many years to come.

A friend said to me recently that those who stand against full inclusion should fear, above all, the mothers of young LGBT people. I have seen firsthand the rage that fills a mother when her child is threatened. The anger at flippant pastors who perpetuate fear. The fierce call for justice at church leaders who make careless decisions that hurt the innocent. I believe there is some truth in my friend's statement. As a parent, you have the unique and powerful position of being your child's strongest ally. You have the chance now to gather around you others of the same mind and sit in your pastor's office to demand an explanation and humbly offer a better path forward. Astonishingly, you are poised now to become educators, change agents, and advocates, because you are driven by the powerful forces that urge you to protect your child. You may not feel equipped, and you almost certainly don't have all of the answers. But you have a clarity and insight that few others in this world could ever hope to grasp. Use this. Shape change.

Above all, with great reverence for his power, might I ask that you commit to praying for your child. If they are open, pray with them, and if they are not, pray for them. Pray for clarity amidst darkness, strength within weakness, hope from despair, grace without shame, and joy in the morning. Pray that your child would walk toward Christ. Pray that the church would offer a warm and radical embrace. Pray that your son or daughter would know that their identity is most marvelously and beautifully tied up with Jesus.

Whatever your theological convictions, the task of learning together and gently guiding your child is an immense burden to carry. But it is also one of God's richest blessings. I can't speak for my parents, but I hope that throughout the journey of seeing me grow into a young, gay man of God, I have in some way or another brought them a measure of joy.

And know that the prayers of God's people around the world go up daily for people like you, faithfully seeking to pass on the glorious gospel to the next generation.

Yours,

Joel

An Open Letter to Pastors and Church Leaders

My fellow pastors,

You bear on your shoulders the weight of caring for our flocks. Called into ministry, you lead your people, always careful to watch your life and doctrine closely. No doubt, you recognize the significance of the theological, cultural, and sociological debates that are taking place, and you long to protect the church and its witness. Perhaps like no other, there is gravitas in this movement. You see this. With Christ as our leader, we are called to follow him in all things, faithfully guarding the gospel that we have been entrusted with.

I speak to you now both as a fellow pastor, and as somebody who has spent years reconciling the worlds of faith and sexuality. Our paths may be very different, but our heart, I trust, is the same—that people would grasp the height, depth, and breadth of God's love for them shown in Christ. In seeking to do this, let me remind you of the shape of our history.

Every era in the life of God's people has held its unique theological complexities. In the first century ecclesiastical bodies debated the nature of the kingdom: how were the Gentiles to be the people of God? In the second and third centuries, discussions turned to Christology, the nature of Jesus, fully human and yet fully divine. These debates morphed into councils examining pneumatology and the nature of God, three in one, transcendent and immanent. Theology proper gave rise to passionate debates about ecclesiology, apostolic succession, and monastic paths toward spiritual enlightenment. Dramatically, the Reformation brought soteriology into sharp focus as the complex interplay between faith and works took center stage. In the past few centuries, the debates have morphed once again to examine theologies of revelation and inspiration. There are two ways that this ongoing saga could be framed. On the one hand, we could say that the church has always been under attack. On the other, we could say that the church, guided by the Holy Spirit, has always been seeking deeper understanding. Most likely, it is a combination of the two.

In recent decades, another shift has taken place as theologians and church leaders have been called upon to respond to an increasingly complex world. Ours is a season of reflecting on anthropological understandings. Moral theology is the flavor of the month, and it is into these waters that we as pastors must courageously wade. It is tempting to think that we have drawn the historical short straw, imagining ourselves to have the hardest of the debates. But a cursory glance at history shows that while we may be paving new paths, the task of navigating uncharted territory is by no means a new one.

My task in this letter is not to convince you to change your theology. My task in this letter is to ask a more basic question—how are you making the church a safer place for LGBT people to explore, find, and walk with Jesus? I hope that in reading this book, you have come to appreciate that this is of utmost importance.

To those of you reading this who are unsure of your theology around LGBT people, let me thank you for engaging in the discussion. Breaking the barriers of silence that have for so long been stalwarts of the church is vital in moving forward. Giving space for people to express their doubts, their existential fears, and their experiences of marginalization is key to dialogue that is respectful, Christ-honoring, and edifying to the church. Whilst it is uncomfortable and can feel threatening to open up such conversation, I am convinced it is only once we have heard these concerns that we can honestly and powerfully speak the good news of the gospel into people's lives.

Pastors, this takes courage. This takes a willingness to stand before your congregations and admit that you don't have all of the answers. There is a humility here that is raw and honest, making oneself vulnerable and open to criticism. Many, I fear, do not have this courage. This saddens me because it deeply reveals a pastor's inability to learn from the rich history that has shaped us, and it betrays the fact that many church leaders are so blinded by their adherence to denominational dogma that they forget the very flock that is before them. This is not leadership, and it is certainly not pastorship.

I have spoken with numerous pastors who have deliberately chosen to remain silent on this topic for fear of dissension in their churches. I have spoken to numerous church leaders who have refused to read widely lest they be seen as sympathetic to a minority view. I have spoken to pastors who have found after much research that they cannot hold a traditional theology in this space, and yet remain silent because they are bound by institutions, denominations, and congregations that are unwilling to follow them down this road. Let me call this cowardice for what it is and remind you that your conscience is bound to Scripture above all. What you do with this journey is up to you, but please be aware of the urgency in this message—people are leaving our churches in droves, abandoning faith in Jesus as they go, and as leaders in an age of change, we cannot afford to let traditional practices take precedence over biblical authority.

Having said all of this, I am realistic enough to know that there are some reading this who will never engage deeper with affirming theology. Let me address you for a moment. If your theology in this area is traditional, you may resonate with such books as *Washed and Waiting* (Wesley Hill) and *The Plausibility Problem* (Ed Shaw). Both maintaining traditional stances around sexuality, these two books, in my opinion, provide the best diagnosis for where our church is currently. They attempt to pave a way forward and give honest accounts about how local congregations need to change, examining culture and teaching practices. Having implemented their solutions for a long time, I personally found them theologically unsatisfying and pastorally unconvincing, but I applaud them for their attempts to make the church a better place. If you have closed your mind to further exploring affirming theology (which I pray you have not), please at the very least read these two books.

I'm sure it will come as no surprise that I don't believe that books such as these will sufficiently equip the church for the moral debates of our age. Sadly, I have seen far too many situations where their solutions have been found to be inadequate and, in the end, damaging. But at the very least, I pray that these books will give you an insight into ways that you can mitigate the damage traditional theology is currently wreaking in our churches.

To those of you who have read widely and come to a grounded, affirming position, can I also say thank you to you for your engagement. There are very few who move through this topic without considerable inner turmoil, and as an LGBT person, I am honored that you would take the time to grasp what my existence within the church can and should look like. Your task now however has truly only just begun. My LGBT brothers and sisters need pastors who point us to Jesus, who affirm our standing as children of God, and who hold us accountable to the high standards to which he calls us. We can't afford to have pastors who will "go light" on us, or water down expectations due to circumstances. My prayer is that together we would be able to paint for LGBT people a picture of sexuality that is God-honoring, self-sacrificing, and love-giving. Alongside of this, the greatest gift that you can give us is not your stamp of approval, it is a constant gospel proclamation that draws us ever closer to Jesus. We need leaders who will bring out our best, not settle for where we have landed.

We truly are in an age of change, once again. If writing this book has taught me anything, it has made me more confident of the fact that God is far bigger than I could have possibly imagined, and in that truth, I find a courage to speak up, challenge the norms of tradition, and stare down a history that has marginalized so many. As we move forward, take comfort above all in the fact that it is Christ who builds his church, and no matter where we may think we are leading it, the gates of hades will not prevail.

May you remain forever in the grasp of our gracious King,
Joel

An Open Letter to My Allies

To those who stand alongside their LGBT brothers and sisters, affirming the beauty of our sexuality and pointing us to Jesus, I say thank you. Thank you for your willingness to question the status quo. Thank you for listening to our stories and for revisiting old beliefs. Thank you for standing with us in a journey that is so often dark and lonely.

I do not doubt that for many of you, the process of embracing an affirming theology has involved deep wrestling, sleepless nights, and fierce debate. Hard conversations have been had, and friendships have, perhaps, been damaged along the way. God's word moves us to mysterious places, and aligning yourself with the marginalized is not without its costs.

Having walked the journey I have, I find it difficult to put in to words the impact that you have had. You may not feel it, but your presence is a source of hope for which I am eternally grateful. When I have found myself angry at the church, you have reminded me that change can, and has, taken place. When I have been disillusioned or frustrated with the painful dialogue in which LGBT voices are so often silenced, you have shown me that we are, in fact, being heard. And when I have been tempted to give up the fight and settle for a non-affirming church, you have spurred me on, painting for me a vision of how stunningly inclusive church communities actually are. You, more than anybody else, have taught me that a healthy church is a church in which LGBT people are able to be seen and welcomed.

I know that this journey has cost you, but if I may, I have three requests, knowing full well that the cost may have only just begun. My first request is that you continue to stand with us, creatively and sensitively challenging the dominant narrative in so many of our churches. When we are silenced, be our voice. When we are absent, be our representatives. When we are threatened, speak louder. I am so convinced that God's heart is that none of his children should suffer at the hands of his church, and when you make known to those in authority that you stand alongside us, you stand firmly in the abundant, extravagant love of God.

My second request is that, out of love, you would hold us to the highest of standards. The Bible has a stunning view of what mutual, self-sacrificing love can be, and it is my prayer that LGBT communities across the world would strive toward this level of beauty. There is a movement within Western sexual ethics that teaches that "anything goes," and there is the temptation to allow loved ones to follow this vein, under the guise of freedom. Love does not equate to license. Your truest love will hold us accountable to the types of relationships that God envisages in one-flesh, spouse-honoring marriages. Deep love is prepared, when we go astray, to call us back to the vision of sexuality that the Bible offers. It is willing to speak hard words when necessary, gently but firmly rebuking and correcting.

Finally, I request that you continue to walk with us. We have begun this journey together, and I pray that together we would see it through to its end. By virtue of being a minority within the church, LGBT people will continue to feel "other," and it is your warmness, your embrace, that bridges the chasm that we so often feel. For us, the world can be a scary place, and your companionship as we walk is a light in the darkness.

The history of the church is replete with rabble rousers, change agents, and cries for liberation. The nature of God's kingdom is that cost must be counted, voices must rise, and justice must run like a river. When you stand alongside us, absorbing the stones that are hurled our way, you stand in an ancient history of faithful witnesses who know the heart of God and seek the divine call. For all that you do, you will be richly rewarded.

From the bottom of my heart, and on behalf of my LGBT brothers and sisters, I say thank you. May the Lord bless you and keep you. May he ever equip you with strength and passion for the task he has given you in standing alongside us as allies.

Your brother,
Joel

An Open Letter to My LGBT Siblings

Fellow pilgrims,

People of courage, humble servants of the most high God, dearly beloved and fearsomely faithful. It is an honor to stand amongst you and call you my siblings. It is my deepest privilege in life to walk this path alongside you, carrying one another's burdens and pointing one another onward to glory. To you, my kindred, I offer this reflection.

Like a breath of wind or a wisp of smoke, you and I are fleeting moments, flashes of light in the vast expanse of history. Intricately knitted together in the depths, we shall pass through this world and return to the dust from which we came. Along the way we will endure fire, marvel at beauty, weep with the broken, taste of God's good earth, rest with the weary, and find joy in the hearts of fellow pilgrims. We will fight for justice, stand with the oppressed, and proclaim the gospel.

We, along with countless others, know what it means to be on the margins, to experience this world as objects of mistrust and suspicion. We, along with countless others, know the cry for equal treatment and the desire to be accepted. As we traverse the path laid before us, we must ask ourselves, how will we engage God's people to see change, leaving this world in a better place than we found it?

My prayer is that in all things, we would take Jesus as our great example. Though entitled to equality with God, he made himself nothing, taking humanity upon himself and being obedient to death. Facing down the might of an empire, he did not retaliate with displays of power, but instead subverted their authority with meekness. When those in positions of prominence sought to discredit him, he did not enter their battles, but rather turned his attention to the poor. This man, perfect in his insights, taught us to turn the other cheek, love our enemies, do good to those who harm us.

Above all, he taught us what it means to forgive—to take upon ourselves the pain of another's actions and in an act of divine redemption, to repay evil with outstretched arms, drawing humanity unto reconciliation.

Friends, we have been wounded. We have been maligned and guided poorly. Some of us have faced abuse, others have been shown the door. There is no hiding from the fact that these are great tragedies, and if we were people purely of justice, we would be right to demand retribution.

But we are not simply people of justice. We are also people of grace. So, I must ask, what does this mean for us?

Grace is messy and it is humbling. It does not mean allowing people to hide the hurt they have caused—it is calling their actions into the light, and then extending to them an arm of forgiveness, offering to walk the journey onward together. If we are to make the church a safer place for LGBT people, it cannot mean leaving the church altogether—it must mean transforming the church from within, and in the act of grace there is a wild, Jesus-shaped power that, with time, I believe will be irresistible to those watching.

And as we extend this grace, let me call upon you to share your stories. Share them widely, and share them courageously. People are moved to change when they see the harm that their theology is having. That is how I was slowly moved to re-examine what I had for so long believed and taught. For some of you, you are reading these words and you feel isolated, alone in this task. If it is any encouragement, let me share with you the truth that you are not alone. There is an army of us fighting, always seeking to make this world a warmer place for LGBT people.

But it cannot stop there. As people who know pain, we are in a unique position to speak up for those who are yet to be granted a voice. We live in a world and church stained with hues of racism, marked with the evils of misogyny, and replete with disdain for any who do not conform to the norm. Justice for just us is no justice at all. The call to action is far bigger than our own tribe. As the church, can LGBT people lead the charge in calling forth inclusion and embrace for those who are yet to be fully welcomed and affirmed? We have such a powerful place, and we must, my friends, be ready to speak up for and listen to the margins.

In all honesty, the more I see the state of change in our world, the more I am filled with hope. I know full well that the journey to date has been so hard, and I soberly recognize that there is still so, so much that needs to be done. Perhaps we are still only just beginning. But each day, the landscape is changing. People are coming to see LGBT people in a new light, and the church is making powerful strides in the right direction. We will see many dark nights before this age has past, but I for one am so excited to be a part of the movement that captures God's heart for LGBT people and lives it out courageously.

And so, my fellow pilgrims, fix your eyes on Jesus, the author and perfecter of our faith. Fight the good fight. Demand righteous justice and extend immeasurable grace. For the sake of the kingdom, which shall stand forever more.

Your brother,
Joel